ISLAM

THE VIEW
FROM THE
EDGE

ISLAM

THE VIEW FROM

THE EDGE

Richard W. Bulliet

Columbia University Press

New York

Columbia University Press

New York   Chichester, West Sussex

Copyright © 1994 Columbia University Press

Library of Congress Cataloging-in-Publication Data

Bulliet, Richard W.

Islam : the view from the edge / Richard W. Bulliet.

p.   cm.

Includes bibliographical references and index.

ISBN 0–231–08218–5

1. Islam—History. 2. Islam and state. 3. Ulama—History.
4. Islam—Iran—History.   I. Title.

BP52.B85   1994   297—dc20   94–36360

CIP

Casebound editions of
Columbia University Press books
are printed on permanent
and durable acid-free paper.

Printed in the United States of America

c 10 9 8 7 6 5 4 3 2 1

To my students

CONTENTS

ISLAM

THE VIEW

FROM THE

EDGE

INTRODUCTION

The Messenger of God, God's prayers and peace be upon him, said to his companion Abd al-Rahman b. Samura: "Oh, Abd al-Rahman, do not seek command. For if you are given it because you asked, you will bear the full responsibility. But if you are given it without asking, God will assist you in it."

This saying of the Prophet Muhammad, usually abbreviated to "Oh, Abd al-Rahman, do not seek command," occurs eleven times, twice as often as any of the Prophet's other sayings, in an eleventh-century book devoted to brief biographies of religious scholars from the northeastern Iranian city of Gorgan.[1] I was puzzled when I encountered this wealth of citations because I hadn't encountered this saying in other biographical collections. Could it possibly suggest something specific about Gorgan's medieval history?

I decided to ask around about the saying. I mentioned it to two of my Arab students, both Sunni Muslims from Lebanon. They told me that the sentiment was familiar, though they had not heard it in this phrasing. They further informed me that modesty in seeking public office was deemed a virtue in Arab society, adding that when they first arrived in the United States, they found American election campaigns peculiar and more than a little distasteful. Who would want to be led, they asked, by people continually and bombastically proclaiming their unique and superior qualifications for office? Real leaders surely wouldn't be such braggarts.

Reflecting upon these observations, with which I could not help but have some sympathy, the fifth article to the constitution of the Islamic Republic of Iran came to mind. Despite the widespread notion that this document that formally conferred power upon Ayatollah Khomeini is nothing but a recipe for theocracy, if not fascist dictatorship, there is nothing divine in its justification of Khomeini's elevation. It reads: "[In the absence of God's divinely appointed leader], the governance and leadership of the nation devolve upon the just and pious *faqih* [religious jurist] who is acquainted with the circumstances of his age; courageous, resourceful, and possessed of administrative ability; *and recognized and accepted as leader by the majority of the people.*" No election, no clash of personalities in the campaign, simply acclamation by the mass of the people, or, according to subsequent constitutional provisions, acclamation by a popularly elected committee of experts deliberating on the people's behalf.

I explored this matter further in a conversation in May 1992 with Hasan Turabi, the widely recognized leader of the Islamic political movement in the Sudan. He was quite familiar with the Prophet's words and said that he and his colleagues had spent many hours pondering how an Islamically grounded democratic process could function without self-nomination, self-promotion, and other objectionable aspects of democracy in the Western mold. Advancing the names of "observant" and "God-conscious" candidates for election and informing the voters of their qualifications in a neutral fashion seemed to him to be serious structural issues, issues that should be addressed at a constitutional level rather than left to the vagaries of party politics as in Western democracies.

Though some leaders in the current wave of Islamic political awakening eschew the word democracy because of its Western overtones, they consistently express support for elective, constitutional government, which they see as implicit in the practice of the earliest Islamic community in Mecca and Medina. Critics of Islamic politics often dismiss this putative precedent as a distortion of historical fact to fit present-day political needs, but the potency of Muhammad's words in stimulating modern thinkers to ponder an aspect of "democratic" process that is not only neglected in Western political thought, but sometimes frustratingly dysfunctional in practice, proves that words thought to have been uttered in Arabia in the seventh century, and frequently reported in an Iranian town in the eleventh century—though I still don't know exactly why—can profoundly influence a modern political force espousing the virtues of electoral politics and constitutional government.

There is nevertheless a stark contrast between this apparent Islamic ideal of the leader as a modest and reticent individual who does not actively court adulation and a much better-known Middle Eastern pattern of egregious self-promotion and vainglorious display. Secular leaders from Turkey's Mustafa Kemal Atatürk and Tunisia's Habib Bourgiba, to Egypt's Gamal Abd al-Nasir and Anwar al-Sadat, to the late shah of Iran and such potentates of today as Muammar Qadhdhafi, Hafiz al-Asad, and Saddam Husain have accustomed three generations of Middle Easterners to seeing the image of their august leader majestically adorning every public place, and usually the front page of every newspaper. Modesty and reticence have been as rare in modern Middle Eastern politics as reluctance to seize power without being asked.

This gap between religious aphorism and secular political practice prompts a question: how have religious political ideals that have lain unexpressed for generations regained their potency at the end of the twentieth century? As a historian of Islamic history, with as much right and aptitude as any other person to reflect upon and try to reimagine the human past, I maintain that, whether or not they ultimately live by the ideals they espouse, today's Islamic activists have inherited from their historical tradition a claim to authority quite different from that of the familiar Middle Eastern monarchs and dictators, a claim that holds substantial promise of restructuring the political, cultural, and moral atmosphere of the Middle East.

The authority I see them wielding is the ability to answer the questions raised by believers in a fashion that convinces the believers of their correctness. A nationalist governor or party leader might attempt to answer people's questions, too, of course; but lacking a grounding in religious authority, his answers will always ring hollow compared with those emanating from people to whom questioners have turned because of their manifest piety, religious learning, or other sign qualifying them for religious leadership. Nationalistic answers that once seemed heady and progressive, buttressed by a purported superiority of cultural and intellectual values originally imported from the West, now fall flat before the whispered—or shouted— suspicion that they are actually symptoms of the malignancy of cultural imperialism. By contrast, answers that purport to be rooted in Islamic tradition, even when the reading of that tradition departs substantially from anything that has gone before, have a much stronger likelihood of winning the questioner's confidence and loyalty.

This description of the popular acclamation of religiously credited leaders that undergirds today's Islamic activism will be illustrated and elaborated in the final chapter of this book, wherein I will try to explain why I believe that the future of the Muslim world lies with the Islamic political alternative. But it would be pointless to enter upon such a discussion without first explaining how, why, and when this particular structuring of religious authority came into being. This will require more than a historical summary, however, because the history of Islam as commonly narrated leads in the wrong direction. One must look with different historical eyes to see the pattern that seems to me most significant. The purpose of this book is to provide this different view of the past, primarily for its own sake but also to help clarify a different view of the present.

These chapters culminate my twenty-five years of involvement with nontraditional sources for Islamic history and are inspired by a deep dissatisfaction with the usual way of recounting that history. We are living in a crucial period of Islamic history, arguably the most intellectually and spiritually vigorous of the last thousand years. Muslims around the world are looking to their illustrious past for solace and guidance in changing times, and non-Muslims are scrutinizing that same history for clues to the nature and fortune of contemporary Islamic movements. Both are incompletely served by the histories at hand.

The story of Islam has always privileged the view from the center:

In 611 A.D. a man in Mecca heard a voice that he considered—as do the 800 million Muslims who today accept him as God's messenger—to be revealing God's word. Some three years later, Muhammad began to recite the growing body of revelation in public, and the handful of close friends and family members who believed in him grew into a small community.

In 622, hostile pressures from unbelieving Meccans forced Muhammad and his community to relocate to the nearby oasis community of Medina. The people of Medina, along with a growing stream of converts from Mecca and from surrounding Arab tribes, swelled Muhammad's community. They called themselves Muslims—those who make submission, Islam, to the will of God.

By the time of the Prophet's death in 632, Islam had reached into almost every part of Arabia. But according to God's revelation, Muhammad was to be the last of His messengers. So who could fill the void he left behind? Experimenting as they went, the Prophet's closest friends and family members invented a new political institution called the caliphate. The caliph succeeded to Muhammad's leadership, but without the sanction of divine communication and without a mandate to deviate from the Prophet's words or practice. The revelations were collected and standardized in book form—the Quran (Koran)—to preserve them from inadvertent corruption.

After a shaky start, in which the first caliph confronted tribes that tried to abandon their earlier allegiance to the Prophet, the caliphate presided over one of the most remarkable episodes of conquest in world history. By 711, Spain had been conquered in the far west, and southern Pakistan to the east. There had also been a change in caliphate. A civil war over the succession to the assassinated third caliph ended in 661 with the Umayyad dynasty, based in Syria, supplanting the caliphate in Medina. The crux of the civil war was a political split between the Umayyads and the Prophet's first cousin and son-in-law Ali ibn Abi Talib. The supporters of Ali and his descendants developed, over the succeeding two centuries, a religious rationale for their allegiance and thus formed the Shi'at Ali, or "Party of Ali," better known as the Shi'ite sect of Islam.

In 750 the Umayyads crumbled before an onslaught from eastern Iran, and the Abbasid family took over the caliphate, moving their seat of government a few years later to their newly built capital of Baghdad. Abbasid power and wealth eclipsed all that had gone before, but within two hundred years their realm, too, was disintegrating. Military insubordination by slave soldiers, financial disarray, bureaucratic corruption, and the opportunistic secession of one province after another led to Baghdad's takeover by rude Iranian tribesmen led by the Buyid family.

For a century the Abbasid caliphs chafed under Buyid rule, their temporal power gone, and their religious authority in question because of the Buyids' adherence to Shi'ite beliefs. Then a new force from the east, the Seljuq Turks, chased the Buyids out of Baghdad and liberated the caliph. But liberation really meant the substitution of Seljuq, albeit Sunni, domination for Buyid. Not until the beginning of the twelfth century did discord within the Seljuq family permit the caliphs to attempt a modest revival. They had scarcely gotten on their feet again when yet another eastern invader, this time Genghis Khan's Mongols, struck the lands of Islam. In 1258, Genghis Khan's grandson Hulagu sacked Baghdad and put the last Abbasid caliph to death.

With that, the view from the center evaporates, at least temporarily. Though a simulacrum of the Abbasid caliphate was soon resurrected in Cairo, it served only to legitimize the pretensions of the warlords of Egypt and Syria, the Mamluk generals who originated as imported slaves and commanded armies of Mamluk slaves. No historian considers the Abbasid caliphate in Cairo a proper continuation of what existed from 632 to 1258 because, unlike the earlier caliphate, it made no plausible claim to being the universal government of all Muslims.

Many accounts of Islamic history end at this point. Almost all recognize a major break between pre- and post-Mongol history. The later history is dominated not by the central focus of the caliphate, but by its pale reflection in the histories of the Ottoman

Empire, governing Turkey, the Balkans, and, after 1516, most of the lands of the Arabs; and the Shi'ite Safavid Empire in Iran. Though prosperous, at least in their heydays, and powerful militarily, the rulers' lack of religious authority prevented them from recovering the aura of the caliphate. The view from the center follows their dynastic trajectories without reading into them the larger meanings ascribed to the vicissitudes of the caliphs.

Then comes the modern world: Napoleon's invasion of Egypt in 1798; the nineteenth-century reform and Europeanization of the Ottoman Empire, foreshadowed by that of its quasi-independent Egyptian province; financial and military disarray late in the century; and finally World War I and the dismemberment of the sultan's realm. After the war, a plethora of new or reconstructed countries clutters the historical narrative, forcing historians to concentrate upon one or another favorite theme—the Arab-Israeli conflict, Arab nationalism, Turkish republicanism, Iranian monarchy, etc.

Only with the Islamic Revolution in Iran in 1979 does a central drama reemerge, the struggle of Muslim activist movements, seeking to recenter society and politics around Islamic values, against dictatorial rulers struggling to maintain control. Back on center stage after centuries of playing only a supporting role, Islam makes claims that thrill millions, and curdle the blood of millions more.

And that, more or less, is the view from the center down to today.

What, one might ask, is wrong with telling the story this way? No one can deny the glory of the caliphate, the might of the Ottomans, or the transformative impact of modern Europe. Nor, indeed, do I intend to deny these things. This book is intended to complement, not replace, the view from the center. The caliphs and sultans—at least some of them—deserve their fame. Epic conquests and tragic defeats are too much the stuff of history to be shoved aside. And above all, the story of Muhammad and his early followers has been a linchpin of Islamic identity for fourteen centuries.

Yet the view from the center leaves too many questions unanswered. Where did all those Muslims come from? Why did they develop a coherent culture or civilization while Europe, despite its Christian homogeneity, was so fractious and diverse? If their society is legitimately tagged with a religious label, what is the role of religion in that society? Whom do people follow? Who responds to their needs?

The view from the center portrays Islamic history as an outgrowth from a single nucleus, a spreading inkblot labeled "the caliphate." But what other than a political label held Islam together? And why did its political cohesion evaporate after little more than two centuries, never to reoccur?

The view from the edge holds out the possibility of addressing questions like these. It starts from the fact that most Muslims outside the Arabian peninsula proper are not the descendants of the Arabs who participated in the Islamic conquests. When their ancestors made their confession of faith that there was no God but God, and that Muhammad was the Messenger of God, they did not do so on the basis of personal familiarity with the Prophet's own community in Mecca and Medina, or even on the basis of familiarity with the Quran. Most of them learned about Islam after they entered the community, not before; and what they learned never assumed a homogeneous character, though from the fourteenth century on there was a strong impulse toward normative homogeneity.

For its first five centuries, despite the nominal inclusion of all Muslims in a single conceptual community called the umma, Islam was divided into many communities, some doctrinal, some ritual, some geographic. The view from the center, in seeking to explain the apparent homogeneity of Islamic society in later centuries, itself something of an illusion, projects back into the days of the caliphate a false aura of uniformity, leaving untold the complex and strife-ridden tale of how Islamic society actually developed.

Where the view from the center starts with a political institution, watches it expand mightily, and then observes its dissolution, the view from the edge does the opposite. It starts with individuals and small communities scattered over a vast and poorly integrated realm, speaking over a dozen different languages, and steeped in religious and cultural traditions of great diversity. From this unpromising start, an impressive measure of social, institutional, and doctrinal cohesion slowly emerges, the product of immense

8

human effort, but even more of historical currents beyond contemporary perception or control.

At the center of the story seen from this angle are the ulama, today called mullahs in Iran or hojas in Turkey, that remarkable body of religious scholars and moral guides holding the conscience of Islam in its grasp down to the present day, though not without serious challenge from new sources of religious leadership in the late twentieth century. But the ulama are not present as the tale begins. The view from the edge is very much the story of when, how, and why this group of people came into existence, destined, as they were, to be the instrument of drawing Islam together and, today, of helping to guide it through a new and dangerous period of change.

Though the view from the center focuses upon a succession of great capital cities, almost to the exclusion of the countryside, the view from the edge is not that from a geographical (or political) periphery. The edge in Islamic history exists wherever people make the decision to cross a social boundary and join the Muslim community, either through religious conversion, or, under modern conditions, through nominal Muslims rededicating themselves to Islam as the touchstone of their social identity, or recasting their Muslim identities in a modern urban context.

For the first two centuries the edge was virtually everywhere. Non-Muslims were the majority. The problems and contributions entrained by their adoption of Islam were felt from the Pyrenees to the Indus River. But they weren't felt uniformly. Each locality had its own microhistory of Islam. Each one was a spring; over the centuries, some springs went dry, others were stopped up, and still others were channeled into larger streams. Even those who might be inclined to conceptualize Islam in later times as a single grand river can benefit from contemplating the variety of its sources, and contemplating the dry courses of channels not taken.

This being said, it must also be apparent that the view from the edge can never be seen whole. There are too many fragmented stories, too many different locales, and, most important, too little data. The richness of Islamic historical sources favors the view from the center. The lives and deeds of Muhammad and his companions have been preserved with great piety and detail. Annalists beholden to caliphs and sultans have dutifully chronicled their political patrons' acts. Others have deliberately written the history of Islam as a centrally focused narrative, partly to convince pious readers of the reality of divine providence. And those few original documents that survive speak either of governmental business, or reflect fragments of dealings that are too private or parochial to provide a broad historical context.

Were it not for one genre of literature, the view from the edge for the early centuries would be impossible to grasp. While most of the ulama busied themselves with studying and writing books on law, theology, Quran interpretation, and the traditions of the Prophet, a few devoted much time and energy to compiling biographical dictionaries (the character and evolution of these often voluminous works will be discussed in chapter 7). It suffices here to note that the names of hundreds of thousands of individuals have been preserved in these works, along with varying amounts of data relating to them. The scope of these compilations varies. Some are devoted to a particular profession or religious orientation. Some are more general and reflect the compiler's literary aspirations. Those that lie at the heart of this book are devoted to the notable people, usually, but not exclusively, male religious scholars, who lived in, came from, or passed through particular cities. Many of these local biographical dictionaries were compiled from the tenth through the twelfth centuries, particularly in Iran; only a few have survived.

The data in these books are varied, unpredictable, and tantalizingly incomplete. Though their value as historical sources has slowly been recognized over the past three decades, they are still rarely used. My own previous writings include one book that attempts to cobble together a profile of the religiously oriented society of the Iranian city of Nishapur[2] and another that essays a portrayal of the course of conversion to Islam based on a quantitative study of the names preserved in biographical dictionaries.[3]

However, years of contemplation of these works has gradually persuaded me that they contain glimpses of a far broader history than that of a single city or social process. They emanate from milieus far removed from caliphal courts and government offices. Though they tell no more about village and rural life than the conventional sources, they do reflect the lives of ordinary, albeit educated, families. Moreover, in their near-systematic disregard of governors, commanders, and administrators, they seem almost to advertise the existence of a history that does not revolve around the central government.

Decocting an alternative view of Islamic history goes far beyond simply tapping the information in local biographical dictionaries. Education, urbanization, economics, demographics, migration, and institution building form major topics of this book. But whatever the other sources called upon to illuminate the view from the edge, its inspiration and many of its insights go back to biographical dictionaries, particularly those of the Iranian cities of Isfahan, Gorgan, and Nishapur.

Is the view from the edge, then, an Iranian view? Within the context of this particular book, the answer must be a qualified yes. But the processes analyzed were undoubtedly mirrored in other locales, too, albeit in different ways. I maintain that Iran played a unique and crucial role in the origination and diffusion of institutions that eventually contributed to the centripetal tendency of later Islamic civilization, but other areas were important, too. My hope is that the approaches suggested here will prompt other historians to investigate the views from other edges.

My purpose in writing this book goes beyond stimulating a new kind of historical enterprise, however. As mentioned at the outset, it is also intended for readers concerned with the contemporary resurgence of Muslim political and social activism. A cardinal failure of the view from the center is its inability to explain how and why Islam became so rooted in the social structure of the Middle East and North Africa, not to mention those parts of Asia and Africa to which Islam spread after the tenth century. The rise and fall of the caliphate and of the Ottoman Empire leaves untold the story of the emergence and institutionalization of the ulama and, in the post-Mongol centuries, of the tug of war between local religious custom and the ulama's determination to promote their own more homogeneous version of the faith. Closer to hand, the history of the disempowerment of the ulama and the erosion of their institutional base by the centralizing, modernizing regimes of the nineteenth and twentieth centuries conveys the false impression that Islam's claim to service the needs and aspirations of the community of the faithful was thereby fundamentally and permanently reduced.

Readers unaccustomed to searching deeper than the nineteenth century for the roots of our modern condition may not credit an assertion that the eleventh century is as, if not more, important for understanding the origin of today's political and social forces than the nineteenth. It is the burden of this book to persuade them that this is so. The nature of Islamic religious authority and the source of its profound impact upon the lives of Muslims—the Muslims of yesterday, today, and tomorrow—cannot be grasped without comprehending the historical evolution of Islamic society. Nor can such a comprehension be gained from a cursory perusal of the central narrative of Islam. The view from the edge is needed, because, in truth, the edge ultimately creates the center.

1

ORALITY AND AUTHORITY

*Whoever has lied in the transmission of
hadith, let him take his seat in the hellfire.*
—Hadith quoted in HAMZA AL-SAHMI,
TA'RIKH JURJAN

In the year 1146 a religious scholar from northeastern Iran named
Abd al-Karim al-Sam'ani completed a book on proper conduct in
teaching and studying *hadith*. A hadith[1] consisted of a statement
made or a description of an act performed by the Prophet Muhammad, preceded by a list of names of varying length called an *isnad*.
The names in the isnad recapitulated a series of educational events:
"I heard from A, who said he heard from B, who said he heard from
C, who said he heard from the Messenger of God, God's prayers
and peace be upon him." Every isnad was thought to bespeak a history of transmission in which each person listed heard with his or
her own ears, from his or her predecessor, the words ascribed to the
Prophet or the description of his actions.

Since the divinely revealed Quran, the only Muslim document
generally (though not universally by non-Muslim scholars) recognized as dating from the Prophet's lifetime, seldom makes more
than indirect reference to events in Muhammad's life, almost everything Muslims knew and know about the Prophet's life and behavior was preserved in the form of hadith, or in the hadith-based
"biography" of Muhammad, called the *Sira*, which in its current
form dates from two centuries after his death. Yet at the time of al-
Sam'ani, and implicitly even today,[2] no hadith was considered
authoritative without its accompanying isnad. "The isnad is the

13

believer's weapon; when he has no weapon, with what will he fight?" said one famous hadith reciter. "Every religion has cavalry, and the cavalry of this religion are those who appear in isnads," said another.[3] This does not necessarily mean that isnads reflecting actual oral transmission were systematically attached to every hadith during the first several generations. But later scholars and students believed they were, and this belief conferred authority upon both the text and the transmitter.

This system of preserving and transmitting religious lore was an oral tradition, not a memory tradition. Though many hadith transmitters did commit to memory the texts and the isnads they pronounced in their classes, their students usually wrote down every hadith verbatim, including its isnad. Al-Sam'ani testifies to this in the section of his book devoted to the tools for taking notes in class: inkwell, pen, pencase, penknife, ink, and paper.[4] And the fame of certain hadith scholars was symbolized by mention of how many inkwells (as many as a thousand) were put out for their class,[5] or how many pens were broken in mourning for them.[6]

By al-Sam'ani's time, boys with sufficient family encouragement and command of Arabic usually began to attend hadith sessions between the ages of five and ten.[7] The teacher normally held a class once a week, but several teachers were likely to be active in any sizable town so a student could pursue his hadith study more or less intensively. Taking down hadith from a teacher's dictation formed the core of early education in prosperous, religiously oriented families, a group probably amounting to fewer than four percent of the total urban population.[8]

Older students sometimes traveled to different cities to learn what the teachers there had to report. However, by their early twenties, most young men had turned their attention to business and family matters. In the northeastern Iranian city of Nishapur, only 166 local hadith teachers became sufficiently prominent between the years 929 and 1120 to have as many as three students mentioned in the 1080 scholarly biographies that include the names of teachers.[9] This left only the most leisured or the most strongly motivated to go on to more advanced and intellectually challenging studies, such as Islamic law, theology, Quran interpretation, and, of course, sophisticated higher criticism of hadith. Fewer still went on to study such secular subjects as medicine, philosophy, and astronomy.

The habit of attending hadith classes persisted, however. Though older attendees did not always write down the hadith they heard, unless they were assisting a son or nephew who was not yet able to take dictation for himself,[10] they delighted in gleaning new information about the Prophet and were particularly apt to attend hadith sessions given by scholars passing through town from distant places. Several instances are recorded of the religious scholars of a town honoring visiting political figures by convening a class for them to recite hadith.

On the occasion of an embassy from a petty ruler, Manuchihr ibn Qabus, to a mightier ruler, Mahmud of Ghazna, passing through the city of Nishapur in 1015, the order in which the visitors presented their hadith is preserved so that one can see that the ambassador who was the *ra'is*, or "head," of the city of Gorgan, outranked the city's judge (*qadi*), who in turn outranked the third member of the party, even though the third member almost certainly knew more hadith than either predecessor.[11] The religious elite turned out to listen to the visitors' recitations of a few hadith in the way that today people go to hear speeches by visiting dignitaries. The import of the particular hadith recited, as of today's visiting dignitary speech, was less important than the honor the local people were able to show their visitors by attending.

The association between religious authority and the oral transmission of sacred lore that was forged early in the lives of the urban social elite thus persisted as a model of authority in later years. Learning a hadith from a book was far less authoritative than hearing it directly, even read aloud from a book—providing, of course, that the person you heard it from had heard it personally from someone earlier. Consider some of the categories of people whose transmission was deemed false and unacceptable by the sophisticated hadith scholars called *muhaddithun*:

> People who heard . . . books which had been written coming from shaikhs whom they had met, but who had not written down what they heard when they heard it and took little account of it till they were advanced in years and were asked

15

for traditions. Then ignorance and cupidity incited them to recite those books from books which were bought, which they had not heard and which they had no right to communicate, yet they imagined that they were truthful in their transmissions.[12]

People who wrote down traditions, traveled in search of them, and had a reputation in the subject, but whose books were destroyed in different ways, by being burnt, worn out, plundered, lost at sea, or stolen; yet as often as they were questioned about traditions they recited them from other people's books, or from their memory by conjecture.[13]

This stress on the authority of oral transmission mirrored the priority given to oral testimony over documentary evidence in the Islamic law courts and carried over into matters that had nothing to do with religion. For example, a certain Ja'far ibn Ahmad al-Makki al-Jurjani said: "I heard Yahya ibn Khalid al-Barmaki [a famous vizier] say that he heard his father [another famous vizier] say that he heard Ibn al-Muqaffa' [another famous vizier] say that the vizier of Kisra [the pre-Islamic Persian shah Khosrow II] said: 'Proper manners [adab] are made up of ten things: three from the category of urbanity [shahrijīya], three from generosity [mihrijiya], three from Arab-ness ['arabiya], and one from birth [mawlida]. As for Arab-ness, the three are poetry, horsebreeding [sabaha], and casting the lance.' "[14] Here the isnad consists of a string of famous viziers, or chief administrators, serving the caliphs of the Abbasid dynasty in the late eighth century. Their alleged testimony to the fact that their pre-Islamic predecessor actually made the remark quoted gives the text its authority. The form of the report, in other words, derives from hadith, but its substance does not even pertain to Islam. That the story is preserved in a biographical dictionary devoted to the lives of religious scholars confirms the association.

Al-Sam'ani's manual on teaching hadith illuminates the extraordinary power of oral authority in its description of the etiquette a teacher should observe in preparing for class. "Let him begin with using a toothpick, for Abu al-Karam Nasr Allah ibn Muhammad ibn Muhammad ibn Makhlad al-Azdi related to us in Wasit, that Abu Tammam Ali ibn Muhammad ibn al-Hasan al-Wasiti the Judge

16

related to him, that Abu al-Fadl Ubaid Allah ibn Abd al-Rahman al-Zuhri related to him, that his father related to him, that Muhammad ibn Muhammad ibn Sulaiman al-Baghandi related to him, that Muslim related to him, that Bahr ibn Kaniz al-Saqqa' related to him, that Uthman ibn Saj related to him, from Sa'id ibn Jubair, from Ali ibn Abi Talib, God's mercy be upon him, that he said: 'The Messenger of God, God's prayers and peace be upon him, said: "Your mouths are the paths of the Quran, so purify them with a toothpick." ' "15

In every succeeding stipulation about the teacher's behavior al-Sam'ani similarly cites the words or deeds of the Prophet, complete with the requisite isnad, to demonstrate the authoritative precedent for the behavior. In this way he demands of the teacher the following:

> Let him trim his fingernails if they are long. . . . Let him trim his mustache. . . . Let him smooth his messed up hair. . . . Let him put on white clothes. . . . Let him wrap on a turban. . . . Let him comb his beard. . . . Let him use some perfume if he has any. . . . Let him look at himself in a mirror. . . . Let him walk at a moderate pace in going to class. . . . Let him begin by greeting whoever of the Muslims meets him. . . . Let him give a general greeting to all the Muslims, including the young boys and the adolescents. . . . When he has arrived at class, let him restrain whoever was sitting from standing up for him since neglecting this is one of the banes of the soul.16

By citing the words or deeds of the Prophet in support of each behavior he stipulates, al-Sam'ani is essentially instructing the teacher to model his personal behavior on that of Muhammad when he is preparing to recite for his students the Prophet's words. This tone similarly pervades the portion of the book devoted to the behavior of students in class, whom he bids to be sober and reverential in manner. He cites a seven-step isnad going back to a particularly punctilious hadith reciter named Waki'. "I was with Waki' [says the earliest transmitter] when he heard some words and movement among the hadith students. He said, 'Oh students, what is this movement? You are people; you should act with gravity.' "17 It should be noted that in this, as in many other instances in al-

Sam'ani's book, the isnad is attached to the words and deeds of someone other than Muhammad. Technically, therefore, this is not a hadith. However, the chain of oral transmission lends the story greater authority than would have been understood from an unadorned statement of what Waki' had said, no matter how distinguished and well known he was.

The inescapable conclusion proceeding from a consideration of al-Sam'ani's book on classroom etiquette is that he saw the transmitter of hadith confronting his students as the Prophet's surrogate, mimicking the Prophet's actions in preparing for class, repeating the Prophet's words, and ritually reciting the names of all those who had performed the same act of pious transmission before him. Given the youth of the students and the gravity of the class situation, it seems apparent that the students accepted as true whatever the teacher said, and that they accepted the procedure by which the transmission of lore took place as normative. Doubting the truth of the teacher's words under these circumstances would have been unthinkable.

Yet there was no real assurance that every hadith was factually true. Specialists on hadith scholarship, the muhaddithun, recognized that there were many ways in which a hadith could be defective.[18] It might be outright fraudulent, something invented by someone seeking to impart authority to a political, doctrinal, or ritual position he espoused; or it might simply have an incomplete or faulty isnad. An example of an incomplete isnad might be one that contained steps in which the hadith reciter was not fully identified, like "I heard from a man of the tribe of Tamim. . . ." A faulty isnad, on the other hand, might allege that A had heard the hadith from B while a muhaddith would know that B died before A was born. In this case, the hadith might actually be true and the inconsistency the result of a name being left out in the transmission of the isnad, but a scrupulous muhaddith would reject it anyway. Then again, there were certain individuals who were reputed to be liars or fabricators.[19] One of their names appearing in an isnad would invalidate the hadith.

The muhaddithun divided all hadith into weak (*da'if*) and sound (*sahih*), with many in-between categories and nuances; and in the ninth century, some two hundred and fifty years after Muhammad death, some of them prepared collections of the sound hadith they had winnowed from the vastly larger body of hadith then in circulation. During this same period the idea became widely accepted among legal thinkers that sound hadith should be considered a source of law second in authority only to the Quran.

This evolution of hadith culminated in the general acceptance, by the thirteenth century, of six books of sound traditions as canonical, at least for the Sunni majority of the population.[20] Shi'ites recognized four other collections as canonical. By that time, Islamic law had become heavily dependent upon the scholarly consensus as to which hadith were sound. What is less evident in this well-known evolution is the educational conflict that arose as a result. Once it became generally accepted that most hadith were weak, and that definitive collections of sound ones could be found in books, the system of oral transmission inevitably came into question.

Was a student supposed to listen to his teacher as a skeptic and write down only those traditions he deemed to be valid? Obviously not. The teacher was standing before him in the persona of the Prophet himself. It would have been unthinkable for a child or a teenager who had never studied the science of isnad analysis and verification of hadith to doubt the truth of his teacher's words. But wouldn't the student be better informed about the faith by memorizing one of the books of sound traditions? Perhaps so, at least in the eyes of the legal specialists; but reading something in a book was not authoritative. According to the teaching protocol outlined by al-Sam'ani, you had to hear it read aloud to you, and read to you by someone who had heard it read to him by someone else who had had it read to him, and so on, back to the compiler of the book.

For example, the *Sahih* collection of al-Bukhari, one of the six that eventually became canonical, was well-known in Nishapur in the tenth century. Nevertheless, fifteen people (a sizable number in comparison with known students of other teachers) are known to have made the two-hundred-mile journey from Nishapur to the village of Kushmaihan near Marv to hear the text read aloud by a man named Abu al-Haitham Muhammad al-Kushmaihani. By the year 1050, it seems, al-Kushmaihani was the last man still living who had

19

copied the book as his own teacher had dictated it, reading from the copy he had made in a class taught by al-Bukhari himself.[21] Someone wanting simply to know what was in al-Bukhari's *Sahih* could have stayed in Nishapur and read a copy, but anyone who aspired someday to teach the text had to hear it read aloud by someone whose isnad reached back to the author.

This conflict between the authority inherent in a book written by an important scholar and the authority conferred by a chain of oral transmission was not sharply articulated. Al-Sam'ani might warn against someone reciting "rare" hadith, i.e., ones that probably could not meet the standards for being sound because of having an isnad that could not be fully verified; but biographical data on hadith transmitters specify that some of them took special pride in collecting precisely such rare hadith. Similarly, students might be warned that a hadith with a "high" isnad, that is, with only a few names intervening between the Prophet and the final hearer, was no more likely to be sound than one with many names, assuming the many names were of reputable reciters; but people still sought to have very young students listen to very old men in an effort to obtain high isnads.[22]

But rare hadith and high isnads gradually became less important as, over a three-hundred-year period, the canonical collections of sound hadith became increasingly authoritative, and hadith classes came to be devoted primarily to teaching them and a few other established written texts. Orality in hadith teaching persisted, but by the sixteenth century, the best isnads were considered those that stretched back to the author of a book, or to a particularly famous teacher, rather than to an individual reciter of unanthologized hadith, as in al-Sam'ani's day. Most hadith deemed by the muhaddithun to be weak died away, and with them dwindled the prominence as teachers of individual reciters with personal isnads going back to the Prophet. After all, if the only worthwhile hadith were those in the books, even including those hadith collections that continued to be consulted occasionally in addition to the six canonical works, what place remained for the scholar who had collected hadith a few at a time on his own?

Al-Sam'ani's almost pleading insistence on the absolute necessity of oral transmission in the introductory part of his book betrays the fact that by the early twelfth century the earlier pattern of oral transmission was already fading. After saying that "the soundness [of the words of the Prophet] cannot be known without a sound isnad, and soundness in isnads cannot be known except by transmission by one reliable source from another, by one honest witness from another,"[23] he goes on to quote various famous hadith reciters to the effect that "your hadith are worth nothing without a control and a seal, that is, an isnad" [al-Zuhri], "the isnad is the ornament of hadith" [Sufyan al-Thawri], "someone who seeks the matter of the faith without an isnad is like someone who would go up to the roof without a ladder" [Mubarak], and "isnads are part of religion; if it weren't for isnads, anyone could say whatever he wished" [Abd Allah ibn Mubarak].[24] These attestations to the absolute necessity of isnads fly in the face of the fact that by al-Sam'ani's time the authoritative collections of sound hadith were already nearly three centuries old, and the system of education he was recommending already becoming obsolete.

The upshot of this process was the development of a homogeneous corpus of authoritative Islamic texts that contributed greatly to a growing uniformity of Islamic belief and practice throughout the vast area in which Muslims lived. But there was also a certain loss, not only of sound traditions that had to be discarded because their isnads had become flawed with the passage of generations, but the loss also of local versions of Islam that had previously been supported by weak traditions transmitted within a specific locality.

The student who in the year 1000 had sat at the feet of an elderly hadith reciter in his home or shop and learned what Islam was all about by hearing him intone the words of the Prophet that he had personally collected was succeeded by the student in 1300 who was more likely to be living and studying in a building dedicated to education, a *madrasa*, and hearing a professor read out loud, with an isnad that went back to its compiler, one of the accepted books of sound traditions. Concomitant with this transition in education was a weakening of the linkage between orality and authority. The Prophet's words still carried ultimate authority in the later Islamic centuries, but they carried authority because they were "true,"

21

whether read in a book or learned in a class. The aura attached to their oral transmission and the chain of authority tying them direct-ly to Muhammad did not entirely fade, for students still prided themselves on receiving their teachers' permission to teach specific books; but its glow became diffused as the sense of personal con-nection with the Prophet receded.

In writing the history of Islamic education, scholars have almost invariably looked backward from this later period and searched for its roots in earlier times.[25] They have not often recognized that things were fundamentally different before the proliferation of new educational institutions late in the eleventh century. Nor have they appreciated that, in some ways, the impact of education on society was stronger in that earlier period, when oral authority resting on personal hadith transmission gave a distinctive tone to elite urban society, than in the later period when learning became cluttered with buildings, professorships, stipends, and competition for acad-emic preferment.

In the following chapters I will seek to explain how the relation-ship between religious authority and society developed in the early Islamic centuries, how that relationship changed between the eleventh and the fourteenth centuries, and what the consequences of the change were for later periods. Finally, I will address the importance of this relationship to any understanding of today's cur-rent of Islamic activism.

2

PROPHET, QURAN, AND COMPANIONS

The Messenger of God, God's prayers and
peace be upon him, said: "Whoever slanders
my Companions, upon them shall be the
damnation of God, and of the angels, and of
the whole people."
—Hadith quoted in HAMZA AL-SAHMI,
TA'RIKH JURJAN

The origins of oral authority in Islam date back to the time of the Prophet Muhammad. The Quran, after all, originated as an oral document, Muhammad's recitation of the words he heard when in a state of receiving revelation. How to interpret Muhammad's role is debatable, however. Muslim tradition, over the centuries, has constructed Muhammad as the "perfect man," the unique communicator of God's final word to mankind. Counterposed to this, and to even more idealizing Muslim viewpoints, is an array of constructions put forward by non-Muslims working in the Western historical tradition. Increasingly in recent years, these constructions have concentrated on a quest for a historical Muhammad, a kind of "demythologized" Muhammad put forward on debatable grounds by non-Muslims as a better, more factual alternative to the Muslims' traditional, piety-bound understandings.

Entering deeply into this debate would be fruitless for the purposes of this book.[1] Nevertheless, it is necessary to state that despite the questions raised by the demythologizers, and the evidence of spurious hadith and invented transmitters, I cannot imagine how so

23

abundant and cohesive a religious tradition as that of the first century of Islam could have come into being without a substantial base in actual historical event. Concocting, coordinating, and sustaining a fantasy, to wit, that Muhammad either did not exist or lived an entirely different sort of life than that traditionally depicted, and inculcating it consistently and without demur among a largely illiterate community of Muslims dispersed from the Pyrenees to the Indus River would have required a conspiracy of monumental proportion. It would also have required universal agreement among believers who came to differ violently on issues of far less import.

Being entirely unconvinced by the evidence brought forward by the demythologizers, I shall assume that Muhammad did exist, that he was the vehicle through which the Quran came to be known, and that he did gather around himself a community in Mecca and Medina that perpetuated its existence after his death. As for the tens of thousands of details that adorn this historical skeleton, I shall proceed on the premise that the Muslim representations of Muhammad, and his community, however changing and various they may have been, are the most important and valid for present purposes because, at any given point in history, they have constituted the operative reality for the Muslim community, just as they do today for most Muslims.

What is important here is not so much what Muslims have thought about the Prophet, as how they arrived at their understanding in the early centuries. After all, if the hadith came to be the paramount extra-Quranic source of authoritative Muslim lore, and the hadith relate the words and deeds of Muhammad, the bases of this phenomenon are of great significance. Not being a divine person, Muhammad's words and deeds while not in a state of receiving revelation might be considered theologically ambiguous. They certainly did not enjoy the same status as the divine revelations collected in the Quran. On the other hand, they unquestionably merited special attention since Muhammad was the founder of the umma and God's chosen vehicle for His final revelation to mankind. But how much special attention did they deserve? Who was to decide?

Since a paucity of verifiable contemporary evidence makes problematic almost any positive assertion about the first century of Islam, aside from the rudimentary narrative skeleton, my concern will be more with establishing the social parameters within which the understanding of Muhammad's role as a human guide to pious behavior developed rather than with trying to prove or disprove the authenticity of any particular hadith or body of hadith. After all, any hadith that was understood by a pious listener, at any point in time, to be authoritative became ipso facto a "true" biographical datum about the Prophet.

Take, for example, the following hadith embedded in the eleventh-century biographical dictionary of Gorgan: According to the authorities listed in the isnad, Ali, Muhammad's first cousin and son-in-law said, "The Messenger of God, God's prayers and peace be upon him, ordered me to eat garlic. He said: 'Were it not that the angels send down [revelations] to me, I would eat it.' "[2]

There are several ways of approaching this as a potential historical datum. First, there is the way of the hadith specialists, the muhaddithun: examine the isnad and determine whether every person in the chain of authority is known, considered reliable, and plausibly connectable with the persons on either side, that is, overlapping in lifespan. Then see whether the same hadith is reported according to one, or preferably more, entirely independent isnads. If these conditions are fulfilled, and there is no intrinsic contradiction in the message (for example, the nonexistence of garlic in the Arabian peninsula), then the hadith is sound, and Muhammad should be considered to have held the indicated opinion concerning garlic.

A second approach, arising out of the Western critical method, would be to assume that there is a strong likelihood that this tradition was interpolated into the body of Muslim lore, all possibly spurious, at some specific time for some specific reason. One might look at the chain of authorities and try to identify some invented individual or person suspected of fabrications in other instances, or possibly to pin down the locale or milieu in which the hadith was fabricated. More likely, however, one would focus upon the substance of the hadith rather than the isnad and ask whether there is any reason why garlic might have been considered a questionable food for the Prophet but not for his son-in-law and, by implication, for ordinary Muslims.

One reason for basing a permissive attitude toward garlic in hadith, for example, might be to legitimize some local, non-Arabian preference. A historian bent on arguing in this fashion could turn to the story of the mid-tenth-century Iraqi who tried to pass as a Dailami, one of the tribesmen from the mountains of northern Iran who had just taken power in southern Iraq.

> I used to eat garlic and take nothing to stop the exhalation, enduring it in order not to depart from the practice of the Dailemites; then I would come and mount among the people who were standing until I got close to the head of Abu'l-Qasim, who would be nearly killed by my poisonous breath; nevertheless I rose in his favour and he would have a chair placed for me as a member of his staff. When I sat down I would set about catching and killing the flies in his presence, after the style of a genuine Dailemite. This would make him cry out: Do release me, some one, from this truly hateful, stinking Dailemite, and take twice the pay.[3]

Alternatively, the historian might cite certain prohibitions in Indian culture on members of elevated castes eating garlic and from this conclude that the appearance of this hadith in a text from northeastern Iran represents not an effort to legitimize local custom but rather a bit of lore from Indian religious culture, elevating the status of the Prophet, sneaking into the Islamic orbit by means of a borrowed isnad and spurious attribution to Muhammad.[4]

I prefer a third approach, however. This holds that for those students who heard this hadith at the feet of a venerable teacher in the city of Gorgan in the eleventh century, there could have been no question as to its being a true representation of Muhammad's views on garlic, such was the authority of the oral transmission of prophetic lore. Questions of soundness and weakness were left to specialists and to the centuries-long winnowing of the vast corpus of tradition. Questions of inherent plausibility or cultural borrowing would have seemed irrelevant and presumptuous, if not downright impious.

How, then, were images of Muhammad's thought and behavior built up? Leaving aside the scant biographical references in the

Quran and the probability that some documents, such as the reported pact between Muhammad and the people of Medina, may once
have existed in written form, we are left almost exclusively with oral
transmission of lore. Yet the lore that was transmitted was clearly
selective in its depiction of the Prophet. Hadith about eating garlic
and lizards have been preserved, but one could also draw up a long
list of foods about which the Prophet's preference is unrecorded.
That he drank water standing up may be known, but not necessarily his posture for drinking milk.[5]

What lies beneath the selective character of the hadith used by
Muslims to construct the Muhammad of their tradition is a manner
of eliciting information. Some individuals did try to compose narratives covering major episodes in the life of the early community.
The *Sira*, the traditional "biography" of Muhammad by Ibn
Hisham (actually a collection of lore about the earliest Muslim community more than a personal biography in the Western understanding of the term), embodies this effort. But tens of thousands of
hadith came into circulation outside the framework of such narratives, and there is little to indicate that they are merely fragments of
what were once sustained narratives or descriptions put together by
the people who knew Muhammad personally. They appear most
often, rather, to be answers to questions.

A question-and-answer approach to authoritative knowledge is
an element in the elaboration of Islamic civilization that remains of
crucial importance down to the present day. Many people in Mecca
and Medina knew Muhammad. A few were close friends and relatives. All of them were capable of saying something about him. Yet
there is little to indicate that any of them sat down to compose a sys-
tematic narrative of his life and practices. Instead, they seem to have
lived after him as sources of lore for Muslims who had not known
the Prophet well, or at all. Some answered questions directly, or had
question-answering stories told about them, without reference to
the Prophet, on the basis of the authority they personally enjoyed as
important early Muslims. Much more often, however, those who
knew Muhammad, or claimed to have known him, or claimed to
have learned something from someone who claimed to have known
him, seem to have anchored their answers in the Prophet's words or

27

deeds. Who but Muhammad, after all, was likely to have known how God wanted people to behave?

One can easily imagine the sort of questions that would necessarily arise. What did Muhammad do to mark the end of the month-long fast of Ramadan? Did Muhammad ever say whether abortion was permitted or prohibited? How did Muhammad feel about wearing fine and expensive clothes? Questions of this sort arise in most religions. They are answered daily by priests, rabbis, and other sorts of religious counselors. But in early Islam, unlike early Christianity, where Jesus's disciples, out of all the people who must have heard Jesus preach, enjoyed special consideration as authoritative sources of his teachings, there was no accepted way of designating some people who had known Muhammad as more reliable sources of answers than others. If someone had known the Prophet and observed his behavior, he or she was equipped to answer at least some questions on that basis, and others, perhaps, on the basis of personal opinion buttressed by the prestige of their early conversion and long association with the Prophet.

Sahaba is the term used for those people who knew the Prophet personally. The standard translation of the term is *companions*. Later specialists made fine distinctions in defining this category, excluding those who knew him only as children, for example, or those who saw him only once. But the circulation of traditions going back precisely to individuals in these excluded categories, or to people who were merely contemporaries of the Prophet, or of traditions not going back to Muhammad at all, but to one of his closest companions, proves that the thirst for answers to questions about Islam and the early community was not limited by these later refinements.[6]

Many people who accepted Islam during the Prophet's lifetime never saw him because they lived in other parts of Arabia. Many others, including most of the people of Mecca, accepted Islam only during the final years of Muhammad's life and may have seen him only during his final pilgrimage to their city in 630. Moreover, after the beginning of the conquests outside the Arabian peninsula around 634, many Muslims, including some who had known Muhammad well, took up residence in the conquered lands and never again experienced life in Mecca and Medina. As the conquests proceeded further, many Arabian tribespeople became involved without ever having personal contact with life in the Hijaz, the part of western Arabia where Mecca and Medina are located.

As a consequence, an increasing problem developed as to how these latecomers, or even geographically remote earlier Muslims, could learn how to behave as Muslims. The only step taken by the caliphate, the government established after Muhammad's death in 632, was the collation and standardization of the Quran, which had never been put together as a single book during the Prophet's lifetime. The Quran was standardized by command of the second and third caliphs, Umar (634–644) and Uthman (644–656), and both authoritative texts and individuals who knew the Quran by memory were distributed among the various Muslim centers outside Mecca and Medina.

But the Quran does not contain much detail about ritual observance, and it concerns itself with only selected areas of social life, such as marriage and inheritance. Moreover, as already mentioned, it says almost nothing about Muhammad himself. Furthermore, most people could not read, and most who knew by memory some parts of the Quran did not know it all. One tradition maintains that only six Medinans learned the Quran during Muhammad's lifetime.[7] Nor does it seem likely that most Muslims sat at the feet of a Quran reader long enough to hear him go through the entire text. In short, it is hard to imagine that the hundreds of thousands of mostly illiterate, geographically dispersed Arabs who identified themselves as Muslims knew much more about the Quran than a few favorite passages and prayers, or certain selected verses that were reiterated as proof texts in political and doctrinal disputes.

It is striking that in the rare historical references to conversion to Islam during its first century, there is virtually no mention of learning the Quran or of knowledge of its contents being a condition of conversion. One conversion report from the Prophet's lifetime reads: "The people of Tabalah and Jurash surrendered/converted [the Arabic verb *aslama* has both meanings] without a fight. So the Messenger of God . . . let them act freely in their surrender/conversion. On the people of the Book [Christians and/or Jews] in the two places he imposed a tax."[8] According to another, Muhammad

29

"wrote to [the people of Yemen] stipulating what they should surrender (*aslamu*) of their wealth, their land, and their precious metal;
and they surrendered/converted (*aslamu*). He sent them his emissaries and governors to familiarize them with the laws of Islam and
his practices and to collect their alms and the poll tax on those of
them who remained Christians, Jews, or Zoroastrians."[9]

Another type of conversion story focuses on government appre-
hension that opportunistic conversions might adversely affect tax revenues by relieving the converts of the obligation to pay the poll tax
demanded of Christians, Jews, and Zoroastrians. In the year 728,
almost a century after the death of the Prophet, an order went out to
the chief tax official of Samarqand, in Central Asia, stipulating that he
should grant tax relief only to converts who underwent circumcision,
fulfilled Muslim ritual requirements, and knew at least one chapter of
the Quran.[10] Since the prayers recited five times daily by observant
Muslims embody the first chapter of the Quran in its entirety, the last
stipulation means that converts to Islam were expected to know no
more of the Quran than was required for prayer. Presumably, however, some didn't even know that much since the purpose of the order
was to tighten up on conversion requirements.

In contrast to the scant prominence the historical sources give
to the Quran and people who were able to recite it,[11] the Companions are ubiquitous in early Islamic history. Particularly noteworthy is the special attention later authors of local histories gave
to the names and circumstances of the Companions who visited,
dwelt, or died in their communities.[12] The abundant mention of
the Companions in local histories from regions far distant from
Arabia, even if they are occasionally spurious, should be contrasted
with their silence regarding the name of the first person in the
locality to know the Quran by heart, or to own or copy a text of it.
Moreover, the body of literature that grew up in the third Islamic
century collecting lore about the early generations of Muslims,
works like the *Tabaqat* of Ibn Sa'd (d. 845) and the *Ansab al-
ashraf* of al-Baladhuri (d. 892), or about the Companions in particular, such as the *Fada'il al-sahaba* of Ahmad ibn Hanbal (d.
855), has no early parallel in collections of lore about Quran mem-
orizers or copiers.

From this it may be cautiously hypothesized that in terms of the daily functioning of the early Islamic communities, the Companions were more important as sources of guidance than the Quran. For the Companions were the people who were most able to answer questions authoritatively. And after their generation passed away, the caliphate taking no firm action to supply more official or reliable sources of religious authority, in the next generation, those people who had learned from the Companions by asking them questions and remembering the answers continued to be the preeminent sources of religious knowledge. However, this following generation, known as the *Tabi'un* or Followers, did not inherit the prerogative some of the Companions had exercised of answering questions solely on the basis of their personal authority; for they could not plausibly claim to have had personal experience of the early community's practices, or to know more about how things should be done than they had learned or extrapolated from the stories they had heard from the Companions.

Understandably, a concern for the authenticity of traditions arose very early. Anyone, after all, might assert anything and allege it reflected the words or deeds of the Prophet, the only intrinsic control being the possibility of other Companions or Followers asserting the opposite. Some people began to interrogate those who recited traditions about which Companions they had heard them from, and notice was taken of the existence of fabrications.[13] This concern grew with the passage of time and the expansion of the number of people reciting hadith. Thus were sown the seeds of the later science of hadith criticism.

My concern here, however, is not with the intricacies of early hadith study, but with what the burgeoning of hadith recitation and collection reveals about the growth of the Muslim community. Just as scholars studying the history of Judaism through an examination of the corpus of rabbinical opinions called responsa have found it valuable to analyze what questions are asked of the rabbis at different times and in different situations for clues about changing community concerns, so it is possible to discover something of the character of the early Islamic community by looking at the sorts of questions the hadith seem to be responding to. Since hadith collections are often grouped by topic, a general picture is fairly easy to formulate.

Out of the 7,077 hadith included in al-Bukhari's *Sahih*, one of the six canonical collections, over 2,000 are devoted to ritual matters like prayer, ablutions, fasting, and pilgrimage to Mecca; another 500 explicate specific verses in the Quran. Marriage and divorce are covered by 286 hadith, food and drink by 251, clothing by 178, and medical matters by 129. Business and agricultural matters are also well covered, as are issues like holy war (*jihad*) and fighting against unbelievers and apostates that were of particular interest to the very early community.

In sharp contrast with this overwhelming concentration on topics that were meaningful for individual Muslims in their daily lives, a meager thirty hadith touch on criminal matters (*hudud*), and another eighty on issues of governance (*ahkam*), all contained in the final portion of the collection after the topics mentioned above. Hence it is clear that to the degree that hadith can be considered answers to questions, and the canonical collections can be considered representative, most of the questions they responded to dealt with personal matters of ritual and behavior, exactly those areas of greatest concern to new Muslims trying to integrate themselves into the community.

It would be desirable, of course, to refine this picture by discovering which hadith circulated most frequently in which regions since it is unlikely that every group of Muslims asked the same questions. For example, it would be interesting to determine whether hadith concerned with issues of personal ritual purity were more commonly reported in Iran, with its heavily Zoroastrian population. Zoroastrianism concerned itself greatly with such matters, and converts from Zoroastrianism might be expected to have had more questions on this topic. But this degree of refinement is not generally feasible. So we are left with the unrefined conclusion that the corpus of hadith that eventually comes to be judged most sound responds particularly to implied questions of personal behavior and ritual practice.

This finding is in keeping with the situation of a dispersed, poorly indoctrinated, largely illiterate religious community in which most individuals had not directly experienced the life of the primitive community in Hijaz. Knowing that they were Muslims, and that as Muslims they might hope to share in the immense prestige and wealth of the caliphate, it was vital for them, whether they were Arabs or non-Arab converts, to understand what was expected of them as Muslims. And in the absence of formal instructors or official religious leaders in their own community, they could only find out by observing and asking. Many questions about standard rituals could easily be answered by any observant Muslim. Other questions, however, would be new, either because of new circumstances or because new converts brought with them concerns and questions that the earlier Muslims in their vicinity had not entertained.

The likelihood of new questions being posed was presumably greater among non-Arab converts to Islam than among the Arabs themselves. After all, Muhammad and virtually all of the Companions were Arabs who shared a common language, a common culture, and the lifestyle of the cities of the Hijaz. If, for example, it was commonplace for all Arabs to wear gowns and sandals, it would probably not occur to Arab Muslims to ask whether such a costume was appropriate or necessary for Muslims. However, Iranian converts from northeastern Iran, accustomed to boots, baggy trousers, and emboidered coats, might well ask such a question. For them, the underlying issue would be whether dressing like an Arab was a necessary component of dressing like a Muslim. As late as 840, during the inquisition of a Central Asian prince and commander in the Abbasid army on charges of apostasy, a witness quoted him as saying, "Truly I have given in to these people [the Arabs] in everything I hated, even to the extent that because of them I have eaten oil and ridden camels and *worn sandals*."[14]

In the case of new questions deriving from different local customs, of course, there might not be an explicit hadith. But there might be one that could be interpreted as being applicable. Or a pious person might attempt to answer the question in the manner that seemed best to him. In the latter case, he might further lend authority to his answer with an altered or invented hadith. One might take the case of the Zoroastrian purity law that requires women to retreat to huts behind their houses during their menstrual periods. How might a pious Muslim have responded to a question from a new convert on the propriety of this practice, which was unknown in Arabia? The answer is contained in the following hadith: "Aisha [Muhammad's favorite wife] said: 'I asked the Prophet, God's prayers and peace be upon him, for permission to build a hut to stay in during my menstrual period, but he did not permit it.' "[15] Leaving aside the question of the authenticity of the isnad, it is not unduly skeptical to suspect that someone invented this hadith in order to give religious sanction to the common custom of the Arab Muslims and to allay the Zoroastrian convert's feelings of impurity.

Referring to such concocted hadith as forgeries, as is done in the back-and-forth debate between Muslim and non-Muslim scholars on the "authenticity" of Islamic tradition,[16] conveys a highly pejorative impression and clouds the fact that the expansion of the corpus of hadith was a vital, healthy, and probably necessary part of the growth of the early Muslim community. The person who learned a hadith became more knowledgeable about his or her own faith and practice, and the assurance that the hadith represented the words and deeds of the Prophet made that person's faith and practice firmer and more positive.

If by learning and following a concocted hadith a person did something that was not part of, or even contrary to, Muhammad's practice, but did it with full piety and religious self-assurance, one might say that that person followed a nonstandard practice; but it would be harsh to say that he or she was impious, or a bad Muslim, or an unbeliever. Since it is well known that millions of Muslims today engage in "nonstandard" practices, and it is safe to assume that millions always have, no special onus should be put upon those people who were misled by fabricated hadith in the early centuries.

It seems reasonable, therefore, to see the expansion of the corpus of hadith as a natural way for the growing Muslim community to respond to the ever-increasing volume of questions raised by believers. From the point of view of the muhaddithun who eventually undertook to prune the overgrowth of the corpus, those individuals who had concocted or altered hadith, or attached to them erroneous isnads, were culpable and strongly condemned. But viewed more abstractly, with an eye toward the community's need for guidance, their piously intended sins had the salutary effect of helping to structure the lives of the believers. As the Prophet reputedly said, "Mendacity will spread after me. So when someone relates a hadith from me, test it according to the Quran and sunna; it if agrees with them, then it is from me, regardless of whether or not I have actually said it."[17]

For the person who was anxious about eating garlic or how a menstruating woman should behave, it was a positive value to have the issue decided, even at the expense of using hadith to lend authority to the solution. And where else could such a person go for an authoritative decision? The governors, tax officials, and military officers dispatched to the provinces by the caliphs had no religious credentials; and the religious judge, the *qadi*, was restricted in his official capacity to ruling on legal cases. For the religion to answer people's needs, there had to be someone who could authoritatively answer questions, and the transmitter of hadith was an obvious choice.

In sum, the Quran was God's word, but it did not give explicit guidance as to how Muslims should behave in all of the matters that concerned them. God's choice of Muhammad as His messenger to mankind marked him as a "perfect man," and this divine favor came to be seen as transforming his every word and deed into a model of proper Muslim thought and behavior.

As membership in the Muslim community expanded and the Prophet's influence became geographically extensive, personal contact with Muhammad, or with daily life in Mecca and Medina, became less and less likely for individual Muslims. Consequently, the Companions, particularly after Muhammad's death, became revered as repositories of knowledge about the Prophet. The stories attributed to them provided crucial answers to questions arising from every quarter, and they became particularly important for non-Arab converts who did not share the language, culture, and background of the earliest Muslims.

When the generation of the Companions passed away, it was succeeded, according to the formal schematization of later hadith scholars, by a generation of Followers, and they were succeeded by a generation of their own followers. Whether matters were actually so neat as this may be questioned, but in various ways some substantial part of the corpus of hadith did originate with the Companions and was transmitted to later generations; and the importance of isnads grew ever stronger as confirmation of oral transmission took the place of personal relationship with the Prophet in buttressing the authority of the generations after the Companions. This entire process was assisted by the incapacity or unwillingness of the caliphate to institutionalize alternative means of giving authoritative answers to religious questions.

As a consequence of this process, a dispersed and uninstitutionalized locus of religious authority grew up outside of caliphal jurisdiction or control during the first two Islamic centuries. Ultimate authority resided in the Quran as God's word, but hadith transmission provided the primary mechanism for answering the questions and responding to the spiritual needs of a growing community of Muslims spread from Spain to Pakistan.

This was only one factor in the socialization of Muslims into a religiously based community, of course; but with time, it became a crucial factor, especially for people living at society's edge. The Prophet's family and Companions, the general populace of Mecca and Medina, the Arab tribespeople who joined the outward movement of conquest and became the mainstay of the nascent caliphate, all of these groups, to varying degrees, belonged to the core of the new society of Muslims. But around this core, living on the edge of Muslim society, and only fleetingly glimpsed in the historical sources, was a much larger population of non-Arabs. It is to their view of the new historical force of Islam that I now turn.

3

THE VIEW FROM THE EDGE

Abu Taiba related from Abu Zubair, [who
related] from Jabir, who said: "The Messen-
ger of God, God's prayers and peace be upon
him, said: 'Whoever believes in God and the
Last Day, let him not enter the public bath
without a loincloth . . . let his wife not enter
the public bath [at all] . . . let him not sit at
the table around which circulates the cup of
wine. . . . Whoever has become rich from
trade or pleasure, God shall dispense with
him, for God enriches the praiseworthy.' "
—Hadith quoted in HAMZA AL-SAHMI,
TA'RIKH JURJAN

Studies of early Islamic history rarely incorporate the view from
the edge. Primary sources concentrate overwhelmingly on descriptions of the communities in Mecca and Medina, the succession of
caliphs, the exploits of the Arab tribes, and the lives of prominent
Arab Muslims. Remote places are most frequently mentioned with
reference to their conquest, or to the activities of the Arabs who settled in them. Non-Arab Muslims, when mentioned at all, are more
often portrayed in the aggregate than as individuals.

Yet the shape Islam came to take was greatly affected by the needs
and questions of non-Arab Muslim converts from lands more or less
remote from Mecca and Medina. Though the paucity of direct reference makes it difficult to trace the course of conversion to Islam

in detail, a rough picture of the overall process can be obtained through a quantitative examination of the onomastic material preserved in later biographical dictionaries, a genre that proliferated in the Islamic world from the tenth century onward.

The procedure in making this examination rests, essentially, upon the expectation that non-Arabs would adopt Arabic names when converting to Islam. For example, a fourth-generation Muslim from Isfahan reports that the famous religious scholar Sufyan al-Thawri had an encounter with the informant's father concerning his slave camel-driver Bahram: "Sufyan said to my father, 'Change his name,' [Bahram's] name being Persian. I [sic] said, 'Name him.' He replied, 'His name is Hizzan.' "[1] Given a sufficiently large sample of specific cases in which such changes of name occurred, and the approximate date of their occurrence, a graph can be constructed that portrays the relative frequency of conversion in the area from which the data derive[2] (see figure 3.1). The S-shaped curve represented in figure 3.1 of conversion in Iran, and on analogous graphs for other regions, is, mathematically, a logistic curve. It occurs frequently in studies of social and technological change, and it reflects a fairly simple dynamic process. New things cannot be adopted until people have heard of them, and in nonliterate societies in the era before the development of mass media, most information traveled by word of mouth. Hence change begins slowly, with a comparatively small number of informants spreading the word about the new thing, in this case a religion.

As the number of people adopting a new thing grows, the number of potential informants multiplies proportionately. This chain reaction leads to a brief period of very rapid growth, which I shall refer to as the "bandwagon" period. On the graph of conversion to Islam in Iran, the bandwagon period is represented by the steepest slope on the curve, between 791 and 864. After the bandwagon period, new adoptions gradually taper off because people who have not been exposed to the innovation in question become more and more scarce. Thus, eventually the wave of adoption, or in our case conversion to Islam, comes to a close, usually with some proportion of the population, those resistant, for whatever reasons, to the pressures leading their neighbors to convert, still adhering to their non-

Figure 3.1   Conversion to Islam in Iran

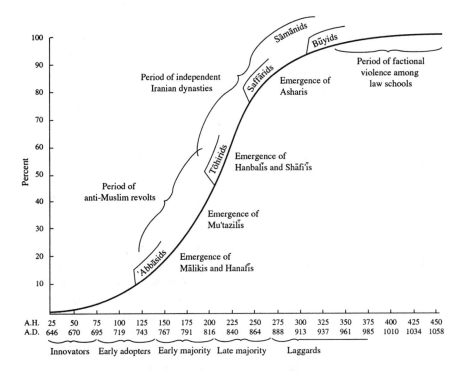

Muslim religious traditions. This residual unconverted population, the size of which varies from region to region and is difficult to estimate, may prove susceptible to a second or third conversion wave in subsequent centuries.[3] For our purposes, however, I am concerned only with the first and primary surge of conversion to Islam in the Middle East.

The post-conquest world, at least through the first two centuries of Islam, was one of geographically dispersed, largely illiterate communities of Arab Muslims constituting the ruling stratum of a multilingual, multiethnic, overwhelmingly non-Muslim empire. The caliphate established in Medina at Muhammad's death in 632 moved twenty-five years later to Syria, where a prominent family belonging to Muhammad's Meccan tribe of Quraysh held sway for a century. This Umayyad dynasty relied upon Arab manpower for its army even while utilizing administrators and administrative practices from the defeated Byzantine and Sasanian empires to collect taxes and keep the government functioning. Down to the end of the Umayyad period in 750, when a revolt surging out of northeastern Iran climaxed with the installation of the Abbasid family, descendants of one of the Prophet's uncles, as the new caliphal regime in Iraq, fewer than ten percent of the non-Arab populace had converted.

The pace of conversion was undoubtedly influenced, at least on the local level, by governmental measures conferring benefits upon, or withholding them from, new converts.[4] The friendliness or animosity of the local Arab Muslims, most of them still organized by tribe, was surely also a consideration.[5] At a deeper level, however, the overall process of conversion, as suggested by the methodology outlined above, was largely governed by access to knowledge. People simply could not become Muslims if they didn't know what Islam was.[6] How, then, were they to find out? The history of Christianity and Buddhism, indeed, the later history of Islam itself in other parts of the world, would lead one to look for stories of missionaries or preachers; but there is no evidence that such directed efforts at proselytization took place during the first century or two of Islam. In their absence, access to information about Islam would normally have come about in one of the following ways:

First, potential converts might have been members of a besieged community that was given the choice of accepting Islam, retaining their Christian or Jewish allegiance, or being destroyed. For example, after conquering the town of Qinnasrin in northern Syria and making a peace settlement, the Arab commander Abu Ubaida "called [an Arab tribe] to Islam, and some of them converted." But others persisted in their Christianity.[7] In these cases, converts probably became Muslims first and slowly found out afterward what that implied by observing the Muslim Arabs' behavior and asking them questions.

Second, they might have been captured in battle and, as part of the booty, been distributed as slaves to one of the Arab combatants. In this case, they would have learned about Islam by living among

Arab Muslims as slaves and quickly come to realize that conversion would greatly enhance the possibility of manumission. The words of the Quran (sura 24, verse 33) on the matter were generally taken seriously: "And those of your slaves who desire a deed of manumission, write it for them, if ye have a good opinion of them, and give them wealth of God, which he has given you."

Third, they might have lived in proximity to a group of Arab Muslims and observed their behavior, very possibly discovering that imitating them enhanced their acceptance and gained them a livelihood purveying goods and services to them. This possibility would have been limited, of course, by the fact that a large proportion of the Arabs in the conquering armies settled in large, widely separated cantonments (*misr* pl. *amsar*), as dictated by a caliphate that was fearful of dissipating its military strength by allowing the tribes to disperse throughout the conquered countryside. Some cantonments, such as Basra and Kufa in Iraq, Fustat in Egypt, and Qairawan in Tunisia, grew into major cities and seats of provincial government; others, notably those in Syria, did not. In any case, however, the lives of the Arabs in these and other garrison and governing centers were quite remote from those of the dispersed mass of villagers, who probably accounted for over three-quarters of the conquered population. As in the first two cases, the number of people falling into this category was initially quite limited, even allowing for migration to the Arab governing centers by people seeking jobs.

Fourth, they might have encountered some bilingual Muslim capable of explaining to them at least some aspects of the Arabs' religion. Assuming that the number of bilingual individuals in the Muslim community during Muhammad's lifetime was comparatively small, most bilingual informants would have emerged through one of the first three processes, assuming new converts learned Arabic, or, more likely, as the offspring of Arabic-speaking Muslim men and non-Arab wives or concubines. Bilingual Muslims of the generation of the Companions, moreover, were more likely to have been able to communicate with the linguistically related Aramaic speakers of Iraq and Syria (not then Arabic-speaking lands) than with the Persians, Egyptians, and Berbers, who spoke very different languages.

It might be noted in passing that historians who have suggested that part of the Arabs' military success stemmed from the perception by religious minorities among the conquered population that Islam was more tolerant than the ruling cults of the Byzantines and Sasanids make a completely unwarranted assumption about the extent to which the conquered population knew anything about Islam. They may have known who the Arabs were, but most of the villagers living at the time of the conquests probably never set eyes on a Muslim Arab and could not have communicated with one if they had.

In the earliest stages of conversion, most non-Arab converts probably entered the Muslim community through the first three processes listed above; but over time, the fourth surely came to predominate. Individuals with missionary outlooks eventually did appear, even though they were not formally authorized by the caliphate. In one example from the late eighth century, Abd Allah ibn al-Mubarak, a non-Arab of partially Turkish parentage, came to the city of Nishapur and resided for a while on Isa Street. There he used to see an elegant young man ride by who turned out to be the son of Isa ibn Masarjis. Isa (Jesus), in all likelihood the man for whom the street was named, seems to have been the son of a Christian bishop (Masarjis = Mar Sergius). When Abd Allah found this out, he called upon Isa's son to accept Islam, and he did so, changing his name to Abu Ali al-Hasan and becoming the progenitor of one of Nishapur's most illustrious Muslim families.[8] While on occasion whole villages, tribes, or localized religious communities probably entered Islam en masse, either following the example of their customary leaders, or responding to missionary appeals,[9] the graphs of conversion derived from name data indicate that the overall model of conversion best fits the hypothesis of an immense number of individual choices to identify with the Muslim community.

The flow of converts into the Muslim community varied somewhat from region to region, in part because of the different dates of conquest, e.g., Syria and Iraq in the 630s and Spain in 711. However, by the early tenth century in Iran, the most rapidly converting area outside the Arabian peninsula, and the late tenth century in Iraq, Syria, and Egypt, the first great wave of conversion was largely complete, though in some areas, particularly remote rural locales, very substantial non-Muslim minorities remained to be affected by other surges of conversion in later centuries.

The quantitative model represented by the graph in figure 3.1 not only portrays the growth of the Muslim community through conversion as a phenomenon that stretched over three or four centuries, but draws attention to the ninth century—the earlier part of the century in the case of Iran, and the later part for the other Middle Eastern provinces—as the bandwagon period when conversion was taking place most rapidly with perhaps half of all conversions during the first four centuries taking place in a period varying from 73 years in Iran (791–864) to 121 years (840–961) in Iraq, Syria, and Egypt. The sense of religious change during these two to four generations must have had a powerful psychological and social impact, comparable, perhaps, to the impact we and our children would feel if Mormonism, now about as old as Islam was in 791, were to become the religion of half the American population by 2065. I will return to a discussion of this bandwagon phase of conversion in the following chapter.

However, as useful as a quantitative model is for suggesting the overall picture of how an important historical change came about, and for directing attention to certain key time periods, it is of little help in envisioning the real-life experience of those early converts, particularly those who did not reside or settle in an Arab community and therefore left virtually no trace in the historical record. Where did they turn for knowledge about Islam? How did they relate, after conversion, to their non-Muslim friends, neighbors, and family members with whom they had previously shared a religion? What personal examples did they set for others who might be thinking of converting? How did conversion change their behavior?

The differences between one convert's experience and another's in these particular areas must have been enormous. But so little information has been preserved about the process of conversion as a whole, much less about individual cases, that generalized characterizations, however plausible logically, will always remain unproven. Take, for example, the following stories:

Sul [the local ruler of Gorgan][10] said to Yazid ibn al-Muhallab at the time Gorgan was conquered: "Is there in Islam someone more illustrious than you at whose hands I might convert to Islam?" Yazid replied: "Yes, Sulaiman ibn Abd al-Malik [Umayyad caliph from 715 to 717]." Sul said: "Then dispatch me to him so I can convert to Islam at his hands." So [Yazid] did. When Sul arrived, he said to Sulaiman what he had said to Yazid. Then Sulaiman said: "There is not now among the Muslims anyone more illustrious than I, but the tomb of the Messenger of God . . . has more." "Then I shall convert to Islam there," said Sul. So Sulaiman sent him to Madina, and he converted to Islam at the tomb. Then he returned to Yazid ibn al-Muhallab and became his companion and managed his expenditures until Maslama ibn Abd al-Malik killed him on the day of al-Aqr when he killed Yazid ibn al-Muhallab.[11]

Some of [the children of the founder of a Muslim family in Isfahan] relate that Mushkan [the founder] was originally from Isfahan. When captivity was imminent, his mother took her son, who had earrings in his ears, and placed him in the house of a weaver so that he would not be recognized. For he was called Prince. They go on: So he was taken prisoner from the house of that weaver, and it was afterwards said that he was his son.[12] [He was transported to the Arab cantonment of Basra where he converted and became an adoptive member (*mawla*) of an Arab tribe there.]

Conversion stories like these from the early centuries of Islam say much more about social backgrounds and about the aspirations or pretensions of descendants than they do about religious belief, or behavior as Muslims.[13] The fact that this sort of story is virtually all that survives, at least at the level of the individual, from the first wave of conversion reinforces the notion that the movement of converts into the Muslim community was generally unremarkable, occurring gradually, without institutional mediation, in myriad different localities. This does not mean, however, that it had no effect upon social patterns and structures. Quite the contrary. Nothing influenced the emerging shape of Muslim society and culture so much as the massive influx of new Muslims who had no prior experience of life in Arabia, or of the culture of the Arabs. Their view is

44

the view from the edge, and it is one I shall explore through the story of a single family, leaving the resumption of my more general analysis for the following chapter.

One extraordinary text has survived that conveys a flavor of life on the edge of the early Islamic community. It is a collection of stories about four generations of a single Iranian family, a family whose first Muslim member converted within twenty-five years of the death of the Prophet. It is contained in the Ta'rikh Jurjan,[14] a biographical dictionary of the city of Gorgan at the southeast corner of the Caspian Sea, but the family originates further to the east. The stories in the collection are strikingly atypical within the genre of local biographical dictionaries. They contain some clearly nonhistorical, folkloristic elements, but they also have a peculiarly authentic tone that suggests that they actually do reflect very early conditions on the eastern edge of the Islamic world.

Although the stories cover the period from the reign of Uthman, the third caliph, to that of the Abbasid al-Ma'mun, the twenty-third caliph, it will be instructive to give the text in its entirety and comment on it since the passage of generations reflects the social evolution of a convert Muslim family in that region.

[Introduction]

Abu Taiba Isa ibn Sulaiman al-Darimi al-Jurjani [Arabic pronunciation of Persian al-Gorgani]. He was one of the religious scholars [ulama] and ascetics [zuhhad]. He recited hadith from Kurz ibn Wabra, Ja'far ibn Muhammad, Sulaiman al-A'mash, and others. His two sons Ahmad and Abd al-Wasi' recited hadith from him, as did Sa'd ibn Sa'id and others. His mosque [masjid] was inside the walled inner city [qasba] on the street named for Abd al-Wasi' ibn Abi Taiba, his son. His house was beside his mosque. He had manifest benefices [ni'ma] in the form of estates and lands. He established trusts [awqaf], which are known by his name down to the present day, on behalf of his children, his grandchildren, and his relations in Juzjanan, in a town known as Ashburqan, to which was added some trust property they had in Gorgan and Astarabadh. His grave is beside the Taifur canal [nahr] at the edge of Sulaiman-abadh cemetery.

45

I learned in Ahwaz from Abu Bakr Ahmad ibn Abdan al-Hafiz, who learned from Muhammad ibn Sahl, who learned from Muhammad ibn Isma'il al-Bukhari the following: Isa ibn Sulaiman ibn Dinar Abu Taiba al-Darimi al-Jurjani died in the year 153. He heard hadith from Ja'far ibn Muhammad.

Commentary

Thus far, this is a typical entry from a local biographical dictionary of the eleventh century. Local biographical dictionaries were normally composed of brief notices concerning religious figures who either lived in or passed through the community. An important criterion for an individual's inclusion was his or her—a few women are included—appearance in an isnad known by the compiler or contained in scholars' notebooks in the compiler's possession or in the collection of local mosques. Along with the transcriptions of the hadith they heard in class, scholars kept notes on the teachers they had heard hadith from in order to keep straight in their own minds what material had come from whom, and under what circumstances. This was important because forty years might well elapse between the time they attended the class and their undertaking to teach hadith from the notes they took in their youth.[15]

The second paragraph reflects the transmission, with isnad, of exactly this kind of lore, which was very important for authenticating isnads. There is a separate biography of Abu Taiba's son Abd al-Wasi' that confirms, with different wording, the information about the street, mosque, and property.[16]

The Story of Dinar, the Grandfather of Abu Taiba

I found among the things my uncle Asham ibn Ibrahim wrote down by dictation the following: Abu Sa'id Abd al-Wasi' ibn Abd Allah ibn Abd al-Wasi' related the following from her mawla [client, dependent] Abd al-Wasi' Abu Sa'id [sic]:

Commentary

It is apparent that the author of the *Ta'rikh Jurjan*, Hamza al-

46

Sahmi, had a written text that his uncle had taken down by dictation from some source. In a separate biographical entry on his uncle, al-Sahmi makes it clear that whatever learned matter he had from him was taken from his books and not from personal conversation.[17] The chance of the story having become greatly garbled in either al-Sahmi's memory or his uncle's is therefore slight.

His uncle's source was the great-grandson of the Abu Taiba who is the ostensible subject of this entry in the biographical dictionary. The modern editor of the published text proposes to emend the apparent confusion of the text before or after the word mawla to indicate that the ultimate source of the stories may have been a slave concubine of Abd al-Wasi', the grandfather of the narrator Abu Sa'id Abd al-Wasi', but this is by no means certain. The separate biographical entries on the earlier Abd al-Wasi' and his brother Ahmad, the two sons of Abu Taiba, contain none of the following stories as they appear here. As will be noted later, Ahmad's biography confirms one of the stories with an independent isnad.[18]

[The First Generation]
The story of Dinar, the grandfather of Abu Taiba, is that he was a rural landowner [dihqan] from Marv. He was taken prisoner during the raid on Khurasan of Sa'id ibn Uthman ibn Affan and fell into the part of the booty that went to a man named Ja'far ibn Khirfash from the Banu Dirar ibn Amr [subsection] of the Banu Dabba [tribe]. He lived with him for a time, and then [Ja'far] manumitted him. Ja'far died without any heir other than Dinar. So [Dinar] took possession of [Ja'far's] wealth. Then he married, and a son Sulaiman, the father of Abu Taiba Isa, was born to him.

Commentary

The Sasanid imperial army that faced the Muslim Arab invaders in Iraq and Iran was largely composed of cavalrymen drawn from Iran's petty aristocracy, designated by the term *dihqan*. The city of Marv was on the eastern edge of the Sasanid empire bordering on Central Asia, which was then divided into a number of small principalities with local ruling dynasties. After the fall of the Sasanids, Marv became a principal Arab garrison center and the seat of Muslim government in the east from which further campaigns were launched against the petty dynasts and Turkic tribes further eastward still. Sa'id ibn Uthman was the son of the third caliph, and his raid into Khurasan probably dates to the year 676.

Being taken prisoner in battle, Dinar, whose name denotes a gold coin in Arabic, though it may conceivably be of non-Arabic origin, became a part of the booty. He was given as a slave to a member of an Arab tribe. When Dinar converted to Islam and gained his freedom is uncertain, but he must have been a Muslim by the time his master Ja'far died because only a fellow Muslim could legally have inherited Ja'far's property.

By giving his son the name Sulaiman (Solomon), Dinar followed a practice that was common in the early period of conversion to Islam in Iran.[19] Names like Sulaiman, Ibrahim (Abraham), Musa (Moses), and Yusuf (Joseph) that occur in both the Quran and the Bible protected the bearer from too obvious a display of his Muslim affiliation. Dinar may have been trying to protect his son from social discomfort in an environment in which very few Iranians had as yet converted.

[The Second Generation]
[1.] Sulaiman left Marv for Juzjanan and settled. There he married a woman named Talha, and she bore to him his son Musa.

Commentary

Juzjanan, also known as Juzjan, was a district of northern Afghanistan some 250 miles away from Marv traveling along the most likely route up the Murghab River.[20] It had been conquered in the year 654, only twenty-two years after the death of Muhammad, so it had probably been under Muslim control for less than twenty years when Sulaiman ibn Dinar arrived there. Where Sulaiman settled in Juzjanan isn't stated, but the introduction mentions family trust property in a town called Ashburqan. This place is not otherwise known and may be a town in Juzjanan. Alternatively, the phrase "in Juzjanan" in the introduction may refer not to where the property was located but to continued residence of Sulaiman's descendants there generations later. Since al-Sahmi does not preserve a biography of Sulaiman's first son Musa, it is possible that some family remained in Juzjanan after Abu Taiba, Sulaiman's second son, departed.

Geographers report that the main town of Juzjanan was known as al-Yahudiya, "the town of the Jews." In light of this, it is notable not only that Sulaiman named his two sons Musa (Moses) and Isa (Jesus), the latter being Abu Taiba's given name, but that there are evident traces of Jewish tradition in some of the lore reported about the family, as will become clear presently. Since Sulaiman's wife Talha was a local woman, and her name is an improbable one for a Muslim woman, Talha being not only a man's name in Arabic but the name of one of Muhammad's closest companions, it seems likely that she was either a Jew or a Christian. One must keep in mind that it was probably difficult for the earliest non-Arab Muslim converts to find Muslim spouses if they did not live in one of the Arab governing centers.

[2.] *Later, while pregnant with Abu Taiba Isa, she had a dream: a chain [silsila] dangled down from the sky to the earth where a group of people was standing. They jumped at it to grab it, but they couldn't reach it. Then her son, who was in her womb, jumped and didn't reach it. A second time he jumped and didn't reach it. But the third time he jumped he caught it. As if it were a dust cloud it lifted, and Sulaiman [the unborn child's father] was wrapped up in its folds [ad'af] and raised into the sky.*

After this happened, she told her dream to her husband. He said to her: "If your dream is true, you will give birth to a virtuous [salih] son. [My good reputation] shall be preserved by him [ihtafizi bihi], and I shall be granted martyrdom, if God wills.

Commentary

The dream about Abu Taiba jumping for the chain from heaven while still in his mother's womb belongs to a very broad category of tales forecasting the future of unborn heroes. I don't know of any direct model for this version, but the chain hanging from heaven is somewhat reminiscent of the biblical story of Jacob's ladder.

*[3.] Later, the people of Juzjanan were struck by famine and a
cessation of heavy rains. They went out into the desert to pray for
rain, but it didn't rain. So Sulaiman, with a group of his ascetic
friends [nussak], went out. They prayed for rain, and it rained. It
became known in the city that God had granted them rain through
Sulaiman. The people came to him [ikhtalafu] and blessed him. But
a governor named Abu al-Haft, who was in authority over them,
denied this and threw Sulaiman in jail. Then the people of the city
became angry and stopped him from doing this. They expelled their
governor from the city and freed Sulaiman from prison. They said to
Abu al-Haft, their governor, "You have oppressed a man through
whom God has granted us rain and imprisoned him. You have
sought our destruction." So he promised that he would not repeat
such an action, and they took him back as their governor.*

Commentary

The story of Sulaiman and his pious or ascetic friends praying for
rain suggests that Sulaiman became the center of a small group of
other Muslim converts in Juzjanan. Communal prayers for rain are
well attested in northeastern Iran in Islamic times, and people of all
religions commonly joined in. The statement that the people attributed the success of the group's prayers to Sulaiman indicates that he
was the principal figure in the group. It is noteworthy that neither
here nor anywhere in the stories of this generation is there the
slightest mention of anything specifically Islamic. Sulaiman appears
as a local person speaking the local language and bearing a name
that would presumably have been normal in a place named al-
Yahudiya. He is a notably pious person with a group of followers,
and he gains a minor reputation as a wonder-worker.

The governor Abu al-Haft has a peculiar name. "Haft" is not an
Arabic name, but rather the Persian word for "seven." Thus his
name means "Father of the Seven." What this may mean is unclear,
but the action he takes against Sulaiman is certainly out of keeping
with his being either an Arab or a Muslim. An Arab or Muslim governor would presumably have supported a saintly local Muslim. In
this case, his persecution of Sulaiman for appearing to be instru-

mental in ending the drought indicates a fear of his popularity and a desire to suppress the local Muslims. Since the Arab conquerors relied on non-Muslim local administrators in many smaller or more remote locales, charging them primarily with assuring tax collection, it seems likely that Abu al-Haft was a non-Muslim. The persecution of Sulaiman was probably repeated in many other cases in communities in which Muslims were few, non-Arab, and lacking in power.

> [4.] Immediately Sulaiman went out on a raid with ten of his young men [ghilman] to Saghaniyan. He encountered one of the Turks and they fell into battle. He and nine of his followers [mawali] were killed. One was left, and he brought the news back to [Sulaiman's] wife and son.

Commentary

Fighting as a holy warrior (ghazi) on the frontier of Islam was a pious undertaking that zealous young men engaged in for centuries. Saghaniyan, a river valley to the northeast of Juzjanan, was an appropriate frontier for that period, and the Turks an appropriate enemy. The size of his retinue indicates that Sulaiman must have been a man of wealth and position. The terms used for them, ghilman and mawali, are puzzling, however. Ghilman (sing. ghulam) literally means "young men," but it later became a common term for the military retainers of Muslim rulers, retainers who, by the end of the ninth century, were often purchased slaves. Mawali (sing. mawla), on the other hand, indicates a devoted follower in late eighth-century usage. Before that, it more often denotes a non-Arab Muslim convert living as a client and adoptive member of an individual Arab or an Arab tribe.

Since Sulaiman was not an Arab, the early meaning of mawla would make no sense here, nor would a slave retainer usually be referred to as a mawla. The terminology is probably less important, in any case, than the portrayal of Sulaiman as a wealthy man of aristocratic (dihqan) social origin comporting himself very much in the fashion of the pre-Islamic Iranian rural aristocracy by taking his per-

51

sonal retainers off on a military raid without being part of a larger army.

[The Third Generation]

[1.] [Sulaiman's] wife Talha stayed in Juzjan until Abu Taiba reached puberty [taharraka]. When it was Friday and he was free from school, he used to hide from his mother so she couldn't see him. She condemned this activity and followed him one Friday until he came to a thicket. There he stood and performed devotions [ta'abba-da]. So she returned home. When it was evening and her son came home, she said to him: "I saw your place, and I am frightened for you because there might be a lion in that thicket. I will not permit you to go there." He replied: "Since you know my place, there is no need for me to go there." And after that he performed his devotions in the courtyard.

Commentary

Though the language of this story is not always clear, the import seems to be that as a youth Abu Taiba felt a need to worship privately. The school (*kuttab*) he was attending was almost certainly religious and non-Muslim so he was apparently being indoctrinated into some other religion. Since his worship was taking place during the daytime on Friday, however, it was obviously Muslim worship. Yet the word used to describe his devotions does not bring to mind any specific Muslim practice. Moreover, the fact that he stood to do his devotions seems to rule out his performing the prostrations of the normal Muslim prayers.

Since he reportedly felt no further need to worship in secret after his mother spied on him, the implication seems clear that his need for secrecy was related to her. The precise meaning of the word translated as "reached puberty" is uncertain, but it probably implies that Abu Taiba was an infant or young child when his father was killed. Thus he was left to be brought up by his mother who, as suggested earlier, was almost certainly not a Muslim by birth, and may not have become one after marriage. Therefore, Abu Taiba was probably trying to carry on his father's religion despite his mother's real or possible disapproval. He seems not to have known exactly what to do as a Muslim, and there appears to have been no one for him to learn from, even though his mother agreed to tolerate his behavior once she found out about it.

This story highlights the isolation Muslim converts, or in this case their descendants, could experience if they lived in largely non-Muslim communities.

[2.] When he reached the age of reason, [Abu Taiba] went away to seek knowledge, and he happened into the land of Gorgan. He encountered the army of Yazid ibn al-Muhallab and met in it Kurz ibn Wabra. He became his companion up until the army conquered Gorgan. He marked out [ikhtatta] the place for his house in Gorgan and settled there.

Commentary

This story embodies a key phrase of medieval Muslim society, *talab al-'ilm*, "seeking knowledge." *'Ilm*, the modern Arabic word for science, denoted religious knowledge in medieval Arabic unless otherwise specified. In slightly later usage the phrase "seeking knowledge" referred to students and adult scholars traveling from city to city in search of hadith they had not previously heard, or even already familiar ones they might hear transmitted with different isnads. In this story, however, the quest for religious knowledge is more primitive. It is a quest for knowledge about what Islam is and what Muslims do.

Abu Taiba heads west on his quest toward the Islamic heartland. On his way he encounters an Arab army led by Yazid ibn al-Muhallab. Since he is in some sense a Muslim, he travels on with the army and becomes the companion of a man named Kurz ibn Wabra. This new situation suits him so well that he stays with the army until it conquers Gorgan and then settles there.

Who, then, is Kurz ibn Wabra? According to al-Sahmi,[21] "Abu Abd Allah Kurz ibn Wabra al-Harithi [from the tribe of Harith] [al-]Kufi [from the Arab cantonment city of Kufa in Iraq] entered Gorgan as a religious warrior [ghazi, just like Abu Taiba's father] with Yazid ibn al-Muhallab in the year 98 [717 A.D.]. Subsequently he

53

became a resident of Gorgan and established there a mosque near Sulaimanabad, where it remains to this day beside his grave. He . . . was known for asceticism [*zuhd*] and piety [*'ibada*]. He recited hadith from . . ." Here al-Sahmi lists the names of seven prominent early hadith reciters. Then come the names of ten people, headed by Abu Taiba, who recited hadith on Kurz's authority.

Al-Sahmi proceeds to give some examples of Kurz ibn Wabra's asceticism. "Kurz did not raise his head to the sky for forty years out of shame before his Lord, the Most High."[22] "Kurz ibn Wabra, may God have mercy upon him, was the most pious of the people of his time. He used to refrain from eating until no more flesh could be found on him than on a sparrow. He used to fast for many days. When he commenced praying, he would glance neither to the right nor to the left. He was among the lovers of God."[23]

Kurz ibn Wabra was also one of the group of four, including al-Sahmi's great-great-grandfather, who determined the direction of prayer for the first congregational mosque in Gorgan.[24] Like Abu Taiba's father, Kurz had his own followers (mawali), though since he was a pious Arab Muslim capable to receiving the conversion of non-Muslims, these were probably new converts who served him and enjoyed his patronage rather than military followers.

From the isnads of the many hadith al-Sahmi gives that were transmitted through Kurz, it is apparent that he was well versed in the traditions of the Prophet. Most of his sources were Followers who had heard hadith from the Companions, but some were themselves Companions.

In view of Kurz ibn Wabra's piety and great store of hadith, it seems understandable that becoming his follower could have been a turning point in Abu Taiba's life. Though he was already a third-generation Muslim, until meeting Kurz he knew nothing about Islam except what little had come down to him from his father, and possibly the few other Muslims in Juzjanan. Through Kurz he suddenly became part of the main current of Islamic lore passing from Muhammad, through the Companions and their successors, to those who wanted to know what Islam was all about. Moreover, Kurz was an ascetic and, as we shall see, a wonder-worker, like

Sulaiman, Abu Taiba's father. It is no surprise, then, that Abu Taiba never returned to Jujzanan, where, as mentioned above, he probably owned property. Once he had found the Muslims, he never wanted to leave them.

*[3.] Abd al-Wasi' said: "Al-Sabu' related to me that when the black force [i.e., the Abbasids] arose in Khurasan, people were afraid of them and kept to their homes in the Gorgan region. Abu Taiba was among those who stayed at home. [Al-Sabu'] said: 'I saw the Prophet, God's prayers and peace be upon him, in my sleep as if he were entering Gorgan from the region of Astarabadh.' He said: 'So I followed him, and he went straight from street to street until he entered Abu Taiba's street, which I did not recognize until later.' He continued: 'Then he came to the door of Abu Taiba and knocked. It was opened for him, and he entered. I entered behind him, and there was Abu Taiba standing in a line with the Messenger of God, God's prayers and peace be upon him, in its middle and Abu Taiba in front of him. Then he knelt before the Messenger of God, God's prayers and peace be upon him. Then I said: 'Oh messenger of God, God's prayers and peace be upon him! Verily, we have encountered this social disorder [*fitna]. What do you command of me in it?' He continued: 'And he said to me: "I have advised Abu Taiba. You do what he does." '*

"Then I woke up and when morning came, I went to the road where I had seen the Messenger of God, God's prayers and peace be upon him, walking. I did not stop following it until I entered the street of Abu Taiba. I knocked on the door. It was opened to me so I entered. There he was, standing in the line where I had seen the Messenger of God, God's prayers and peace be upon him. He was praying. When he noticed me, he quickly finished his prayer and received me. I greeted him. Then he said to me: 'What do you want?' I told him the story of my dream. Then I said to him: 'What do you command of me? For the Messenger of God, God's prayers and peace be upon him, has ordered me to follow you.' And he [Abu Taiba] said to me: 'Keep this dream secret and keep to your house.' [Al-Sabu'] said: 'So that's what I did.'"

Commentary

Since Abu Taiba came to Gorgan in 717, this story must reflect his position some thirty years later when the movement to overthrow the Umayyad caliphate became publicly known in the East. A hallmark of the movement was the use of a black banner and black clothing, possibly with eschatological connotations. The fact that the political beneficiary of the movement was the Abbasid family, the descendants of one of the Prophet's paternal uncles, was not revealed until 750 when a new caliphate was established in Iraq. The leaders who were visible at the start, when this anecdote seems to take place, were Arabs and Iranian converts to Islam living in the vast northeastern frontier province of Khurasan and in the still contested lands beyond the Oxus River.

While historians of the Abbasid movement have often remarked on the popular support it enjoyed in Khurasan, particularly among Iranian converts to Islam, this story makes it apparent that this support was far from general. Being a descendant of a very early convert, and having thrown in his lot with the Arabs who settled in Gorgan, Abu Taiba may have felt apprehensive about a challenge to the existing order. After all, most of the population of Khurasan was still non-Muslim in the mid-eighth century, and the potential for anti-Arab, anti-Muslim rebellion was significant.[25]

The story itself portrays Abu Taiba at a pious and blessed man, but not as a well-known religious leader. The narrator, after all, seems to have been unfamiliar with him before his dream. What is important in the story, for present purposes, is the pattern it reflects of a local Muslim who finds himself in a quandary, in this case political, and turns to a local pious man rather than to any government official for an answer to his dilemma. This is in keeping with the importance of questions and religiously authoritative answers discussed in the previous chapter.

The anticlimactic character of Abu Taiba's answer robs the anecdote of any obvious political partisanship but, paradoxically, lends it greater credibility thereby. I recently asked a ninety-five-year-old member of my own family (now deceased) what my ancestors in southern Indiana did during the Civil War. He said, "They didn't like slavery, but they didn't like Negroes either; so they took the horses and headed for the hills." Whether true or not, this kind of story, in which the specific activities of the ancestor are the focus and not the ancestor's political position, sounds more like family lore passed down through the generations than the fabrication of someone wishing to put his ancestors retroactively on the side of the angels.

[4.] Abd al-Wasi' said: "Then there came a time when a man named Husain al-Sajjada ruled Gorgan as governor. The people asked him to appoint for them a religious judge [qadi]. He asked them: 'Who would satisfy you?' They agreed that they would be satisfied by Abu Taiba so they asked for him. The people at that time used to wear a black headdress [qalansuwa] called a Muhammadiya and did not come before the civil authority [al-sultan] without it."

He continued: "The virtuous people [sulaha'], when they wanted to approach the civil authority, carried [their Muhammadiyas] with them in their sleeves. When they reached the gate, they took them out and put them on their heads. Then they went in."

He said: "So Husain summoned [Abu Taiba] to persuade him [rawada] into the judgeship. [Abu Taiba] put his Muhammadiya in his sleeve and walked to [the government building]. When he reached the gate, he took it out, put it on his head, and went inside. The prominent people [nas] celebrated and came together in the assembly [majlis] of the civil authority, with the common folk ['amma] at the gate. They awaited Abu Taiba's emergence as the qadi over them.

"When [Abu Taiba] entered unto [Husain], [Husain] greeted him and drew him near his majlis. Then he said: 'Truly, I have sent for you, oh Abu Taiba, to empower you as qadi, for the people are satisfied with you, and there is no denying them a judge who shall establish their laws.' "

[Abd al-Wasi' the narrator continued]: "[Abu Taiba] replied: 'Oh Amir, truly I am not fit for this post.'

"[Husain] replied: 'There is no escaping it. The people have not found anyone else.'

"[Abu Taiba] said: 'Then give me time to put my personal affairs in order and to finish off some of my work. Then I'll be free for this job.'

"[Husain] said: 'How much time do you want?'

"[Abu Taiba] replied: 'A year.'

"[Husain] said: 'Out of the question.'

" 'How about ten months?' said [Abu Taiba].

"[Husain] said no. And they continued to haggle until they got to one month. [Husain] said: 'Okay then, but keep yourself busy.'

"'God willing, I shall do so,' said [Abu Taiba]."

[Abd al-Wasi'] said: "Then he left and went home and met his friends and brothers. He greeted them and bade them farewell. He freed them from any obligation to him, and they likewise freed him [istahallahum wa istahalluhu]. Then he went into the bathhouse and used a depilatory and shaved his head. He went out, and on the morning when the word came to him of the end of the contracted period, he dressed himself in his shroud and put on embalming ointments. Then he went to [Husain]. The people gathered with the civil authority for the elevation of Abu Taiba to the post of qadi."

[Abd al-Wasi'] said: "So [Abu Taiba] came to [Husain], and [Husain] said to him: 'Oh Abu Taiba, the contracted time which we agreed upon is over. Go forth to the people as a qadi and judge among them.'

"Then [Abu Taiba] fell to his knees in front of Husain and said: 'By God of which there is no other God than he, I shall never govern for you [la walitu laka] or for anybody else. You may do whatever you want.' "

[Abd al-Wasi'] said: "Then Husain got angry with him and did not know what to do about the matter. He remained silent with downcast eyes for a long time. Then he said to an aide: 'Show him out by the private gate so the mob won't realize what has happened between us.' And [Abu Taiba] went out and returned to his home."

Commentary

The history of Islamic law (another view from the center) teaches us that the power to appoint a qadi rested with the caliph in early Islam and that the Abbasids regularized the appointment procedure with the key role in selecting appointees being played by the chief qadi in Baghdad, the Abbasids' new capital city in Iraq. Here, however, we find the appointment being proposed by a local governor at the behest of the populace. Yet the ultimate

58

political authority is still clearly the Abbasid caliph since the unpopular official headdress is black, the symbolic color of the Abbasids.

The motif of a pious man refusing to serve as qadi arises early and lasts long in Islamic history. As one supposed hadith put it, "Whoever is appointed qadi, truly he is sacrificed without a knife."[26] Sharing responsibility for the possibly sinful acts of government and accepting a salary derived from possibly sinful taxes are the usual reasons for refusing to serve, but disrespect for the ruler and his capricious choices also plays a role. One anecdote concerns Bishr ibn al-Walid al-Kindi, a judiciary official under the Caliph al-Ma'mun. "Umar ibn Isa al-Anisi, the judge, said to us, 'One day, when we were at the court of al-Ma'mun, there passed by us Ibrahim ibn Ghiyath, whose intimacy al-Ma'mun had purchased, providing him with a judgeship. Then Bishr said, "We have seen an adulterous judge, a judge used for sodomy, and a judge committing sodomy, but now behold us observing a judge who is hired [as a pimp]!" ' "[27] In later times a person's first refusal to serve is often followed by reluctant acceptance. Abu Taiba's actions in preparing for death, however, indicate a willingness to be executed rather than accept the post. When he successfully wards off the appointment, he disappoints not just the governor, but even more his fellow Muslims. Significantly, his final refusal is couched in the language of governing [*la walitu*] rather than judging, which suggests the degree of perceived complicity in governance that the qadis labored under.

The passage about releasing friends and "brothers" from legal obligations as if he were about to die is obscure but suggestive. Since there is no other evidence that Abu Taiba had any brothers in Gorgan, and no later collateral descendants show up in al-Sahmi's biographical dictionary, it seems likely that "brothers" here is used in a religious sense. If so, given that Abu Taiba seems to have had some sort of legal connection with these "brothers," this may imply a small band of devoted disciples or retainers just as his father and his mentor Kurz ibn Wabra seem to have had.

[5.] Abd al-Wasi' said: "At a later time Kurz ibn Wabra al-Harithi asked God . . . to vouchsafe to him his greatest name. He stood for a year praying for this. While he was standing in his prayer niche [mihrab] praying, there fell upon him a piece of paper with Hebrew writing on it. He took it and read it. Verily, on it was God's greatest name."

[Abd al-Wasi'] said: "So [Kurz ibn Wabra] hid it and told no one about it except Abu Taiba."

[Abd al-Wasi'] said: "Then Abu Taiba asked to copy it so he would have it, too. After his son Abd al-Wasi' [i.e., the grandfather of the narrator] was born, he being his oldest son, and [Abu Taiba's] own death was imminent, he called him to him and gave that name to him, ordering him to keep it safe. When death was nigh for Abd al-Wasi' [the inheritor of God's greatest name], he called my father to him one day around noon and gave him a sealed and stoppered glass bottle. In it was a folded piece of paper. He gave it to him and said: 'Take this bottle, son, and throw it in the Sulaimanabadh canal. Note what you see when you throw it in and report back to me about it.'

"Abd al-Wasi' said [quoting here the words of his father]: 'I disapproved of the business of the bottle and the Sulaimanabadh canal, so I reported to my maternal aunt about it. She blessed me and wished me well. Then she said: "I was thunderstruck [ibsabtu], son, when you told me about that bottle. Do you know what that bottle is, son?"

" 'I said: "I don't know."

" 'She said: "Verily, in it is God's greatest name. Your father feared your losing it so he ordered what you have related. Give it to me so I can save it for you, and [you] go back to him. Tell him: 'I threw it.' When he says to you, 'What did you see?,' say, 'I saw as if a white bird rose from the water into the sky.' " '

"Abd al-Wasi' said [still quoting his father]: 'So I returned to my father and reported to him that I had thrown it into the water. He said to me: "What did you see?" I reported what my aunt had ordered me to tell him. He said: "I was thunderstruck [ibsabtu]." ' "

Commentary

This, the most peculiar story of the entire collection, is also the only one referred to elsewhere among al-Sahmi's biographies. In his entry on Kurz ibn Wabra he relates: "Muhammad ibn Ahmad ibn Ibrahim informed me that he heard from Abu Ja'far al-Warraq, who heard from Isma ibn Ibrahim, who heard from Muhammad ibn al-Hasan, who heard from Ahmad ibn Ibrahim, who heard that Abu Uthman Sa'id said, 'I heard Ibn Uyaina say that Ibn Shabrama said: "Kurz, may God have mercy on him, asked his Lord, the Great and the Glorious, to give him the greatest name in return for which he would ask for nothing more in this world. So God gave it to him. Then he asked to have the power to read the whole Quran through three times in a day and a night." ' "28

The completely separate isnad of this other version of the story indicates that Kurz ibn Wabra's reputation for working wonders was widespread. Crafting a version of the story to show the fruit of Kurz's piety being passed on in the family of his close follower Abu Taiba would be better understandable as an act of family aggrandizement, however, if it told what happened to the bottle once it fell into the possession of Abd al-Wasi's aunt, and if it did not hinge upon the narrator's father's blatant disobedience to his father Abd al-Wasi.'

It is noteworthy that God's greatest name was vouchsafed in Hebrew characters. Al-Sahmi's biography of Abd al-Wasi' relates, with isnad, that "Abd al-Wasi' ibn Abi Taiba al-Jurjani said: 'It is written in the Torah that al-Day [corrected by the editor to al-Rayy, a major city in northern Iran] is one of the gateways of the lands [al-aradin], and [leading] to it is the route mankind follows for trade.' "29 The purport of Abd al-Wasi"s words is most unclear, but they are worth mentioning here because they suggest that he was remembered as someone who knew something of the Torah, conceivably reflecting the possibility that, in childhood, his father Abu Taiba may have gone to a Jewish school at al-Yahudiya in Juzjanan. There was also a Jewish district in Gorgan, however, known as Bab al-Yahud (Gate of the Jews).30

[The Fourth Generation]

[1.] Later Zuwaid compelled Abd al-Wasi' ibn Abi Taiba to take the post of qadi. He resisted. So [Zuwaid] let him surrender it and compelled his brother Ahmad to take it. He too resisted, but [Zuwaid] made things hot for him [ahraqa 'alaihi babahu], and the people refused any qadi except him.

[Abd al-Wasi'] said: "He made him go out and sit in the court of judgement wearing black and the insignia of office [zina], and litigants came for him to judge between them. Ismail ibn Mus'ab, then the commander of the Amir's guard, came to him and said: 'Oh Qadi, the Amir orders you to judge between these two men.' So he went about asking them the matter of their dispute, and tears flowed down into his beard while he judged between them."

Commentary

This is the first generation in which distinctively Muslim names appear, though the earlier practice of giving biblical names survived with Abu Taiba's least-known son Nuh (Noah).[31] Abd al-Wasi' is a rare name meaning Servant of the Comprehensive One, al-Wasi' being one of God's epithets. Al-Sahmi's biography of Ahmad ibn Abi Taiba, the first entry in the *Ta'rikh Jurjan*, confirms that Ahmad served as qadi of Gorgan.[32] Here again we see the unexpected role of popular choice or acceptance in the appointment of a qadi. The theme of a pious man refusing to serve as qadi reappears here for both brothers, but they served anyway. Mention of wearing black as a sort of stigma of office reflects the anti-Abbasid tone noted in the previous generation. The Amir is presumably the local Abbasid governor.

[2.] Abd al-Wasi' said: "In Gorgan there was a secretary (whom Abd al-Wasi' named) who owned [an estate called] Valashjird and a slave girl named Abath, who played the rabab, which is a harp-like stringed instrument [chang]. Her sale price was 50,000 dirhams. [The secretary] was greatly smitten with her, and he was a friend of the Amir. Now the Amir approached him about selling his estate Valashjird and his slave girl Abath, both of which the Amir would buy from him. [The secretary] said to him: 'Oh Amir, Valashjird is my benefice [ni'ma] from which I cannot part, and Abath [holds] my spirit in her bosom.' [The Amir] continued to harass him with requests, and the man refused. [The Amir] kept trying to outwit him, but the man was wary of him until [the Amir] invited him one time and served him wine and got him drunk. Then he ordered that his stomach be trod on, and [the man] died. Then he sent to Ahmad

[ibn Abi Taiba, the qadi] and advanced the idea of selling Valashjird and Abath."

[Abd al-Wasi'] said: "The man had little children by his lady."

He continued: "So Ahmad said: 'He has little children, and a sale against their interest is not possible.' "

[Abd al-Wasi'] continued: "So [the Amir] denied that he would do anything that was not in their interest."

He continued: "Then Ahmad got mad at the Amir and said: 'Oh enemy of God, information has reached me that you killed the man and now you want to possess his wealth. No! You have no consideration.' "

He went on: "So [the Amir] said to him: 'Then I depose you.'

"[Ahmad] replied: 'We accept that and willingly.' And he gave up his position."

[Abd al-Wasi'] said: "The Amir appointed in Gorgan a qadi named Zakariya' al-Raffa'. He bribed him 6,000 dirhams for the sale of Valashjird and Abath, and he accomplished it."

He continued: "The people became upset with the Amir. They said: 'We do not want anyone but Ahmad judging over us.' "

He went on: "So the Amir deposed Zakariya' al-Raffa'."

He continued: "Then [the Amir] sought repayment of the six thousand dirhams and sent to Ahmad [now, apparently, reappointed as qadi], pressing him for a judgment. [Ahmad] refused and left town in disguise by the Qumis road heading for al-Ma'mun [the Caliph], who was at Marv. When he reached his court, he had there a friend, named Kathir ibn Shihab, who was one of al-Ma'mun's chamberlains. He asked permission to see the Caliph and praise him and raise his issue with him. So he entered al-Ma'mun's presence. [The Caliph] greeted him and bade him come near his majlis. He said to him: 'What brings you here?' So [Ahmad] complained of the wrongdoing of the governor of Gorgan and mentioned the harm [reading adhat for adhah] done him. So [al-Ma'mun] said to him: 'Then indeed we shall depose him from you and from the people of your town, and he shall have no power against you.'

"Kathir ibn Shihab said to [Ahmad] in the presence of al-Ma'mun: 'Truly the Commander of the Faithful shall grant you sixteen boons, so ask.'

"[Ahmad] replied: 'The first of them would be granting me relief from the judgeship.'

"[Kathir] replied: 'He shall not grant you such relief because the Commander of the Faithful has trust in the likes of you.'

"[Ahmad] said: 'Over someplace other than Gorgan, then.'

"[Kathir] said: 'Choose any city you want other than Gorgan.'

"[Ahmad] said: 'I shall choose Qumis since it is close to my home city.'

"[Kathir] said: 'I shall appoint you as judge over it. Now what of the rest of your needs?' "

[Abd al-Wasi'] said: "So he asked for certain things that were granted him. He did not ask for anything for himself, but made all of them out of a spirit of charity. So [Kathir] made him qadi of Qumis and gave him a written document for the deposition of that governor."

He continued: "So he went to Gorgan and deposed [the governor]. Then he brought him before the court of administrative misdemeanors [mazalim], and they purchased from him Valashjird and Abath."

[Abd al-Wasi'] went on: "As for Abath the slave girl, if she had been left until these fatherless children were grown, she would have gotten out of practice and some of her value would have eroded. So [Ahmad] sent her to Baghdad, and she was sold there. He went to Qumis as qadi over them and remained there until he died."

Commentary

In Ahmad's own biography the following is related on the authority not of his grandnephew Abd al-Wasi', but of Abd al-Wasi's brother Abd al-Rahman:[33] "Ahmad ibn Abi Taiba went to al-Ma'mun in Marv and asked him to dismiss him from the qadiship of Gorgan. So he dismissed him on condition that he should then appoint him as qadi elsewhere. He chose for himself the judgeship of Qumis, and [al-Ma'mun] appointed him to it. Then he went there and stayed there until he died. He was buried in Qumis."[34]

The Abbasid caliph al-Ma'mun fought a war of succession against his brother al-Amin between 809 and 813. His seat of power was the province of Khurasan and his capital Marv. After his victory, he became caliph but remained in Marv until 819. Thus, this story must date to the period 813–819. Ahmad died in 831. Apparently, despite the central appointing power of the caliph's court, the disposition of the office of qadi in a second-echelon city such as Gorgan fell to the governor. But the ability of the qadi to go directly to the caliph and secure the governor's deposition and his own appointment elsewhere shows that the caliph unquestionably retained the ultimate power of appointment.

From the family point of view, this story demonstrates well that in the fourth generation after conversion the descendants of Dinar had become pillars of Muslim society in Gorgan. Ahmad's personal friendship with one of the caliph's chamberlains and his service as judge for the next decade in the nearby city of Qumis serve to confirm this.

> *[3.] Abd al-Wasi' said: "I made the pilgrimage to Mecca with my father shortly after the year 200 [816 A.D.]. When I entered Damghan, there [Ahmad] was, with his ghulam Najah, standing in the road waiting for me. When he saw me, he said to me: 'Your uncle says to you, "Oh my son, why didn't you tell us you were coming?" ' "*
>
> *He continued: "So I stayed for a while with him."*
>
> *He went on: "When I wanted to leave, he gave me some good advice. Among those pieces of advice, he said to me: 'Oh my son, never, ever, enter a town at night or leave it at night; and never, ever, enter a desert without taking water with you.' "*

Commentary

The mundanity of this closing story of a young man meeting his aged great-uncle in another city reinforces the impression conveyed by the whole collection that these were tales that passed down through the family with no discernible tendentious editing.

Is the history of the descendants of Dinar in any way typical of life on the edge of Islamic society? It is impossible to say. The survival of these family stories is certainly *atypical*, but there is no apparent reason to doubt that they are what they seem to be, a collection of tales about ancestors, some of them fanciful, passed down within the family for no purpose other than informing later generations about their forebears.

Nevertheless, I would not have told the story of Dinar's family at such length if its historical value lay simply in its quaintness, or in the possible truth of each episode. The glimpse of the edge that it affords is not only rare, but suggestive of the life trajectories of others in similar situations. In the following chapters I will reflect back on the history of the family of Dinar in the context of describing the evolution of local religious authority and its relationship to the central institutions of the state. It should be noted, however, that the stories in this collection played no role in the formulation of the ideas I shall use them to illustrate.[35] Their fortuitous discovery and extraordinary convergence with the topics I intended to develop here simply reconfirm my conviction that history is the last refuge of serendipity.

4

ISLAMIC URBANIZATION

Those who believed and left their homes and
strove with their wealth and their lives for
the cause of Allah, and those who took them
in and helped them, these are protecting
friends of one another. And those who
believed but did not leave their homes,
you have no bond with them till they
leave their homes.

—QURAN 8:72

Until now, the educational, intellectual, and emotional life of the early Muslims has held center stage in my narrative. However, their drama was not without a setting. Therefore, I must digress to describe the physical locale in which the main action takes place, the nascent urban communities that developed most strongly during the second, third, and fourth centuries of Islam. Once the origin and characteristics of the all-important cities of medieval Islam have been delineated, our discussion can return to the religious authority that developed among these cities' educated and spiritual elites.

The family descended from Dinar originated with a rural aristocratic landowner being enslaved in Marv as a prisoner of war. Though Dinar is described as a dihqan of Marv, his son moved to the district of Juzjanan, where he seems to have followed the life of a minor aristocrat. In addition, the family seems later to have had property there. This strongly suggests that whatever property Dinar may have had around Marv, he also had property in Juzjanan that remained in his possession despite his capture and temporary enslavement. A similar case of recovery of real estate, years later, by an Iranian taken prisoner during the conquests and led off to Iraq is specifically recorded for the city of Isfahan.[1] Yet Dinar's grandson Abu Taiba becomes a prominent figure in Muslim circles only when he moves from Juzjanan and settles permanently in Gorgan, a small city greatly enlarged by becoming a garrison center for Muslim Arab tribespeople guarding the desert frontier just east of the Caspian Sea. The relocation of Abu Taiba from Juzjanan to Gorgan exemplifies a pattern of migration by new Muslims that was crucial to the growth of Islamic urbanization.

Cities and urban culture are the hallmark and glory of medieval Islamic civilization. But the roots of Islamic urbanization differ significantly from those of other major episodes of urbanization in world history. Widespread urbanization, at least in the medieval and modern periods, has normally been accompanied by a significant change in the efficiency of agricultural production as well as, in most cases, an overall population increase. The reason for this is that there is a limit to the number of agriculturally nonproductive urbanites that can be fed by the surplus drawn from any region's farms and agricultural villages. If agricultural production goes up, either because the rural labor supply grows or because new crops or techniques improve the efficiency of production, more people can be supported in cities. A greater surplus, in either percentage or gross production terms, does not create larger cities; but it is a sine qua non.

Large-scale import of food can produce the same effect, but given the great expense of premechanized land transportation, that possibility was reserved for cities like Rome, Constantinople, Alexandria, and Venice that could be serviced by sea or river transport. The only major Islamic cities of the medieval period that were supplied primarily by water were Baghdad, Kufa, and Basra on the Tigris-Euphrates system, and, on the Nile, Cairo, the capital established in 969 by the newly triumphant Fatimid dynasty alongside the early Arab cantonment (misr) of Fustat.

In the case of Islamic urbanization in general, there is little to indicate either a major improvement in agricultural efficiency or a substantial increase in the overall population, nor is there any evidence of large-scale food importation from distant lands. Even the large riverine cities of Iraq and Egypt relied upon food produced elsewhere in the same region rather than imported from abroad.

Andrew Watson, in his book *Agricultural Innovation in the Early Islamic World*,[2] has mustered the case for an opposing viewpoint. He observes that many new crops, including cotton, citrus fruits, bananas, watermelons, spinach, artichokes, and eggplants, were cultivated more widely during the Umayyad and Abbasid caliphates than before, and he gleans from the few surviving medieval agricultural treatises some indication that important techniques, such as summer cropping and crop rotation, became more widely known in the early Islamic centuries. He notes, furthermore, that Islamic law gave tax abatements to people who brought new land under production and thus encouraged canal digging and other irrigation works, and the cultivation of virgin land that these projects made possible.

On the other hand, most of the crops he mentions could not have had the kind of major effect on calorie production that, for example, the later spread of potatoes and maize from the New World had. Three crops he discusses, sorghum, rice, and hard wheat, are, indeed, staples; but sorghum has never been a popular food in the Middle East, rice requires too much water for most regions (it was cultivated in Mesopotamia before Islam anyway), and hard wheat simply substitutes for soft wheat. Furthermore, one of the most successful of his new crops, cotton, could only have decreased the amount of agricultural land and labor devoted to food production, for a steady growth in popularity of cotton fabrics is well attested. As for technological changes, Watson's data are at best equivocal for early Islam since the Islamic agricultural manuals he uses date mostly from the tenth century or later, well after the onset of large-scale urbanization, and the extent to which the techniques they describe were implemented is left unstated.

Finally, the new lands brought under production have to be balanced, as Watson recognizes,[3] against a retraction in the area under cultivation in other areas, most drastically in the region around Baghdad, the Abbasid capital.[4] Moreover, unlike in temperate

69

Europe where an increase in the market price for grain could stimulate the plowing of virgin land and an overall increase in cultivated acreage, most arable parts of the Middle East are dependent on some sort of irrigation. Given the substantial investment in building the requisite canals and other irrigation systems, therefore, the inclination of entrepreneurs to open new lands for production cannot be considered to have been an automatic function of tax abatements or fluctuating market prices. The availability of capital and labor, the stability of the political climate, and the conditions of rural security were important additional considerations for investors looking to fructify dead land. Instances of new lands being opened during the heyday of the Islamic caliphate cannot be generalized either geographically or chronologically.

Given the questionable and circumstantial character of the evidence regarding crops, technology, and taxes, the strongest argument for a substantial increase in agricultural productivity during the early Islamic centuries boils down to its customary historical association with urban growth. Though Watson mentions a few instances of apparently high rural population densities in widely scattered areas, often using for comparison modern rather than pre-Islamic densities, it is mainly the undeniable evidence of urban growth from which he infers that there must have been an accompanying revolution in agricultural efficiency. "Indeed," he writes, "it is likely that in the early Islamic world the proportion of the total population living in the cities rose. This increasing urbanization of the population, if it occurred, implies a rising productivity of the agricultural labour force: those who tilled the soil could produce not only enough to feed themselves and other rural dwellers but also a surplus big enough to provision cities whose populations grew more rapidly than total population."[5]

Yet if urban growth is the best indicator that new crops and techniques did, in fact, have a widespread impact on agricultural efficiency and population growth, the argument remains inconclusive since there might be other explanations for the growth of cities. In particular, I contend that it is more plausible to associate the burgeoning of cities with the establishment of Arab rule, and the subsequent growth of the Muslim community through conversion and rural-urban migration, than to attribute it to a massive improvement in agricultural productivity or a region-wide growth in population.

The proposition that religious conversion was the most important mechanism of urban growth rests on two types of evidence: first, indications that the most explosive urban growth was disproportionately Muslim and synchronous with the timetable of conversion to Islam; and second, indications that an accelerating depletion of the rural population eventually led, in at least some areas, to a Malthusian crisis of maldistribution of population in which certain overlarge cities outstripped the food-producing capacity of their hinterlands. The body of evidence dealing with the growth of cities will be explored in this chapter. The remaining part of the argument, dealing with hyperurbanization and demographic crisis, will be discussed in chapter 8.

Historians agree that cities grew phenomenally during the early centuries of Islam. However, they usually leave the chronology of growth unspecified and neglect the differences between types of city. Iraq's great cantonments of Kufa and Basra, established in the first decades of the caliphate, grew rapidly into major cities, partly because they almost adjoined and gradually absorbed the preexisting cities of al-Hira and Ubulla, respectively. The early history of Islamic urbanization focuses upon them both because of their importance as governing centers and jumping off points for conquests in the north and east, and because of a heavy concentration in the chronicles upon the acts of their governors and tribes.

Kufa and Basra were not typical, however. Ramla and Qinnasrin, contemporary cantonments in Palestine and Syria, did not grow into major cities; the urbanization of Fustat in Egypt and Qairawan in Tunisia, also military cantonments, was less rapid and less culturally dynamic. Baghdad alone, founded in 762 as the Abbasid capital and cantonment for their army from Khurasan, paralleled Kufa and Basra in dynamism and speed of growth, yet even then, Baghdad's growth was at the expense of nearby Kufa's decline.

Urbanization of the cantonment, or misr, type depended overwhelmingly upon the settlement, partially coerced as a stipulation of army enrollment and pay, of large populations of Arabs. Kufa and

71

Basra bordered the Arabian desert and were the natural destinations for tribes migrating to join in the conquests. Fustat and Qairawan were farther away and did not have so steady a stream of new arrivals. Garrisons more distant still, such as those in Iran and Central Asia, depended more upon sporadic tribal resettlement commanded by the caliphs than upon steady Arab migration.

Later in Islamic history, forced resettlement of civilian populations plays an important role in populating new capital cities with the talents needed to make them flourish. Tamerlane swelled his capital of Samarqand this way in the fourteenth century; Mehmed the Conqueror did the same thing for Ottoman Istanbul in the fifteenth century; and Shah Abbas similarly made Isfahan the capital and showcase of Iran in the seventeenth century. By comparison, there is scant evidence of any deliberate transplantation of non-Arab populations into the early Islamic amsar. Their flowering or decline was more a function of proximity and attractiveness to Arab warriors and non-Arab civilians bent upon catering to the Arabs' needs than of a specific caliphal policy of building cities. The cantonment of Wasit, founded in 702 by the Umayyad caliph Abd al-Malik halfway between Kufa and Basra to keep those two cities from rebelling, never developed extensively as a city. Even Baghdad was designed primarily as a circular, walled cantonment for the army from Khurasan that had brought the Abbasids to power. The rapid growth of a huge civilian population living outside its walls seems comparatively unplanned.

A second type of city includes such historic names as Damascus, Aleppo, Antioch, Jerusalem, and Alexandria. These had been great cities for many centuries. In none of them did the caliphs quarter a major army. In certain cases, however, they did recognize their symbolic importance as traditional centers of political or spiritual authority by building grand Islamic monuments like the Dome of the Rock in Jerusalem and the Umayyad Mosque in Damascus. Some cities in this category, notably Damascus and Aleppo, eventually shared in the burgeoning of Islamic urban culture, though Alexandria and Antioch sank into comparative decline. The periods of greatest growth of the former, however, were substantially later than the first three Islamic centuries.

72

A third type of city displays more clearly than the other two the importance of rural-urban migration in the growth of Islamic cities. This type is most visible in the piedmont and mountain valley communities around the central Iranian deserts. Though numerous city names are mentioned in Iranian and Greek sources of the pre-Islamic period, archaeological evidence and Islamic geographical texts indicate that most of these so-called cities were very small, consisting of little more than a fortress adjoining a walled area at least partially designed as a refuge for nearby villagers in times of unrest. These small "cities" guarded trade routes and provided strongpoints for local protection, but they were comparatively unimportant as population, manufacturing, trade, or cultural centers.

The comparison underlying the word "unimportant" is with many of the same cities three hundred years after the Arab conquest. Nishapur, the paramount Islamic city of northeastern Iran, for example, grew from 1,700–3,500 inhabitants before the Arab conquests to 110,000–220,000 at its peak, around the year 1000.[6] Rayy, outside of modern Tehran, was by then almost as large, though its small inner city of pre-Islamic vintage had become delapidated.[7] In the west, Isfahan consisted of two communities in pre-Islamic times, a larger one, apparently of Jews, called al-Yahudiya, and a more typical fortress town about a third its size two miles away. Their combined population might have been 14,000–20,000. However, if the wall of the tenth-century city was more than 15,000 paces around, as is reported, its population then could by then easily have exceeded 200,000.[8]

Further examples would only reinforce the point that the scale of urban growth in the Iranian highlands was enormous. But where did the population come from? Arab tribespeople displaced by caliphal order from the climatically more congenial provinces of Iraq, Syria, and Arabia usually formed the nucleus of Muslim settlement, but steady and continuous Arab migration seems unlikely. Instead, the Arabs provided the attraction for the non-Arab converts to Islam who migrated to the city from other towns and villages.

In Gorgan, for example, Yazid ibn al-Muhallab, who commanded the city's second and definitive conquest mentioned in the story of Dinar, assigned an area (*khitta*) to each tribal contingent for a mosque and settlement. Some of the forty areas were inside the small preexisting city (qasba) and some were in the camping area (*mirbad*) outside.[9] Information preserved about twenty-four of these mosques contains clues to the city's growth pattern. All but two bore the names of Arab tribes, though one was called the Mosque of the Miscellaneous Arabs (*afna' al-arab*).[10] The others were the mosque of the "reds" (*hamra'*), possibly designating a contingent of fair-skinned Iranian troops who joined the Arab army, and the mosque of the mawali, or converts to Islam. The latter mosque was located on Mawali Street, which indicates, perhaps, that it was built within a settlement area reserved for converts.

By the eleventh century, when the local history of Gorgan that preserves the mosque list was compiled, half of the mosques had come to be known by other names.[11] Eight new names came from individuals associated with the particular mosque; one was named for the cotton cloth merchants; and one for the saddlers. The Mosque of the Miscellaneous Arabs had become the Mosque of the People of Basra. The mosque of the Sinan tribe inside the qasba had been renamed for Abu Taiba ibn Dinar, and later renamed again for his grandson Abd al-Wasi'. Another, that of the Qais ibn Tha'laba tribe, had come to be known for another convert, Shuja' ibn Sabih, like Abu Taiba a disciple of Kurz ibn Wabra.[12] These instances show that mawali were not restricted in their place of worship and residence and suggest that some of the Arab contingents were so small that they lost control of their mosques within a generation of the conquest.

Considering that the area outside the qasba is simply described as a camping area at the time of its original subdivision, the locations later indicated for the mosques gives clues to the city's expansion. One was at the New Gate, another on the market square (*murabba'a*) beside the New Gate, and another at the Gate of the Jews. Since the Gate of the Jews district also featured rows of shops for wheat merchants, butchers, and spinners,[13] it, too, seems to have been a commercial area. Thus Arab settlement outside the gates of the qasba provided the space and the customers for market development. The renaming of mosques for the cotton-cloth merchants and the saddlers supports this idea, as does the location of another

74

mosque on the Street of Sandals. One of the most frequently mentioned streets of the city, the Street of the Stucco Workers, was also located outside the walls.[14]

The settlement of Arabs outside the walls of Gorgan and the subsequent development of their settlement area into the bustling core of a new Islamic city fits a pattern replicated elsewhere on the Iranian plateau. The local history of Nishapur, for example, preserves a list of sixty-five villages and locations that were incorporated into the city as it grew, while a later list of forty-seven city quarters repeats twenty names from the village list, confirming their engrossment by the growing city. The main markets, the governor's seat, and the congregational mosque were all in the area built up outside the old walls.[15] Al-Hira, the wealthy market quarter near the walls east of the inner city, was reportedly settled and named by Arabs from al-Hira in Iraq who participated in the Muslim conquest of the city.[16]

Showing that the cities of the Iranian highlands grew around a core of Arabs who settled outside the walls of the small, preexisting cities does not, of course, establish the identity of the people who became the butchers, stucco workers, wheat dealers, sandal makers, cloth merchants, etc. referred to in place names. They must surely have been, for the most part, Iranians, however. Not only was the population of Arabia too small to account for the growth—particularly given the Arabs' preference for living in Iraq and Syria—but down to the second half of the eighth century, the primary occupation of the Arab tribesmen was military service.

This leaves open the possibility that the Iranian migrants may have been predominantly non-Muslims. Yet despite the occasional references to Jewish, Christian, and Zoroastrian inhabitants, the latter particularly noticeable in southwestern Iran, most of the Iranian cities have an unmistakably Muslim cast from the very beginning. Place names, for example, rarely betray non-Muslim residence, except, as in the case of Yahudiya in Isfahan and the Gate of the Jews in Gorgan, when the name dates to the pre-Islamic period. This relative absence of non-Muslims is particularly striking in comparison with Damascus, Aleppo, Antioch, Jerusalem, and Alexandria, where the pre-Islamic Christian presence remains strong and visible in the Muslim sources.

75

Some new converts to Islam moved to an Arab governing center and settled, as was the case with Abu Taiba. In other cases, non-Muslim migrants converted after arriving. In still other instances, non-Muslims stuck to their ancestral faiths. Those newcomers who converted before migrating were probably prompted to relocate partly by the ostracism they felt from their former coreligionaries,[17] partly by the feeling that only among other Muslims could they live a proper life, and partly by a desire to share in the prosperity of the Arab settlements, where the military payroll, periodic infusions of booty, and local expenditure of a part of the tax revenue made life generally comfortable. Though the last of these motivations, economic betterment, seems most plausible today, it may not have been so important in the eighth or ninth century. People who by converting to Islam cut themselves off from their primary social grouping, namely, their religious community, must have found life very difficult in their native town or village if no sizable Muslim community had yet developed. Pressures to apostasize would have been very strong. Similarly, new Muslims who did not have ready access to people who could answer the questions they had about their faith must have felt socially and spiritually deprived. Both of these factors are evident in the stories of Dinar's son and grandson. Economic betterment, on the other hand, may not have been that evident a possibility to converts of village backgrounds whose primary skills were agricultural. People with craft skills, whether converts to Islam or non-Muslims, were probably more influenced to migrate by economic considerations.

This analysis of factors conducive to rural-urban migration would also apply to the urbanizing Arab cantonments and large pre-Islamic cities of Iraq, Syria, and Egypt; but the impact of conversion is less visible there either because of the disproportionate visibility of the much larger Arab populations in the cantonments, or, in the preexisting cities, because many of the early converts came from non-Muslim communities already resident in the city. Only in Iran, with its small pre-Islamic urban nuclei, does the importance of the convert population stand out clearly. It is in Iran, moreover, that the timetable of urbanization best reflects the timetable of conversion: the ninth century witnesses the highest rates of growth in both cases.

If a substantial number of converts chose to migrate to the Arab settlements, then the rate of Muslim expansion in the countryside must have been slower than that in the cities. Fewer Muslim converts remaining where they were meant fewer personal contacts to spur friends and neighbors into making the same decision to convert. Thus, if less than ten percent of the Iranian population had converted by the time the Abbasids seized control of the caliphate in 750, many rural areas of Iran must still have had very few Muslims at all. The test of the new religion as a social system, therefore, came in the cities, and it accelerated as the curve of conversion entered its bandwagon phase in the early and mid-800s.

The ninth century witnessed the most rapid growth of cities in Iranian history.[18] New congregational mosques were built for the enlarged communities. New districts were developed, sometimes by the locally based rulers who consolidated their strength as Abbasid power progressively weakened after 847. And urban manufactures blossomed with a creativity that fused pre-Islamic styles with Muslim sensibilities.[19] In human terms, the average number of eminent religious figures whose biographies are preserved in the local histories of Nishapur tripled from 4.5 per year between 750 and 860 to 12.5 per year between 860 and 950; figures from Isfahan show an even greater rise from 1.4 per year to 10.2 per year. For Iran overall, a sample of 4,039 scholarly biographies drawn from a general biographical dictionary compiled in Syria in the seventeenth century reveals a tripling of Iranian representation between 815 and 913,[20] during which time, according to the timetable of conversion indicated in figure 3.1, the Muslim population of Iran approximately doubled.

The social and religious consequences of urbanization and concomitant Muslim community growth, and of the burgeoning of religious scholarship in particular, will be dealt with in the next chapter. First, however, it is necessary to return to the question of the roots of Islamic urbanization with which we started. How does the evidence suggesting that people migrated to Arab settlements and governing centers for mixed reasons of conversion and economic opportunity stack up against the evidence that a phenomenal rise in agricultural productivity enabled the food producers to support a greater nonproducing population?

That the cities of the Iranian highlands grew enormously during the early Islamic centuries is beyond question, and historians would probably also agree that growth during the Umayyad and early Abbasid periods was less impressive than growth after the year 800. Yet none of the fourteen new food crops chosen by Andrew Watson to argue for an "agricultural revolution" in early Islamic times was newly introduced to the Iranian highlands at this time. Moreover, the changes in irrigation technology discussed by Watson did not affect Iran, where underground canals (*qanat*) had long been the most efficient means of irrigation; and summer cropping, which may have been an important innovation in the torrid provinces of Mesopotamia and Egypt, was meaningless on the Iranian plateau where winters are cold and summer the normal growing season. This leaves only the question of land tenure, but here, too, there is nothing to suggest any significant changes in Iran.

If the Iranian cities did not grow naturally because of greater agricultural productivity, however, it might still be argued that the change in political regimes, in and of itself, prompted growth. After all, the conquering Arabs had plenty of money to spend in their new governing centers, and they needed local people to supply them with goods and services. But world history exhibits many examples of conquests that are not followed by large-scale urbanization, notably the Germanic invasions of the Roman Empire and the later Mongol conquest of much of western Asia. A conqueror's capital might swell in size and exhibit a prosperity derived from collection of booty, but overall urban growth of the sort seen in Iran is truly unusual. Besides, the new cities were Muslim in character from the very outset and remained so even as the initial Arab settlers came to be outnumbered by the new arrivals.

The story of Abu Taiba's settlement in Gorgan provides one example of a Muslim seeking and finding religious guidance in the company of an Arab army. He himself, however, was not a convert, but the grandson of a convert. A similar example can be drawn from the eminent Hamdani family of Isfahan.[21] Ajlan, its founder, was a dihqan holding lands in the rural area outside Isfahan. He was captured by the Arab army that conquered Isfahan and transported to Kufa, where he became a mawla of the Arab tribe of Murra ibn

Hamdan (hence the family name). His two sons were born in Kufa but in adulthood returned to Isfahan. There they reclaimed possession of their father's lands. But instead of living on the land as he had done, they moved into the city where one of their sons became a disciple of the major Muslim legal figure Sufyan al-Thawri, much as Abu Taiba became a disciple of Kurz ibn Wabra.

Two examples, of course, do not make a trend; but given the paucity of data dealing with urbanization, they are surely indicative. There is no way of telling what proportion of the migrants to the cities converted before they moved, or what proportion converted after arrival. But without the inducement of conversion, either prompting people to move to escape persecution or drawing them into the Arab Muslim communities to learn about their new faith and share in the Muslim commonweal, it is hard to see how such dramatic urbanization could have occurred.

This discussion of Iran leaves open, of course, the question of how urbanization occurred in the caliphate's other provinces, an issue that is complicated by the possible significance there of Watson's putative "agricultural revolution" and by the fact that old, large cities and urbanizing Arab cantonments easily accessible to migrants from Arabia make the impact of converts less easy to ascertain.[22] If conversion played a key role in Iran, however, it may well be assumed that it played a similar role wherever else the social and economic pressures inducing converts to relocate obtained. Otherwise, it would be necessary to explain why Iranian converts opted for urban migration at a disproportionately higher rate than converts did elsewhere.

5

QUESTION AND ANSWER:
THE ROOTS OF
RELIGIOUS AUTHORITY

Ustad Sahl Su'luki was seen in a dream,
and was asked, "How has God treated you?"
He replied, "All my litanies and sayings
were of no avail save for the answers (I gave)
to the questions people asked."
—ANONYMOUS, *THE SEA OF*
PRECIOUS VIRTUES

Let us now return to the people who came to the nascent Islamic
cities and chose to make their homes there. How did they come to
conceive of an Islamic society? To what authority did they turn in
seeking guidance on religious matters?

When Abu Taiba was wandering westward from Afghanistan in
search of religious knowledge, he fell in with Yazid ibn al-Muhallab's army and settled with them when Gorgan was conquered.
What convinced him that his search had ended was the presence in
the army of the ascetic Kurz ibn Wabra. Kurz combined some of the
wonder-working attributes of Abu Taiba's own father with a wealth
of hadith about Muhammad. He employed the latter to assure the
young Abu Taiba as to the way he should comport himself as a Muslim. Some of the specific hadith Abu Taiba learned, as determinable
from the phrase "Abu Taiba heard from Kurz ibn Wabra" in their
isnads, are the following:

"When the month of Ramadan [the Muslim month of fasting] comes upon you, the demons are manacled, the gates of hell are locked up, and the gates of paradise are opened. The witchcraft of sorcerers is not permitted in it."[1] (Another recension transmitted from Kurz through Abu Taiba goes on at great length promising, among other things, God's blessings and protection for every hour of the day and his removal of anger from the hearts of sultans and tyrants.[2])

"Whoever fasts during Sha'ban [the month before Ramadan], verily God frees him from all of his sins on the day of Sha'ban that he fasts."[3]

"Whoever fasts in Rajab [the month before Sha'ban], God shall forgive him seventy-fold for each day and shall grant seventy of his needs in this world and seventy in the next."[4]

"Whoever fasts three days in every month . . . his fasting shall be reckoned as of three thousand years; and whoever fasts during Ashura [the tenth day of the month of Muharram], it shall be as if he fasted for eternity and was resurrected."[5]

"On the twenty-fifth day of Dhu al-Qa'da [the eleventh month], God bestowed upon Adam the Ka'ba [the cubical building in Mecca toward which Muslims face in prayer]. It was the first blessing that God sent down from heaven. So whoever fasts on that day has forgiveness of sin for seventy years."[6]

From these hadith, and from the stories related about Kurz's asceticism, one might conclude that Kurz had an inordinate interest in fasting. As so he might. But none of the many hadith known to have been transmitted from Kurz by other reciters ever mention fasting. One hadith from Kurz, for example, condemns the sect of the Qadariya as God's enemies. It was so popular that it occurs three times in slightly different form, but each time the isnad goes back to someone named Muhammad ibn al-Fadl rather than to Abu Taiba.[7]

What seems most plausible is that Abu Taiba, who was well known as Kurz's disciple, shared Kurz's interest in fasting and self-denial. Therefore, the guidance he got from Kurz fed his personal needs and interests. The unknown Muhammad ibn al-Fadl, on the other hand, was probably interested in the issue of free will in Islam, the focus of Qadari doctrine, and Kurz answered his need for guidance as well. In Abu Taiba's case, one can deduce the source of his interest in asceticism from the stories told of his father leading a band of ascetics in Juzjanan. No information about Muhammad ibn al-Fadl has been preserved, however.

To get a sense of what the religious atmosphere of these early Muslim communities in remote places must have been like, one must multiply the above examples by tens of thousands. Wherever people converted to Islam, they had questions about what they should believe and how they should behave, questions that could not be answered from the Quran, even if they knew Arabic and had access to the Quran. Some, like Abu Taiba's father, lived their lives among unbelievers and probably never had a very clear notion of how their religion was observed in its Arabian homeland, or even in the nearest Arab garrison, for that matter. But others, like Abu Taiba himself, migrated to a city with a Muslim community.

In the boomtown informality of recently settled Gorgan, Abu Taiba probably met personally both the military commander, Yazid ibn al-Muhallab, and the former Iranian ruler, Sul. Both men's families continued to reside in Gorgan for generations.[8] But Sul was a more recent convert than Abu Taiba and thus had nothing to teach him about Islam, and Yazid ibn al-Muhallab, despite his wealth and prestige, was known for only one hadith, and there were dire suspicions about the genuineness of that one.[9] Abu Taiba turned, therefore, to Kurz ibn Wabra and took him as his mentor.

The bond between these two men was not without long-term effects. What Kurz told Abu Taiba, Abu Taiba passed on to his own students or admirers, and they transmitted it to the next generation. Eventually, therefore, this body of lore about fasting became available in hadith class to every youth in Gorgan. Moreover, the authority residing in the teacher was such that whoever heard these hadith believed them to be sound regardless of any reservations that might somewhere have been raised by a specialist trying to winnow out only certifiably sound traditions. This was all the more the case since Kurz and Abu Taiba were two of Gorgan's most famous early personalities, and Abu Taiba is described by al-Sahmi as "a virtuous man whom I do not think ever intentionally lied."[10]

Was this strong orientation toward supererogatory fasting similarly implanted in other Muslim communities? There is no way of telling. Even if each individual fasting hadith were to be regarded as sound, there is no way of knowing exactly where everyone who knew them lived, or whether they, or the people beseeching them for knowledge, were interested enough in fasting to pass them along. Probability dictates against such uniformity, however. The Iranian local historians normally listed all of the Companions, and of the Followers, the people of the next generation who transmitted hadith from the Companions, who set foot in their community. Given that some three centuries elapsed between a city's being conquered and the lore about its leading religious figures being collected, it may be assumed that they missed some names and invented others. But any names they missed were not being passed along in isnads anyway, so their absence is insignificant from the point of view of the local sources for Muslim practices. Likewise, the invention of names in isnads would not have affected the existence, and presumed authenticity, of hadith ascribed to them.

Since the number of known Companions and Followers in Iran was small, and few names overlap between Isfahan, Nishapur, and Gorgan, it must be assumed that each community's reservoir of hadith was initially quite limited. Even though these natural repositories of authoritative religious lore were probably confronted by all manner of religious questions, there was only so much that any one of them actually knew. In time, however, in the ordinary course of things, the local fund of hadith grew larger as new arrivals in each generation of newcomers brought in lore they had picked up elsewhere; but as discussed in the preceding chapter, more and more of the new arrivals were fresh converts who had no Islamic lore to contribute. Ascribing hadith to nonexistent names must also have had a local rather than a general impact since identical names and hadith could not have entered into circulation everywhere at the same time.

To be sure, local people traveled and collected hadith in other cities, and knowledgeable people just passing through were prevailed upon to impart some of the hadith they knew; but most young Muslims learned their hadith exclusively from local sources. For every individual who collected hadith in faraway places, there were dozens who contented themselves with the hadith they could learn at home. Only ten percent[11] of the individual student-teacher contacts noted in al-Farisi's biographical dictionary of Nishapur occurred in some other city.

To pursue this specific example, out of the group of 1,080 Nishapuris for whom educational data are available, over a period of a century only thirteen definitely studied in Isfahan, under two teachers. The number of Isfahanis who are mentioned in that city's biographical dictionary as studying in Nishapur over a similar period is three. Even taking into account the likelihood that a good number of educational contacts went unrecorded, serious scholarly visits between these major cities of eastern and western Iran must have averaged less than one per year. Furthermore, seeing that a visiting scholar had to sit in class and take down hadith by dictation like everyone else, only a small portion of each city's collectively known hadith could have been exchanged in this way. No visiting scholar is likely to have recorded all of the hadith being recited by all of the hadith teachers active at the time of his visit; even if he had, the city's fund of hadith might be augmented at any time because of new lore put in circulation by a new teacher drawing on materials gleaned in his travels.

With cities outside Iran, with the exception of Baghdad and the holy cities of Mecca and Medina, contact was even more irregular. Yemen affords an instructive example. Of the 4,397 individuals mentioned in Nishapur's biographical dictionaries, none is recorded as having visited Yemen. For Isfahan, out of 1,881 known individuals, only two visited Yemen, one of them on business. But no fewer than eight out of 1,194 Gorganis went all the way to Yemen specifically to study. Whether because of tribal connections dating back to the early days of Arab settlement, or for some other reason, Gorgan had an educational contact with Yemen that Nishapur and Isfahan lacked. Its fund of hadith, therefore, must have differed, with regard to lore emanating from Yemeni sources, from that of those other cities.

Scholars from Spain and North Africa almost never visited Iran; Iranians rarely visited Spain and North Africa.[12] More students are recorded trekking the 1,900 miles from Gorgan to Yemen than traversing a third of that distance from Isfahan to Nishapur. Data of this sort make it abundantly clear that most hadith-based knowledge of Islam was local even though the sharing of hadith between communities undoubtedly increased over time. In other words, it is inconceivable that the hadith eventually compiled in the six "canonical" collections of sound traditions were distributed homogeneously throughout Iran, the homeland of the collectors, much less the whole Islamic world, in the early centuries. After all, if they had been, no one would have bothered to travel about in order to discover new sources.

The scholarly practice of bringing together sound hadith from different locations and rejecting the much greater number of hadith that did not meet the rigorous standards the muhaddithun applied in evaluating hadith eventually produced a near-consensus on what the Prophetic lore of Islam contained, but the same practices have made it almost impossible to reconstruct what was earlier understood to be the corpus of Prophetic lore in any particular community. The false image of uniform religious practice and of a uniform corpus of Islamic knowledge thus engendered served well the interest of Muslim scholars in later centuries who believed that, apart from well-attested sectarian splits, the Muslim community had changed little in religious practice and outlook since the time of the Prophet; but it is an impediment to the historical reimagining of localized Muslim communities in the early centuries.

The local history of Gorgan, for example, preserves a body of hadith of indeterminable representativeness that was unquestionably being taught in local hadith classes in the year 1000. In the eyes of the muhaddithun, some came to be considered sound, many others weak; but all were accepted by the students who heard them as authoritative statements about the meaning and content of their religion. In many cases, we can almost hear behind them the questions to which they responded.

When a territory is captured by force and sacked, should the women be killed?
"The Prophet, God's prayers and peace be upon him, prohibited killing women in war."[13]
Are women basically good? Or bad?

"I was raised up to heaven and saw that most of its denizens were poor people; I was raised [sic] into the hellfire and saw that most of its denizens were women."[14]

Now that we are Muslims, can we still have drinking parties where we pass around a ceremonial cup and all drink from it as we used to do?

"Whenever a group of people sit down to drink and the cup rotates among them, the damnation of God rotates among them."[15] Furthermore, "Whoever drinks from a goblet of gold or silver, or one that contains anything of them, surely hellfire gurgles in his belly."[16]

Is it permissible to have social contact with someone while you're urinating?

"A man passed by the Prophet, God's prayers and peace be upon him, while he was urinating and greeted him, but he did not return the greeting."[17]

When you put your hands up while praying, is it all right to touch your beard?

"The Messenger of God, God's prayers and peace be upon him, often touched his beard while praying."[18]

How bad is it to keep a dog as a pet?

"Whoever keeps a dog that is neither a sheep dog nor a hunting dog loses every day one grain of his eternal reward."[19]

Do we really have to learn Arabic? What's wrong with speaking Persian?

"Umar [the second caliph] was walking, and he heard two men speaking Persian. Thereupon he said, 'Switch to Arabic, for whoever speaks Persian is mischievous, and whoever is mischievous loses his manhood.' "[20]

Is it all right for me to shave my head and just leave a topknot?

"The Messenger of God, God's prayers and peace be upon him, forbade shaving the head leaving tufts of hair."[21]

Our nobles are accustomed to wearing expensive brocaded coats made of silk and gold thread? Can they continue this practice?

"Gold and silk are permitted to the females of my community, but prohibited to the males."[22]

The Jews say their religion is older and their prophets said nothing about Muhammad's coming. Are they telling the truth?

"The writing on the signet ring of King Solomon [Sulaiman ibn Daud] said 'There is no God but God, and Muhammad is the Messenger of God.' "[23]

We have just heard (in the year 945) that the Buyids have entered Baghdad and taken control of the caliphate; how serious a matter is this?

"Mu'awiya [the fifth caliph] said to Abd Allah ibn Amr ibn al-As: 'This community will bear fruit for three hundred and thirty years and thirty months and thirty days.' "[24] (The Buyid takeover occurred in the three hundred and thirty-third year since the beginning of the Islamic calendar in 622.)

I converted to Islam before another Persian, not before an Arab; am I a mawla, and if so, whose?

"The mawla of a people is one of them, and the mawla of one of their mawali is one of them, too."[25]

I know we're forbidden to drink wine, but can we sell our grapes to winemakers?

"Whoever keeps back his grapes at the time of harvest in order to sell them to a Jew, a Christian, or a Zoroastrian, or to anyone else whom he knows uses them for wine, surely hellfire has ventured upon his mind."[26]

We've seen that the Arabs have different eating habits. How should we eat our meals?

"Malik ibn Anas said, 'The Messenger of God, God's prayers and peace be upon him, did not eat from a tray, or a bowl, or a flattened piece of bread.' Qatada asked, 'Then from what sort of thing did they used to eat?' [Malik] said, 'From a piece of leather.' "[27] Another tradition relates, "I came upon Harun al-Rashid [the fifth Abbasid caliph] while he was eating date pudding with a spoon. He said, 'Come over here, Sufyan, and eat with me.' I replied, 'Oh, Commander of the Faithful, in interpreting the verse of the Quran "Verily, we have been generous with the sons of Adam," Abd Allah ibn al-Abbas [Harun's ancestor] said, "They eat with their fingers." So [Harun] put down the spoon and ate with his fingers."[28]

Since polytheists are supposed to be offered a choice of conversion to Islam or death, is it permissible to do business with them?

"You do not kill the merchants of the polytheists."[29]

How should we regard the Jews?

"God fought with the Jews. They took the tombs of their prophets as places of prayer."[30]

While some of these and of the other traditions circulating in Gorgan must have been fabricated, for example the ones describing

King Solomon's ring and predicting the Buyid takeover of Baghdad, and some are technically not hadith because they go back to a caliph or someone else other than the Prophet, their substance, collectively, was the substance of Islamic lore in that community. To the extent that this body of lore was particular to Gorgan, the Muslims of Gorgan understood and practiced Islam in their own distinctive fashion. Moreover, despite the concern a few hadith specialists had with authenticity, most Muslims revered the people who transmitted their lore and implicitly trusted what they had to say.

To return to the case of Abu Taiba and Kurz ibn Wabra discussed in chapter 3, it is highly unlikely that the type of asceticism they fostered in Gorgan and sustained by their recitations of hadith coincided precisely with Muslim ascetic inclinations elsewhere. Yet piety and asceticism were important matters in other Muslim communities, as well. In general, the Companions and the Followers are rarely called ascetics (*zahid*, pl. *zuhhad*), though Kurz ibn Wabra was. By the third generation of Islam, however, ascetics and pietists (`*abid*, pl. *'ubbad*) become more visible; and by the latter part of the ninth century they constitute a significant current of Islamic belief and practice. At the same time, several additional words gain currency: *dayyin* (godly), *nasik* (devotee), *wari'* (abstainer), *mujab al-da'wa* (he whose summons to Islam is heeded), and even *rahib* (monk).[31]

Clearly, there were people everywhere who stood in awe of manifestations of piety and self-denial and sought to emulate them. This is hardly surprising given the prominence of such practices in the non-Muslim religions from which people were converting. Those who were psychologically inclined to admire or imitate such behavior as Christians, Jews, and Zoroastrians would naturally gravitate toward the spiritual athletes in the Muslim community. It is noteworthy, therefore, that the rate of occurrence of the terms "ascetic" and "pietist" in both Isfahan and Nishapur doubled during the ninth century when conversion and urbanization were at their peak. Pious excess loomed large in the spiritual life of the booming Islamic cities.

Another type of spiritual venture gained ground more slowly, however. The story of Kurz ibn Wabra and the greatest name of God foreshadows this development. Kurz performed prodigies of

89

fasting and self-mortification, but in one specific instance he prayed for a year to be vouchsafed God's greatest name. In response, a slip of paper floated down from heaven with the holy name written on it. Kurz gave a copy to Abu Taiba, who passed it on to his son as a sacred relic. The relationship between God, Kurz, and Abu Taiba anticipates the spiritual structure of Sufism, often referred to as Islamic mysticism.

In very simple terms, Sufis seek the psychological experience of union with or vision of God through a graded series of ritual and meditative exercises, including asceticism and worldly denial. The earliest Sufis explored this spiritual territory alone, but by the eleventh century it was more common for an aspirant to devote himself to the way of a single master. Once a Sufi was seen to have attained the sought for enlightenment, people regarded him as a vessel of divine grace and believed that a residue of this grace adhered to his tomb, personal effects, and kin after his death.

In the story of God's greatest name, Kurz prays long and intensively and is finally granted direct contact with God. The evidence of his contact survives on the piece of paper, which also preserves God's blessing, as symbolized by the white bird rising from the ripples of its supposed disposal. The story is fanciful, of course, and primitive in its visualization of how man might entreat God directly. It demonstrates, however, the Sufi premise that arduous spiritual endeavor can, indeed, enable man to "see" God. And from this derives an alternative form of religious authority for the Muslim community. As we have seen, a perplexed Muslim looking for answers to spiritual questions might be guided by a hadith transmitted from the Prophet, or follow the example of pious Muslim behavior set by a pietist or ascetic in the local community; but with Sufism came the possibility of following a mentor whose authority derived directly from God. (After the Sufi passed away, of course, the stories about his or her deeds and sayings had to be related with isnads because of the prior establishment of oral transmission as the criterion of authority.)

The absolute number of Sufis mentioned in the local biographical dictionaries does not exceed ten percent until late in the eleventh century; before the ninth century there are none.[32] When Sufism does begin to surge, however, it is apparent that it absorbs the previously independent trends of pietism and asceticism. Though people labeled as pietists and ascetics before the eleventh century never bear the additional label Sufi, these become markedly less numerous as the number of Sufis rises. Then, once Sufism finally takes over as the main form of extreme Muslim piety, its devotees rewrite history to portray the early ascetics as forerunners of the Sufis. Nevertheless, asceticism and pietism clearly originated as tendencies separate from Sufism, though not necessarily from each other.

Even so, no matter how much they might admire otherworldly ascetics and Sufis, most Muslims were not personally inclined toward extremes of religious behavior. The Arab essayist Abu Hayyan al-Tawhidi at the end of the tenth century sarcastically opined, "As for asceticism and those who are known for piety and uprightness, it is claimed of them that bronze takes the form of gold for them, and something else becomes silver; and that God the Great and Glorious shakes the mountains with earthquakes for them, and makes it rain for them, and causes plants to sprout from the earth for them."[33]

Some even went so far as to deplore excessive religious devotion as vainglory and hypocrisy, setting forth a third course, neither scholarly nor mystical, as a model for pious behavior. This current was known as the *malamatiyya*. Being a *malamati* meant "giving up the reputation one might have for being any different from other people in the way they dress, walk, and sit. [It meant] going along with them in the externals of legal ordinances, but secretly standing alone in the perfection of one's fear of God. [The malamati's] external behavior, therefore, did not contradict the external behavior of other people to the extent of distinguishing himself from them; but neither did his internal state coincide with the internal state of other people. [In this way] he assisted them through those practices and habits he decided upon."[34]

The same treatise that thus praises the sobriety and ordinariness of the malamatis also expounds the errors of people claiming to be Sufis. For example, "one group errs by withdrawing, imagining that withdrawal [from society] and taking up residence in caves, or becoming hermits in mountains and deserts, will protect them from the evils of their selves and cause to enter into them what enters into saints. . . . Another group errs in putting on woolen garments and patched cloaks unnecessarily [i.e., without proper Sufi authorization] and taking up ewers and leather bags. They learn a few of the signs and a little of the learning of the [true Sufis] and think that once they've done that, they are part of them."[35]

The malamatis' belief in the pious necessity of remaining religiously inconspicuous made public promotion of their doctrines morally questionable, a contradiction that played a role in the comparative obscurity of this trend.[36] Many people probably shared their feeling, however, that extreme behavior was not the only way to exhibit one's adherence to Islam. As a general rule, people who convert from one religion to another tend to expect or seek in their new religion the values and institutional supports that they are accustomed to, or perhaps more often feel to be inadequate, in their old one. Christians, Jews, and Zoroastrians with a zealous taste for self-abnegation surely looked, upon conversion, for examples of such behavior within Islam; or possibly they were induced to convert by the perception that Islam welcomed such behavior on the part of its ascetics and pietists. But by the same token, stodgy and conservative Zoroastrians, Jews, and Christians, though slower to convert, might not have adopted Islam if they had not seen in it a place for stodgy, conformist, conservatism.

A hint of this may be found in data relating to the rise of legal thought and teaching in the new Muslim cities. Qadis are mentioned from earliest times since the appointment of judges for the Islamic community was a caliphal function deriving from the judicial role of the Prophet himself. But a qadi did not have to be a legal specialist, particularly in the first centuries. His duty in the disputes brought before him was to make a finding of fact based on the rules for oral testimony sketched in the Quran. The qadi had to be male, adult, free, and sound of mind and character. However, if he lacked knowledge of the Quranic verses or Prophetic precedents in some matter, and did not want to impose his own opinion, he was free to consult with someone more knowledgeable. This knowledgeable person might go so far as to issue a *fatwa*, or consulting legal opinion, designed to advise the judge or one of the litigants in a non-binding fashion.

The role of the legal specialist—the fully evolved form of the "more knowledgeable person"—increased over time, both because a growing sophistication in legal reasoning required greater knowledge, and because growing communities generated more, and more complicated, legal disputes. A legal specialist was called a *faqih*, a word derived from *fiqh*, meaning "jurisprudence," which itself went back to a verb meaning "to understand." The presence of *fuqaha* (the plural of faqih) in a community bespoke not just the application of Islamic law, but also the teaching of law and a general awareness of Islam's legal framework.

Though no general discussion of the Islamic religion is complete without the observation that the *shari'a*, the law of Islam, guides the faithful in all their acts from birth to life in the hereafter, such discussions seldom touch on the situation of Muslims living without everyday recourse to the shari'a. (These real-world situations are usually relegated to anthropological studies of tribes and villages.) Yet the importance of the law during the first century or two of Islam seems to have been restricted to fairly small circles within major Muslim population centers. So long as most Muslims were members of Arab tribes, tribal custom and tradition governed many affairs that later became the provenance of the shari'a. And as for the non-Arab converts, some assimilated to the Arab tribes and accepted their customs, and some, like Abu Taiba's father, lived in communities where there were too few Muslims to support a qadi, or perhaps even an awareness of Islam as a basis of law.

With the swelling of the current of conversion in the ninth century came not only the growth of cities, but an expansion of the social domain of Islamic law. This can be seen through the lives of eminent jurists, but equally in the number of fuqaha named in the local biographical dictionaries. There are only two people called fuqaha among those known religious worthies who died before 850 in Isfahan, though some of the qadis during this period may also have been legally erudite. Between the middle of the ninth century and the middle of the tenth century, however, the number rises to 29, or 2.5 percent of the total number of entries. After that, the percentage more than doubles to 5.8 percent. The pattern in Nishapur is strikingly similar: fuqaha account for 1.6 percent of entries before 850, 3.7 percent between 850 and 950, and 8.9 percent thereafter.

This evident relationship between urban growth and an expansion of the legal calling bears comparison with the growth in the number of ascetics, pietists, and Sufis discussed earlier. For the legists, considering that our chronological categories are defined by death dates, the tenth century is evidently the period of greatest growth. For the devotional zealots, however, it is the ninth century. In other words, law gained prominence with the maturing of the Muslim urban communities and provided an alternative model of Muslim religious observance. Doubtless, the conversion of more conservative elements from the non-Muslim communities toward the end of the bandwagon period and later had something to do with this change. But regardless of its cause, its effect must have been a moderation in the tone of Muslim society. It is noteworthy in this connection that Muslim and quasi-Muslim sectarian revolts pretty much disappeared in Iran in the course of the ninth century, only to be supplanted in the following century by urban factional discord focusing on differences between schools of legal thought.

To summarize the argument thus far, religious authority at the local level was complex and fluid in the early Islamic centuries. Initially the Companions and their Followers commanded the field because of their direct experience of the Prophet's community or of his Companions of the founding generation. They alone had a plausible claim to being able to answer the believers' questions. The reports they conveyed about life in Mecca and Medina, including many that came to be foisted upon them by people seeking to gain greater authority for words of their own invention, had a powerful influence locally; each locale had its own supply, which only partially overlapped what people in the next town knew.

The converts to Islam, perhaps even more than the Arabs themselves, revered these living vessels of Muslim sanctity, sometimes faultily remembered. But as generation succeeded generation, the charisma of contact with the Prophet's community in Mecca and Medina waned steadily until little remained but its symbolic evoca-

94

tion in isnads and in the solemnity of the hadith class. In the meantime, new paragons of religious devotion arose to compete for the attention of the new Muslims and their children. Jews, Christians, and Zoroastrians alike were attuned to respecting and emulating notable religious figures living in their midst. Jewish rabbis, Christian clergy and monks, and Zoroastrian priests, titled *mobad* or *herbad*, were different from one another in the qualities that made them admirable, but they shared the characteristic of fitting into established categories of religious leadership.

In imagining the religious life of non-Arab converts from these religions it is hard to avoid picturing them looking within Islam for the kind of exemplary religious figures they had been reared to emulate in their previous faith. The rise to prominence of ascetics and pietists in the generations following the Companions and the Followers bespeaks a type of religious authority based upon pious example rather than contact with the Prophetic tradition.

Other aspects of non-Muslim religious experience were slower to make their influence felt. Christians, Jews, and Zoroastrians had long lived in communities in which law and education were near-monopolies of religious institutions. Once they became Muslims, of course, they recognized the political rule of the caliph, unless they were attracted by one of the many rebels against caliphal authority. But it was evident that the qadis sent by the caliph did not settle disputes on the basis of the caliph's decree. No code of laws came forth from Damascus or Baghdad, and no royal edicts were posted in the markets and public squares to make known the king's law, and then saved to become part of a corpus of royal decrees.

Rather, the laws of Islam were like the laws the new Muslims had known in their old religions. They rested upon divine writ, the holy example of the Prophet, and increasingly sophisticated interpretations of both. They also incorporated venerable local custom, which varied from region to region. It stood to reason, therefore, that those people who specialized in understanding the law moved into positions of religious authority analogous to those held by similar functionaries in the non-Muslim communities. The religious leadership of the fuqaha came not from hadith, though expertise in hadith was an essential part of their knowledge, and not from exemplary personal piety, but from the fact that they were the local representatives and guardians of the sacred law.

Yet hadith, piety, and law do not account for all of the sources of religious authority in the burgeoning Muslim cities. They are just the ones most easily discernible in the local biographical dictionaries, compilations that were devoted to the literate upper crust of local society. At the popular level, recourse to religious authority took a wide variety of forms. Story-tellers and popular preachers relied on the substance of their words to impress and influence their audiences. One ascetic in Nishapur, for example, told the following story:

> In India there was an old man who for seventy years had served an idol [sanam] and acknowledged its divinity. One day an important matter came his way. He prepared himself, put on a shawl, as was their custom, and entered the house of idols. Standing humbly in front of the idol, he cried and prayed long and fervently, beseeching the idol to help him in that work. Then he called to him and said, "O Sanam, you know that I have served you faithfully for the past seventy years and acknowledged you as my god. Now that this consequential task has come up, do make it possible for me to succeed in it." But the idol did not respond or answer him. He repeated his words and said, "O Sanam, take pity on me! Recognize my services to you for the last seventy years!" But to no avail. The Idol did not answer though he repeated his prayers seventy more times.
>
> The old man was desperate. Then Allah the Exalted and Almighty looked into his heart with a look of mercy and compassion. A thought came to the man's mind and he said, "I have served this sanam for seventy years, and I have called upon him seventy times, and he has not answered me. Let me try to call upon Samad [the Eternal One, one of the names of God]; perhaps he will answer me." He raised his head to the heavens and shyly called once, "O Samad!" At once [a voice] was heard saying, "Here I am. O my servant, ask what you wish." The angels, shocked and bewildered, said, "Our Lord! This person, who has turned away from your worship, who has chosen another to adore, spending his life in the service of an idol to which he has prayed and called upon seventy times, without receiving any

answer—how is it that you answer him after he calls upon you only once?" Then Allah, High and Exalted, said, "My angels, this man invoked his idol and did not receive an answer. Then he called upon Samad. If Samad did not answer him, what would be the difference between Samad and Sanam?"[37]

While this can be read simply as an amusing tale designed to show God's mercy, it should be noted that it is attributed to a member of the Karramiya sect, an ascetic movement that had a special interest in drawing converts to Islam.[38] One can well imagine, therefore, that for some listeners this was a tale to take to heart. It told them that no matter how old they were, or how long they had worshipped as non-Muslims, God would turn his face to them as soon as they confessed their belief in him as Muslims. This assurance, however, rested upon no particular authority other than the personal credibility of its teller, in this case an ascetic.

Oblique testimony to the pervasiveness of Muslim religious sensibility and authority in the social life of Iranian cities comes from a long poem by Abu Dulaf al-Khazraji devoted to the informal brotherhood of beggars and confidence men, known as the Banu Sasan, that seems to have thrived in the new urban environments.[39] Court sophisticates in the tenth century reveled in tales of these scoundrels, perhaps because of a certain disdain in ruling circles for the religious values and manners they mimicked and took advantage of. While many of Abu Dulaf's beggars fall into well-known categories, such as people feigning blindness or lameness, many others imitated or exploited Muslim piety in quest of alms. Among the latter were:

> "The one who tells stories about the history and legends of the Jews [i.e., about the prophets before Muhammad], or who relates a series of brief anecdotes one after another" (verse 41).
> "The one who parades in the garb of an ascetic, or who begs on the pretext that he is a pilgrim" (verse 42).
> "The one who makes out that he is fasting almost totally during Ramadan, or who fraudulently claims to be following the divine law, or who wears coarse garments of hair and pretends to be mortifying the flesh" (verse 43).
> "The one who creates a false impression that he is fasting, but

who seeks refreshment in the river, pretending that he is trying
to keep cool" (verse 79).

"Of our number [i.e., of the Banu Sasan] is every ostensible convert to Islam from the People of the Book, who recites volubly
the Gospel and the Quran" (verse 49).

"The one who lifts up his voice during the prayers in the mosque,
in the mornings and in the afternoon" (verse 52).

"A group of people who have with them books of traditions, from
which they recite, and they adjure their audience strenuously
against unnatural vice and wine drinking" (verse 56).

"The one who declaims traditions, indeed, what would fill a
whole book container" (verse 65).

"The person who throws down prayer beads and cakes of sweet-
meats at shop doors. Some of these beggars are not only given
money but have the beads and cakes given back to them"
(verse 73).

"The person who dyes his hands with henna. At the same time,
he shaves off his moustache and thus leaves his upper lip like a
polished washing-bowl and like a woman's plucked puden-
dum. He then claims to be one of the Sufis, the learned and
ascetic ones, and he begs his daily living by means of that"
(verse 82).

"Of our number is every person who adopts a pious mode of life
and a submissive demeanor, like a learned scholar" (verse
131).

From top to bottom, Islam provided the central drama of urban
social life. It is a drama in the course of which Arab immigrants,
non-Arab converts, and the descendants of both created a new society simply by trying to determine how best to live as Muslims. The
many seek anwers to their questions and solutions to their problems. A few, buttressed by varying forms of religious authority, provide the answers. Another few exploit the social piety of their urban
brethren through begging and charlatanry.

The view from the center, however, sees only traces of this drama,
which, from the point of view of princely courts, is mostly performed offstage. There is little here of caliphs and conquests, and
the most illustrious intellectual figures, at least as they are customarily presented, think and write at more elevated levels. Yet despite

the tone of superiority and detached amusement that pervades the stories of popular life retailed in court circles, life in the cities, the true locus of Islam's civilizational greatness, inexorably molded society more forcefully than any caliph or philosopher.

6

ULAMA

Seeking knowledge is a divine injunction
upon every Muslim, but bestowing knowledge
on the wrong people is like putting necklaces
of pearls, gold, and jewels on pigs.
—Hadith quoted in HAMZA AL-SAHMI,
TA'RIKH JURJAN

By the year 1000 the great surge of conversion and urbanization
had reached its peak. The population and prosperity of Iran's cities
plateaued. Within a century they started to recede. I will now look
at the evolved character of social and religious authority in the late
tenth and early eleventh centuries before that recession began.

Seen from the center, the eleventh century was a pivotal period
when the Seljuq sultans, drawing on the might of nomadic Turkish
tribes infiltrating westward from Central Asia, expelled the Buyid
warlords from their principalities in western Iran, gained control of
the Abbasid caliphate in Baghdad, and established an empire that
stretched from Afghanistan to Syria. As Sunni Muslims succeeding
the Shi'ite Buyids, the Seljuqs have sometimes been seen as spon-
sors of a "Sunni revival"[1] that ended a century of Shi'ite dynastic
ambition both in Iran and, late, Egypt.

The view from the edge is very different. Young cities whose fluid
social patterns were dominated by the needs and hopes of a teem-
ing mass of newcomers matured into stable, bustling communities
with established social divisions and strong local identity. The pretensions and ambitions of their leading families, now defined more
by wealth and scholarship than by ascetic behavior or connection

101

with the Arab conquerors, powered a myriad of local political histories that only tangentially related to the histories of the sultans and caliphs. In the long run, however, the religious outlook and social undertakings of these eminent urban lineages had greater impact on the evolution of Islamic society than any Turkish warlord.

We have seen in the family of Abu Taiba a progression from a nominally Muslim holy man living in a remote non-Muslim region, to a principal disciple of an Arab ascetic of the Follower generation in an Arab garrison city, to a judge of that city with connections in the court of the caliph himself. By the second half of the ninth century, however, Abu Taiba's descendants no longer led Gorgan's Muslim community, even though the memory of their pious ancestors continued strong in oral tradition. Newer families, risen to prominence during the most explosive period of conversion and urbanization, provided a new leadership for the city's greatly matured Muslim community.

The example of the Isma'ili family will be developed at length later in this chapter. One peculiarity in the history of the Isma'ilis, however, will serve to introduce the topic of local religious leadership as a whole.

Abu Sa'd al-Isma'ili died in 1007, aged just over sixty.[2] Gorgan's historian, al-Sahmi, knew him well because he had set out with him twice on pilgrimage. The first time, in 994, they turned back before reaching Mecca; the next year they succeeded. Al-Sahmi eloquently praises Abu Sa'd's excellence in law and Arabic, mentioning that he taught law for many years and wrote books on the subject, including one on drinking. He extols, too, his excellent habits and constant preoccupation with religion, finding it particularly commendable that he was as morally upright on the road as he was at home. Piety is mentioned, but not asceticism. The latter would have been out of keeping, perhaps, with Abu Sa'd's unstinting generosity.

The most interesting passage in al-Sahmi's biography, however, is the following: "Among those things by which God blessed him was that when his death drew near, all of what he possessed by way of wealth and estates departed him. He had sent cotton to Bab al-Abwab [Derbent on the western side of the Caspian Sea]; it was all lost at sea. He had goods which were being transported from Isfa-

102

han; Kurds descended upon them and took them. He had some wheat being shipped to him from Khurasan; a group of people fell upon it and plundered it. He had an estate in the village known as Kuskara; Qabus ibn Washmagir [the local ruler at that time] ordered that its trees be uprooted, and they were. The underground canal was filled in and all his property seized."[3]

This is the only indication, among twenty biographies of Isma'ili family members, of where the Isma'ilis got their money, except for one of Abu Sa'd's third cousins being called a silk merchant. In fact, among the 7,472 biographical entries from Gorgan, Isfahan, and Nishapur combined, it is the only extensive statement about the financial resources of any religiously eminent family. To be sure, individuals are surnamed "Merchant," "Druggist," "Saddler," and the like, and fleeting mention is made of estates or family trusts; but al-Sahmi portrays Abu Sa'd as a man of multifarious and far-reaching business and agricultural interests.

Al-Sahmi's calling Abu Sa'd's misfortunes a divine blessing indicates the reason for his, and the other local historians', reticence on financial matters. When the urge to compile lists of local religious worthies came over people, as it seems to have done in most important Iranian cities in the tenth century, it was an urge born both of local pride and scholarly service. Collections of lore about the Companions and the Followers had been made during the preceding century when budding localities far from Arabia did not yet have all that much to show for themselves. But oral transmission expanded geometrically, and within three or four generations many men in every community knew something of the Prophet's words and deeds, the more able and ambitious of them having traveled far afield to learn them.

A peculiarity of hadith education was that while each student took down verbatim the words of his teacher, the pile of folded papers he accumulated in this process was of little use to anyone but himself. His children and grandchildren did not have to write down their own personal versions of the hadith they learned from dad or granddad, of course. Parental copies could do for them because no one would question their having learned their contents orally in the family circle. But even when these texts became accessible in mosque libraries by pious bequest after a scholar's death, no one else could legitimately study hadith from them because they could not claim an oral connection. Nevertheless, people were reluctant to destroy them since they contained the name of God.[4]

So notes and texts accumulated, and some hadith scholars began to realize that however inappropriate it might be to transmit hadith from them, they were nevertheless invaluable as indicators of whom each person had studied with, particularly in those instances when a student who had studied with many teachers listed them in a separate book.[5] Since isnads inevitably got longer with time, and the number of possible hadith transmitters increased so rapidly, these scholars reckoned it a service to their religious profession to collate all of the names and thus make it easier to check isnads.

A perusal of their compilations reveals that urban pride and identity were also motivations sustaining them through their exhausting labors of collation. Why else would the finished works include sections devoted to the city's mosques and quarters? Why else would they describe the extent of the city's rural hinterland? And why else would they detail the circumstances of he city's founding, and of its conquest by the Muslims? The last of these regularly included items points to the importance to the compiler of his city's development as part of the Muslim community. Though the portions of these local histories devoted to urban geography and physical distinction, the founding of the city, and its Islamic conquest are much briefer than the biographical sections, they balance one another: the concrete fabric of the Islamic city against its human and spiritual fabric. It was only appropriate that the latter be given precedence.

Strikingly, none of the biographically focused local histories of tenth- and eleventh-century Iran seeks to go beyond the scope of a single urban center. Though all Muslims were part of a single *umma*, or community, what seemed to count most was the subcommunity of Muslims right there in the town. Those among them who evinced religious authority by virtue of their piety or transmission of hadith, even if they only passed through briefly, constituted the memorable high points of the city's Islamic history, just as its conquest—literally its "opening" to Islam—and the building of its mosques constituted the physical high points of its Islamic history.

Local histories of this sort testify to a city's coming of age as an Islamic community. Hence their pronounced popularity in the tenth and eleventh centuries.

Returning to the story of the Isma'ili family, then, the studious omission of details of worldliness and pelf from the biographies contained in the local histories is hardly surprising. God's forestalling the devastation of Abu Sa'd al-Isma'ili's fortune until he was on his deathbed was a blessing in the eyes of al-Sahmi. If it had not had this religious significance, there would have been no point in mentioning it. In the religious milieu of the time, wealth was praiseworthy when it was devoted to charity or the endowment of religious edifices, but in and of itself it played no part in defining the local Muslim community.

The main factor defining that community by the end of the tenth century was scholarship, and principally, but not exclusively, scholarship in hadith. Just as the word "scientist" derives from the Latin verb *scire* meaning "to know," the Arabic verb for knowing, *'alima*, yields the word *'alim* for a "knower," as well as *'ilm* for "science." In the narrower medieval usage, an alim was a person who was knowledgeable in the "sciences of the faith" (*'ulum al-din*). The plural of alim is *'ulama'*.

In a literal sense, ulama can be said to exist from the earliest days of the Muslim community. There were always some people who knew more about Islam than others. But other terms are more commonly used: Companion, Follower, Quran reader (*qari'*), Quran memorizer (*hafiz*). In time, as more and more specialized terms came into favor—faqih (legal specialist), *mufassir* (Quran commentator), *nahwi* (grammarian)—the need for a general term applying to all religiously learned persons was more strongly felt. Ulama appears more often in sources than alim because at the individual level one or more of the specific terms was usually more appropriate.

As a group, the ulama represent religious authority based on learning. Some were also authoritative as pietists, or ascetics, or Sufis. Some inherited a measure of religious authority by virtue of lineal descent from Muhammad's family (*sayyids* or *sharifs*) or, less importantly, from one of his closest companions. The edges of Islam bubbled with competing claims to religious authority during

105

the first three centuries—not only the main currents I have already identified, but scores of claims by would-be prophets, invitations into secret conspiracies, and calls to pious rebellion. With thousands of people asking questions about Islam, the marketplace of answers was wild and colorful.

Yet it is hardly surprising that knowledge eventually won out. Such is the common course of religious development. Though the Sufis, uniquely claiming direct contact with the divine, competed with the ulama with increasing success as the centuries wore on, from the tenth to the twelfth century the ulama commanded the greatest popular allegiance. They were the great men and heros of Islamic society on both the local and the cosmopolitan levels.

The ulama won the competition for popular allegiance because, as the chronological gulf separating the believers from their Prophet deepened, they alone could credibly connect their coreligionists with the ever more perfect-seeming early community. It is also important, given the constant flux of early society, that throughout the eighth and ninth centuries, almost any male Muslim might become an alim. Arab or Iranian, the offspring of a dihqan, a slave, a villager, or a warrior, a person's aspiration to learn the words of the Prophet was unencumbered by rules and institutions. Hadith were transmitted in mosques, in homes, in shops, and in the street. Whoever chose to sit and learn was welcome. To be sure, only the literate listeners could take down the teacher's words and thus qualify themselves to transmit hadith on their own. But literacy was a matter of time and effort. No ritual qualifications comparable to those of medieval Christianity or of monastic Buddhism stood between the believer and the Prophet's words.

From the late tenth century on, however, it became increasingly apparent that most of the ulama in a community belonged to families with established traditions of learning.[6] The social mobility of the cities of the conversion era yielded to an almost caste-like local domination by families of ulama. Lowly individuals still might study, but the likelihood of their ever teaching or gaining religious preferment steadily diminished. Many, no doubt, returned to their towns and villages and became locally celebrated for their knowledge,[7] but few ever made it in the big city.

No single factor determined the success of the major ulama families; each has a different story. In the case of the Isma'ilis of Gorgan, the pivotal figure is Abu Bakr, the father of the Abu Sa'd al-Isma'ili already mentioned. Whether Abu Bakr al-Isma'ili was of Iranian or Arab ancestry, or both, is unknown. His family tree bears four generations of names, but no fruitful information. He married the sister of a man who left Gorgan to become a teacher of law according to the Shafi'i interpretation in the city of Balkh in northern Afghanistan;[8] and his brother married a woman whose father spent time in Balkh and also espoused the Shafi'i school of law.[9] Abu Bakr's second wife was the daughter of a man, apparently of Arab stock, who lived in the old and prestigious Canal Gate quarter of Gorgan where he owned various shops and warehouses.[10] This father-in-law drew up on parchment a document establishing his property as a trust for his descendants, but he excluded his daughters' children. He stipulated that the administrator of the trust should be a pious man of his own legal persuasion, presumably Shafi'i, and had the document witnessed by a leading hadith scholar of his own generation and by his son-in-law Abu Bakr al-Isma'ili.

Asking a son-in-law, at the time still in his twenties, to witness the act disinheriting his own wife and children must have been rather awkward, unless that son-in-law was already well fixed for money. The rationale for excluding female descendants was presumably to keep the income from the property from falling into the hands of in-laws, but family *waqf* deeds more commonly provided for daughters along with sons.[11] The fact that the report stresses the exclusion of the female line in the transaction serves to enhance the likelihood that Abu Bakr al-Isma'ili inherited wealth from his own family, as does an anecdote indicating that his grandfather was not deeply learned in Islam.[12] It is noteworthy in comparing the Isma'ilis with the family of Abu Taiba discussed earlier that the matter of when any ancestor converted is never mentioned.

The stories told about Abu Bakr himself deal exclusively with his learning and his reputation, which stretched as far as the caliph's court.[13] We see him besieged by scores of visitors and would-be students and leading the funeral prayers for Gorgan's most illustrious citizens.[14] When word of his death reached Baghdad in 982, hundreds of scholars, merchants, and other notables went into mourning. There is even a vignette of an octagenarian Abu Bakr boasting that his seven-year-old grandson has already memorized the Quran and learned some hadith. Yet aside from a note in another biography that he dispatched that person to a border defense colony as judge,[15] there isn't the slightest indication that Abu Bakr held any official position.

This lack is made up in the next generation. Abu Sa'd may have been known primarily for his legal expertise, but Abu Bakr's other son, Abu Nasr al-Isma'ili, became Gorgan's chief (*ra'is*) while his father was still alive.[16] Historians haven't determined exactly the powers and duties of a ra'is in the tenth and eleventh centuries, but it was clearly the highest specifically urban post. On the other hand, it was not a post that led anywhere. Provincial governors and officials in the retinue of caliphs and sultans rarely came up from the level of a ra'is.

Though secular in nature, the office of ra'is often went to a scion of a leading ulama family, probably because many of these families, like the Isma'ilis themselves, had acquired substantial property and business interests along with their learning. In Abu Nasr's case, his learning is attested by the fact that after his father's death, he took his place in the mosque every Saturday teaching hadith. His wealth is attested by the fact that the same ruler who seized his brother's property imprisoned him to extort money from him. It took the intervention of a qadi traveling as an emissary from a neighboring ruler to get him freed.[17]

Little is said of the three sisters of Abu Sa'd and Abu Nasr. The eldest married a Shafi'i legal scholar from southwest Iran and had four sons.[18] The middle one transmitted hadith to two of her nephews and had one son.[19] The youngest had no sons.[20]

It would appear that when Abu Sa'd al-Isma'ili was around fifty, he took all five of his sons on pilgrimage.[21] This gave them all an opportunity to study hadith in Baghdad, Mecca, and other cities en route, although Abu Sa'd had to take the dictation for the youngest of them himself. One of the sons, Abu Mu'ammar, eventually took his uncle Abu Nasr's place teaching hadith in the mosque after his death. Another, Abu Sa'id, specialized in law and took over issuing legal opinions after their father's death.

As for Abu Sa'd's three daughters, two are unknown, but the third married the man who became ra'is of Gorgan following her uncle. Muhammad al-Jaulaki had studied with Abu Bakr al-Isma'ili and some other notable teachers in Gorgan, but he was not an outstanding alim.[22] It must have been his wealth and connections outside the religious arena that qualified him for the office of ra'is, but marrying the granddaughter of Abu Bakr and the niece of the current ra'is brought him into the circle of ulama prominence.

Twice he traveled to Afghanistan as an emissary from the ruler of the Gorgan region to the court of the greatest ruler of the period, Mahmud of Ghazna. On his second trip, in his late fifties, he married a woman in Herat. She became pregnant but died after their return. Al-Jaulaki himself died in the following year, 1019.

Upon his death, his son, Abu al-Mahasin al-Isma'ili, who had substituted for him while he was away, took over the office of ra'is. He was only eighteen years old at the time.[23] Abu al-Mahasin's surname being Isma'ili instead of Jaulaki confirms the superiority of his mother's lineage to his father's. Like his Isma'ili predecessors on the maternal side, Abu al-Mahasin became a noted teacher of law and hadith; but like his father, he also traveled as an emissary. The son of the ruler who had imprisoned his great-uncle to gain his money and seized his grandfather's lands sent him to the court of Mahmud of Ghazna. He was honored along the way by having classes convened for him, and he returned to Gorgan laden with gifts.

Nothing further of substance is recorded of the Isma'ili family. The four generations we know about, however, amply demonstrate the salient qualities of an important ulama family: money, learning, and power. The Isma'ilis were no more great historical figures than are the leading bankers, clergymen, and businessmen of today's middle-sized American cities. Some family members were known outside of Gorgan, but their eminence was essentially local. The contemporary histories of Nishapur and Isfahan yield their own arrays of ulama families, all of them as local in their orbit of influence, aside from the occasional star scholar, as the Isma'ilis.

Hadith study being intrinsically personal, the study tours of young ulama did not often result in lasting interurban connections. The student traveler took home with him his precious dictation notes and some familiarity with the wider world, but ulama careers were not cosmopolitan in nature. The most important connections among the Muslim cities of the tenth and eleventh centuries were not personal but sectarian.

Abu Bakr al-Isma'ili and all of his family adhered to the Shafi'i interpretation of Islamic law. The Shafi'is' primary rival in Iran was the Hanafi school, though a few scholars adhered to less popular alternatives. The Shafi'is and the Hanafis were part of the broad mainstream of Islam known as "the people of tradition and community" (*ahl al-sunna wa'l jama'a*), or Sunnis for short.

Most introductions to Islam and histories of Islamic law describe the technical differences between their ways of deriving legal rulings, but also portray them as mutually tolerant of one another's approach, not to mention of the approaches of the other two Sunni law schools, the Malikis and the Hanbalis. This tolerance, however, only began to set in in the twelfth century as part of a broader recentering and homogenization of Islamic thought and institutions. In the tenth and eleventh centuries, the Shafi'is and the Hanafis were bitter, and sometimes violent, rivals.

The Hanafi interpretive method crystalized early in the ninth century, the Shafi'i half a century later. The ninth also being the century of most rapid conversion and urbanization in Iran, their main battleground, it seems likely that their adversarial relationship was affected by these circumstances. Fragmentary evidence suggests, in fact, that the Shafi'i interpretation, which elevated the hadith to a level of legal significance second only to the Quran, prospered particularly among those ulama families, like the Isma'ilis, that rose to prominence late in the tenth century on the basis of profound scholarship in hadith. This does not mean that early converts and their descendants were invariably Hanafi and later converts invariably Shafi'i. But judging from the steady increase in Shafi'i influence and popularity in the eleventh century, a tendency to divide along these lines seems likely.

The core of the friction between the Shafi'is and the Hanafis was not legal interpretation itself. The Hanafis who most angered the

Shafi'is were those who elevated individual reason over hadith. In Iran this subgroup was usually referred to as the "masters of opinion" (*ashab al-ra'y*), but the word *mu'tazili* is more often used by historians. Someone said to Abu Bakr al-Isma'ili, " 'O Abu Bakr, what about Ibrahim ibn Musa al-Wazduli?' He replied, 'Yes, he used to recite hadith [in Gorgan]. I never wrote any down from him, though, because I never used to take transmission from the masters of opinion; and Ibrahim was a shaikh of the masters of opinion.' "[24] This unusually blunt remark typifies the current of animosity the Shafi'i hadith specialists had for those who did not share fully their veneration of the Prophet's words. The fact that al-Wazduli was a respected reciter of hadith did not temper Abu Bakr al-Isma'ili's antipathy toward his ideas.

Another undercurrent in the Shafi'i-Hanafi rivalry was Sufism. As we have seen, by the end of the tenth century, claims to a mystic vision of God were becoming more popular at the expense of earlier ascetic and pietistic tendencies. Given their direct line to the divine, many Sufis had little interest in legal matters. Of those whose legal affiliation is identifiable, however, most were Shafi'is—twenty-three in Nishapur, for example, compared with only one Hanafi.[25] Hanafi Sufis remained rare well into the twelfth century. Mystic visions simply did not sit well with people devoted to legalism, rationalism, and traditional forms of piety.

Still a third non-legal difference between the competing camps was the much greater interest in local history and biographical compilation shown by the Shafi'is, including the Shafi'i Sufis.[26] Their interest in local communal identity and in defining the parameters of Muslim community was further displayed in the eleventh century by Shafi'i works on Muslim sects that have no counterpart among the Hanafis.[27]

Cosmopolitanism versus localism, rationalism versus mysticism, legalism versus faith in hadith as the best guide to Muslim behavior: the rivalry between the Hanafis and Shafi'is played on a field much broader than legal interpretation per se. Of one Nishapuri it is reported: "He was a Hanafi in law school, but he was a Shafi'i in morals (*akhlaq*) and social relations (*mu'ashara*)."[28] This may refer only to the persons that individual associated with, or conceivably to specific legal subtopics on which he diverged from the main-stream of his school, but the likelihood is that Hanafis and Shafi'is lived their lives rather differently.

Material evidence points to a marked cleavage in popular lifestyle in the tenth century. Pottery had become an exciting new area of expression in the nascent Muslim cities during the previous two centuries. Prosperous communities of recent immigrants provided a market for ornamental, but not luxurious, manufactures that was very different from that afforded by the old Iranian aristocracy based in the countryside. A pre-Islamic dihqan would hire an artist to do heroic wall paintings and purchase lavishly decorated silver dishes from itinerant artisans or merchants. By contrast, the Muslim city folk had less money to spend individually but provided a larger, more concentrated market. In addition, their tastes ran toward the geometric and calligraphic because of their desire to distance them-selves from the traditions and imagery of the non-Muslims.

Styles emanating from Iraq found favor, with local modification, all the way to Samarqand in Central Asia. In fact, Samarqand and Nishapur became famous for their production of white plates deco-rated with ornate, virtually illegible, Arabic writing. The manufac-tures of the two cities were indistinguishable from each other, as well as from others apparently produced in Gorgan.

During the tenth century, however, another ware gained great popularity. Primarily represented by yellow bowls, the rival style fea-tured floral and pictorial ornamentation, including paintings of peo-ple costumed as dihqans and scenes of drinking and hunting. Occa-sional explicitly non-Muslim motifs show that these wares found customers outside as well as inside the Muslim community, but their great abundance indicates that most customers were undoubtedly Muslim.[29]

There is no way of proving that Shafi'is preferred to eat tradi-tional Iranian soups, like *ash* and *ab gusht*, from deep yellow bowls decorated with traditional Iranian motifs while Hanafis supped on fruit and grilled meat served on broad white plates bearing Arabic aphorisms. Yet the bifurcation of styles did coincide with the matur-ing of the urban social structure and the appearance of rival world-views among the major ulama families. Moreover, the new style in

Nishapur is not replicated in Samarqand or Gorgan, much less in the urban centers of Iraq. Like the mental outlook labeled as Shafi'i, it is local rather than cosmopolitan, Iranian rather than Arab.

So the view from the edge, like the view from the center, differs dramatically at the end of the tenth century from what it was a century or two earlier. The central narrative by this time is unraveling. Shi'ite Buyid princes, their power based on mountain tribes from south of the Caspian sea, hold the Abbasid caliphs under virtual palace arrest in Baghdad after 945 and rule western Iran as a group of minor duchies. A rival Shi'ite caliphate, the Fatimids, spread from North Africa to take over Egypt in 969 and the coastal regions of Syria. In Iraq and the Arabian and Syrian deserts, Arab tribes vie for supremacy in the vacuum of power left by the Abbasid collapse. Eastern Iran is left in the hands of a shifting array of warlords for a century. In short, the central narrative of Islamic history aborts in the tenth century; what follows are the separate histories of more or less powerful regional successor states. Neither the Mongol catastrophe of the thirteenth century, nor the rise of the Ottoman Empire in the fifteenth and sixteenth centuries accomplishes a reunification of the Arab, Iranian, and now Turkish realms.

Yet the fall of the caliphate excites little notice on the edge. The story there in the tenth century is of growth and maturity. Ulama families, despite their apparent insignificance in comparison with the petty dynasts who populate the central narrative, provide a locus of local stability and religious authority that runs counter to the prevailing picture of political fragmentation. From the local perspective, the retention by petty dynasts of tax revenues that generations before would have been sent to Baghdad is a boon, and the vagaries of behavior of the warlords cause no more woe than the earlier fights between rebels and caliphal governors. With the growing sense of local urban identity, testified to by the appearance of local histories, and focused by and upon the great ulama families, comes a relegitimation of Persian as a language, and of pre-Islamic Iranian motifs as accepted parts of a Muslim culture.

Iran regains consciousness with the composition at century's end of Firdausi's epic of kings, the *Shahnameh*. But Islam is an inseparable part of the new consciousness. The stories of kings and heroes that Firdausi tells he learned from dihqans whose oral poetic tradition had preserved them faithfully from their forefathers. Some of those same dihqans, however, were ever on the lookout for promising young religious scholars to marry their daughters to.

The view from the edge does not forget that God revealed his ultimate word in Arabic, that Muhammad was an Arab, and that the Arabs brought Islam to the world. But it sees Islam not as an Arab tent or a caliphal palace, but as a house with many rooms. Islam in Gorgan is different from Islam in Isfahan or Nishapur. It differs even more from Islam in Cordoba, Qairawan, Cairo, and Damascus. Local religious authority is embodied in the local corpus of hadith, and even more in the locally prominent families of ulama. To be sure, collections of "sound" traditions are already acquiring a supralocal legitimacy, but the local power, pride, and particularism of the ulama will survive for another hundred years.

7

CALIPH AND SULTAN

When the ruler judges unjustly, or contrary
to the people of knowledge, he is repudiated.
—Hadith quoted in BUKHARI, *SAHIH*

Sometime around the middle of the ninth century, Ubaid Allah ibn Sa'd, a descendant of one of Muhammad's closest companions, journeyed from Baghdad to Isfahan to assume the post of qadi. Actually, he was appointed twice, but it isn't stated whether the incident that follows occurred during his first or second attempt to take up the post. At the time of his arrival, there were one hundred certified legal witnesses in Isfahan.

Given the great weight put upon oral testimony in the Muslim courts, judges scrutinized closely the probity and character of every witness. In many cases, of course, particularly criminal cases, witnessing was a matter of chance. But in contracts, the contracting parties preferred witnesses of known acceptability. Besides, certified witnesses were often skilled in drawing up documents in a legal fashion. Thus, official recognition of a man's integrity was highly valued in the nascent Muslim society, and it was not uncommon for a family to begin a rise to prominence with the certification of a family member as a witness.[1]

In Isfahan, the job of certifying witnesses lay not with the qadi but with a *muzikki*, an "appraiser of purity," possibly because judges coming from out of town were not always in a position to determine who the city's solid citizens were. At the time of Ubaid Allah ibn Sa'd's appointment, the muzakki was also the ra'is of the city and its most important citizen. His name was Abd Allah al-Hamadhani. He had inherited his eminence from an uncle, al-Husain ibn Hafs, whose own sons had predeceased him.[2]

Al-Husain ibn Hafs, in turn, was the son, or possibly grandson, of an Iranian who had been part of the booty taken to Kufa from the city of Hamadhan at the time of its conquest.[3] His father was already established in Isfahan at the beginning of the Abbasid caliphate in 750. He must have been a prominent figure because he married the daughter of Ata' al-Khushk, an Iranian convert to Islam from Isfahan who had become one of the leaders of the Abbasid movement in Khurasan. Ata' al-Khushk established a family in Marv, the capital of Khurasan, but later returned to Isfahan. There he prospered, possibly in real estate development judging from his name being attached to a gate and a city quarter.[4]

Al-Husain ibn Hafs grew up, then, in a wealthy home. Educationally, he retraced his father's steps back to Kufa where he steeped himself in that city's learning. Kufa was then much more sophisticated in Islamic matters than Isfahan so al-Husain ibn Hafs returned home an eminent religious authority in the eyes of his fellow Isfahanis. He became a judge and issued legal opinions according to the doctrine of the Kufans, which later developed into the Hanafi law school. He also enjoyed an income of 100,000 dirhams per year.[5]

His nephew Abd Allah al-Hamadhani was not a profound scholar.[6] Therefore, he succeeded al-Husain ibn Hafs not as qadi, but only as ra'is and muzikki. As Isfahan's ra'is, Abd Allah married the daughter of the provincial governor[7] and corresponded with four successive caliphs, al-Mu'tasim, al-Wathiq, al-Mutawakkil, and al-Musta'in, who altogether ruled from 833 to 866.

Exactly why Abd Allah al-Hamadhani clashed with the new qadi, Ubaid Allah ibn Sa'd, is never stated; but both times the qadi was appointed, the ra'is secured his dismissal.[8] Abd Allah's great-grandson, on the authority of his grandfather, related that Abd Allah once said: "I spent one million dirhams of my wealth for the deposition of Ubaid Allah ibn Sa'd." The reason, the report explains, is that the certified legal witnesses refused to serve the new qadi and rallied around Abd Allah. Every day for six months they congregated at his mansion with their retainers and riding animals, and Abd Allah was bound by the rites of hospitality to feed and support them.

After his second recall, no more is heard of the qadi Ubaid Allah ibn Sa'd in Isfahan. Abd Allah al-Hamadhani's descendants and cousins can be traced for five generations, however. Down to the middle of the tenth century they include individuals who are known for wealth and generosity and who hold the posts of qadi, ra'is, and muzikki.[9] His own son, moreover, in a story reminiscent of the almost contemporary Abu Taiba family in Gorgan, distinguished himself by fleeing Isfahan as soon as a caliphal diploma investing him as qadi arrived from Baghdad. He took refuge in his mother's hometown of Qashan until the caliph relented and appointed a new qadi from out of town.[10]

The incongruity between the father spending a fortune—surely most of it on bribes to Baghdad rather than feeding his guests—to prevent an outsider from taking over the judgeship held for so long by his uncle, and his son fleeing town to avoid holding the same post and not returning until an outsider had been appointed is best understood by assuming that Abd Allah al-Hamadhani's opposition to Ubaid Allah ibn Sa'd took place in the context of the *mihna*. The mihna was an inquisition begun by the caliph al-Ma'mun (813–833) at the end of his reign, continued by his successors al-Mu'tasim (833–842) and al-Wathiq (842–847), and terminated with the accession of al-Mutawakkil in 847.

The ostensible purpose of the mihna was to bar from important religious positions anyone who did not subscribe to the nu'tazili theological creed, but historians have long debated its deeper meaning. The Abbasid dynasty had come to power advertising a return to religious purity after decades of what the Umayyads' opponents considered impious, tribally based tyranny. Delivering upon the promise of a more religious caliphate was difficult, however, especially in the face of revolts from many quarters. Abbasid credibility slipped even further after Harun al-Rashid's death in 809 when his sons al-Amin and al-Ma'mun fought a civil war to see who would be caliph.

Al-Ma'mun, whose mother was Iranian, won the civil war using troops from Khurasan. For six years after the fall of Baghdad and the killing of al-Amin he continued to rule from Marv in northeastern Iran, sending one of his Iranian lieutenants to govern Iraq. Then, in

819, he took the extraordinary step of summoning the recognized chief of the Alid family to Marv to proclaim him heir to the caliphate. The Alids were descendants of Muhammad's cousin and son-in-law Ali ibn Abi Talib and therefore cousins of the Abbasids, who descended from the Prophet's uncle al-Abbas. But a tragic sequence of failed rebellions had turned the Alids and their followers from a vocal party claiming for Ali's descendants a legitimate right to rule into a religious faction, the Shi'a, dedicated to the belief that the Alids' rights were divinely ordained.

Alid sympathies had been strong within the movement that brought the Abbasids to power, and the Abbasids had fought against Alid and Shi'ite rebels. Thus to turn the caliphate over to the Alid leader, Ali al-Rida, was a truly radical step. Al-Ma'mun cemented the new arrangement by disinheriting his own sons and marrying a daughter to Ali al-Rida's son. Then the court began a slow progression back to Baghdad. It had not gone far, however, when Ali al-Rida suddenly died, possibly the victim of poisoning. Al-Ma'mun, his succession plan accidentally or purposely aborted, proceeded on to establish his court in Baghdad. Then, a decade later, when he was in his mid-forties, al-Ma'mun instituted the mihna, only to die before it had been fully implemented.

Some analyses of al-Ma'mun's objective in being the first caliph to declare and enforce an orthodoxy in Islam have focused on nu'tazili dogma. The view from the edge, however, sees his plan primarily as an attempt to extend the power of the center in religious affairs—in effect, an attempt to create a church. Inasmuch as Islam came into being in a religious environment dominated by ecclesiastical bodies and formally invested clergy, it is rather surprising that a church had not arisen earlier. While Muslims now pride themselves on the absence of priesthood and church organization, it must have seemed strange to many converts that the religious community they were joining was able to do without these things. Yet there were enough exemplary religious figures around, starting with the Companions, to fill the need for guidance without falling back on an ecclesiastical structure.

By the caliphate of al-Ma'mun, however, the pace of conversion was accelerating into its bandwagon phase. Muslim cities were growing fast, and the meaning of the caliphate was changing. The caliphate's one clear-cut political mission, discernible from its very beginning, was to protect the Muslim community from attack or dissolution. In the seventh and eighth centuries, this meant not only conquest and defense on the frontiers, but also local protection of the fledgling Muslim settlements set down in the midst of much more numerous non-Muslim populations. This latter rationale eroded steadily as conversion gained momentum. Non-Muslims gradually became a minority, and rebellion increasingly arose within Islam instead of against it.

Al-Ma'mun made his uncertainty about the political and religious role of the Abbasid caliphate apparent by appointing Ali al-Rida as his heir. But whatever he intended by that act did not come to pass. The mihna, therefore, may be seen as a different approach to the same objective, the reformulation of caliphal legitimacy. The network of qadis appointed, or at least confirmed, by the central government provided al-Ma'mun and his successors with the human and organizational core of a centralized church. All that was necessary was to activate it by adding to the qadis' judicial function a doctrinal mission. Had the mihna succeeded, the caliphate would have been well on its way to becoming a papacy or patriarchate.

The failure of the mihna is properly ascribed to the resistance of individual religious figures who preferred jail or even death to abandoning their principles and affirming the nu'tazili creed. Ahmad ibn Hanbal, the eponymous founder of the Hanbali law school in Baghdad, was the symbolic leader of the resistance so historians have detailed the distinctions between his thought, heavily rooted in hadith, and that of the nu'tazilis. But quite apart from intellectual matters, the intrusion of the caliphate into what had developed over the preceding century as local constellations of religious authority was quite sufficient to provoke resistance.

Returning to the conflict over certified legal witnesses in Isfahan, after his first rejection in Isfahan, Ubaid Allah ibn Sa'd would scarcely have been appointed a second time as qadi unless the central government expected him to carry out a specific task, namely, the enforcement of the mihna. Judicial emissaries from Baghdad were al-Mu'tasim's and al-Wathiq's normal instruments in this.[11]

119

Dating his appointment to the fourteen years when al-Mu'tasim and al-Wathiq were enforcing the mihna also illuminates the refusal of the city's certified legal witnesses to come before him. To be accepted in his court they would have had to pass the nu'tazili litmus test by swearing allegiance to the doctrine that the Quran was not coeternal with God, but rather created by God as His first act.

Torn between compliance or dishonorable dismissal as legal witnesses and imprisonment if they stood by their principles, the witnesses sought the protection of the man who had appointed them, Abd Allah al-Hamadhani. Possibly they even considered armed resistance since they gathered at Abd Allah's mansion with their horses and retainers. The stand-off lasted six months, during which time Abd Allah corresponded with Baghdad and used his tremendous wealth to secure the qadi's dismissal.

The crux of this story as it was passed down in the memory of Isfahan's citizens was not theological resistance to an intolerable religious inquisition, but the expression of local power by a major ulama family vis-à-vis the distant Baghdad government. Abd Allah al-Hamadhani was the city's ra'is and the son of its previous ra'is and qadi. After him as ra'is came his nephew, his son, and his nephew's son. Altogether the family dominated the office from the beginning of the ninth century until the second half of the tenth, during which time several family members also served as qadi and muzikki.

An incident in the life of Abd Allah's son Muhammad, the one who fled to avoid becoming qadi, illustrates the family's power locally.[12] Abu Da'ud al-Sijistani, the compiler of a collection of 4,000 "sound" hadith that Sunnis eventually came to accept as one of their six canonical collections, fell into a discussion about Ali ibn Abi Talib while visiting Isfahan. It was alleged that in the discussion he related a story about Ali scratching one of the Prophet's wives. Whether out of jealousy, as one biographer asserts, or simply the desire to save the reputation of their noble ancestor, some Alids charged him before the governor with insulting Ali. Three estimable witnesses, one of them descended from Isfahan's pre-Islamic Iranian military commander, testified against him, and he was condemned to death.[13] Then Muhammad ibn Abd Allah al-Hamadhani stepped in. He testified that one of the witnesses had a

120

history of disobedience to his father, that another lent out money at interest, and that the third was not truthful in his scholarship. As a result, Abu Da'ud was spared.

Such was the power of a muzikki[14] that he could not only certify his fellow citizens' trustworthiness, but also successfully impugn their testimony whenever he felt they were acting dishonestly. Not having been party to the discussion that generated the accusation, Muhammad ibn Abd Allah could not testify that Abu Da'ud had never uttered the damning words; but he could destroy the testimony of three of the city's leading scholars simply by swearing that they were of bad character.

The episode of Isfahan's rejected qadi illustrates the degree to which, irrespective of religious doctrine, the mihna was seen as a threat to local religious authority. Al-Ma'mun's letter promulgating the inquisition charges that people of incorrect belief (in nu'tazili eyes) induce the masses to "incline toward agreement with them and accordance with their evil opinions, by that means getting to themselves honour with them, and procuring to themselves a leadership and a reputation among them for honourable dealing."[15] Honor and leadership on a local basis is the crux of the issue. Had al-Ma'mun's plan succeeded, not only would religious authority have been centralized, but the determination of local social status, as well.

Coming in the middle of the ninth century, when an increasing flood of migrants from the countryside was quickening the ferment of the new Muslim cities, the effort to establish an ecclesiastical structure was doomed from the start. Prisoners of conscience like Ahmad ibn Hanbal sealed its failure, but the pivotal issue was caliphal control and government legitimacy rather than any particular theology. The caliph's right to appoint qadis was never questioned, but qadis who were appointed against local wishes, or who refused to cooperate with the local power structure, were repudiated. In some cities, as the anecdotes in the story of Abu Taiba suggest, qadis were nominated locally, often by heredity, with the caliphal sanction merely a formality.[16]

Al-Ma'mun's mihna is usually described as a unique occurrence, but it had a parallel two centuries later. The differences between the two episodes testify to the changes that took place in Islamic society during the intervening period. The view from the center, as of 1048 when the second episode probably begins, concentrates on the history of the Seljuq Turks, who had by then established their empire in Iran but not yet taken over in Baghdad. Their leader, Tughril Beg, was using the titles Shahanshah and Sultan, the former a revival of pre-Islamic Iranian titulature and the latter, literally meaning "power," connoting a delegation of the caliph's role as a temporal ruler.

The view from the edge, by contrast, sees eleventh-century Iranian urban society as totally dominated by the great ulama families. In selected instances, constellations of these local families may usefully be termed patriciates inasmuch as they attempted, though with only fleeting success, to secure for their cities autonomy from all but the most formal aspects of imperial control.[17]

Tughril Beg and his brother Chaghri, being newcomers to power and to the sophistication of urban society, relied on Iranian advisors and administrators to maintain government functions, just as the original Arab conquerors relied on Sasanian and Byzantine officials. After casting about briefly for the right person to become his vizier, Tughril selected a protégé of the leader of the Shafi'i ulama faction of Nishapur.

For a young man of insignificant parentage from the small town of Kundur, elevation to the peak of government power was a heady experience. However, it had a negative side, as well. Scions of the great ulama families neither sought nor served in government positions, unless they could do so without prejudicing their scholarly independence. The position of qadi was suspect because qadis could be subjected to government influence. Witness the tale told earlier of Abu Taiba's son Ahmad and the man who was murdered for his property and his slavegirl. Being a royal emissary, on the other hand, could be an honor since emissaries were selected for their political neutrality. As for being a vizier, no official was more closely tied to the will of the ruler.

In al-Kunduri's case, accepting the position meant traveling with and serving an uneducated, foreign warlord and his rude tribal army of horsemen. Left behind were his hopes for a prestigious career as

122

an alim; ahead lay possible death on some distant field of battle. Furthermore, he may have had the suspicion that his mentor was getting him out of town partly to make room for the advancement within the Shafi'i faction of his own son, and the sons of some of Nishapur's other eminent Shafi'is. Al-Kunduri himself was a rare example—for the eleventh century—of a small-town lad of no particular family distinction trying to break into the ranks of the major ulama simply on the basis of talent and ambition.

Nishapur's rival Hanafi and Shafi'i factions were verbally at each other's throats in the 1040s with the Hanafis trying to regain some of the prestige they had lost through being only lukewarm in welcoming the Seljuq invaders in 1037–39. Under these heated conditions, al-Kunduri, now known by his vizieral title Amid al-Mulk, "Pillar of the Monarchy," pronounced in 1048 a blanket condemnation of all proponents of Ash'ari theology.[18] The Ash'aris, whose doctrines had developed, ironically, after the mihna as an attempted compromise between the nu'tazili and Hanbali views, were forbidden to preach, teach, or fill any religious office. Al-Kunduri charged them with being heretical innovators, but their doctrines were less important than their local social and political standing. Not only did the Ash'aris all subscribe to the Shafi'i school of law, but their leading thinkers and writers were members of just two or three powerful ulama families in Nishapur—including the family of Amid al-Mulk al-Kunduri's original patron.

The official ban forced hundreds of Ash'aris out of their posts in different cities and put many of them on the road to exile. Arrest warrants were eventually issued for four of Nishapur's leading Ash'aris, including the son of al-Kunduri's patron, who had succeeded his father as head of the Shafi'i faction. The Ash'aris defended themselves by writing tracts and letters of exculpation, petitioning Sultan Tughril Beg, and even breaking out of jail and fleeing to Mecca, which afforded safe haven from persecution. But the ban remained in effect for over a decade, and possibly for as long as the mihna begun by al-Ma'mun.

There are significant differences between al-Ma'mun's mihna and Amid al-Mulk al-Kunduri's banning of the Ash'aris: the former was the policy of a caliph based explicitly upon a claim to absolute authority in religious matters; the latter was the act of a sultan who knew very little about Islamic religious affairs and claimed he was outlawing heresy rather than establishing orthodoxy. The former demanded allegiance to a single doctrine; the latter banned a doctrine but otherwise left people free to believe as they wished, even though the practical effect was to allow Hanafis and nu'tazilis to regain control locally. The former affected the entire caliphate but focused primarily on the capital, Baghdad; the latter had no effect outside Seljuq territory and focused on a major Iranian city, Nishapur, even after Tughril Beg took over Baghdad in 1055.

The view from the edge, however, sees these episodes in the same light. Despite the centrality of the caliphate in political affairs, Islam developed socially without a strong center, at least from the ninth century on. The early community in Mecca and Medina did serve as a social model, its practices being disseminated in varying forms throughout the conquered lands by the Companions and those who transmitted hadith from them (or fostered hadith upon them). But it was an ideal and unevolving model. Even though every year brought tens of thousands of Muslims on pilgrimage to the holy cities, the tales they brought back of current Meccan life carried less authority than the thousands of well-known hadith describing life there in Muhammad's time. By comparison, travelers returning from Kufa, Basra, Damascus, or Baghdad, the major political centers of the first two centuries, were better able to tell people about styles and intellectual trends in those places than about how a model Islamic society actually worked.

Without more detailed studies of the local variants in Islamic lore, ritual, and social practice from Cordoba to Samarqand during the early centuries, it is difficult to erase the image of Islamic social and religious homogeneity that becomes an article of belief in later centuries and suffuses general accounts of Islam and of Islamic history. Yet the particularism and localism visible in the growing Muslim urban communities in Iran, with their increasing coalescence around major ulama families, surely had its counterparts elsewhere. The differences between Nishapur, Gorgan, and Isfahan were only a fraction of those that must have obtained between any Iranian city and the urban communities of Egypt, Morocco, or Spain. In one

124

sense, however, all of these places were alike: they were essentially autonomous in how they derived a pattern of social and religious life from the Quran and the model of the Prophet's community.

For two hundred years this lack of a central authority officially prescribing social practices and structures did not constitute a problem. Conversion gained momentum slowly, and Arab mores stemming from a more or less common cultural formation in the Arabian peninsula exercised a persistent influence conducive to parallel social development from one region to another. The ninth century—or somewhat later in the western provinces—was a time of change, however. Conversion accelerated. Cities mushroomed. Masses of new Muslims looked to local social and religious leaders, increasingly non-Arabs, to define their place in rapidly changing communities. Seen from the political center, things were paradoxically beginning to flourish and to fall apart at the same time.

With a vision made acute by his war against his brother, al-Ma'mun seems to have seen clearly that the center was not holding. Whether he really believed his mihna could succeed in drawing together the caliphate's ever more divergent social currents where his earlier idea of transferring authority to the Prophet's most revered descendants had failed cannot be known because he died soon after its start. Certainly his two less gifted successors did not make the new policy work. The likelihood, however, is that the devolution of religious authority from the Prophet to the myriad of local assemblages of ulama, Sufis, and ascetics was too far advanced for any policy of doctrinal centralization to reverse. Away from the political center, people living on the Muslim community's far-flung social edges saw the mihna not just as an imposition upon their doctrinal freedom, but as an attempted usurpation of their local religious authority, and devaluation of the people they saw as embodying that authority.

Two centuries later, the contradiction between doctrinal pronouncements from the center and the assorted constellations of local religious authority is far more obvious. The ninth-century nu'tazilis constituted a school of thought more than a close-knit community. Al-Ma'mun presumably championed their ideas either because he shared them, or because he thought they would serve best the purposes he had in mind. By contrast, the eleventh-century Ash'aris were clustered within the Shafi'i faction, far from the caliphal center, around a few important ulama families, families of the sort that in every major city commanded great strength in influencing mass opinion for or against the government.

Did Amid al-Mulk al-Kunduri persecute his former religious associates for personal reasons? Or did he do it in machiavellian fashion to rebalance the power of the local factions in the aftermath of a change in regime in which the Shafi'is had gained too much influence by welcoming the Seljuq takeover? There is no way of telling, but the decision to issue the ban was unquestionably more involved with the interplay between central power and local religious authority than it was with al-Kunduri's personal religious beliefs, much less Sultan Tughril Beg's.

Paradoxically, the view from the center, which understandably looks upon the mihna as a failed attempt to assert a centrally dictated Islamic orthodoxy, usually omits all mention of the Seljuq banning of the Ash'aris, yet attributes to the dynasty a successful recentralization of religious leadership under the rubric "Sunni revival." Historians ignore this one unequivocal Seljuq effort to exert religious control during the vizierate of Amid al Mulk al-Kunduri for two reasons. First, they associate the putative Sunni revival with Amid al-Mulk's rival and successor, Nizam al-Mulk; and secondly, they regard it as a revival of Sunnism as a whole vis-à-vis Shi'ism rather than an effort to define Sunnism according to centrally espoused dogma.

Since there is very little to indicate that Shi'ism gained a mass following within the Muslim community during the pre-Seljuq century that saw Shi'ite Buyid warlords take control of Baghdad, and Shi'ites of a different stripe rule Egypt, North Africa, and part of Syria in the guise of the Fatimid caliphate, the idea of a Sunni revival makes sense only to historians wedded to the view from the center. The eleventh century did, indeed, see the waning of Shi'ite political fortunes and a reassertion of Sunni dominion. But the great growth of Shi'ism as a mass religion seems to date from late Seljuq, or even post-Seljuq times. To be sure, the view from the edge in the eleventh century is in most places a predominantly Sunni one, but so it was in the ninth and tenth centuries, as well.

What is termed the Sunni revival is actually the first stage in the dissemination of religious institutions and standardization of Sunni religious norms that becomes the hallmark of later Islamic history. Before describing this historical watershed, however, it is necessary to return to the discussion of Islamic urbanization because the dissemination of social and religious institutions that commences in the eleventh century is closely tied to the decline of the Islamic cities of Iran.

8

CITIES IN CRISIS

*In the middle of the central bazaar, war
broke out—civil war—between the people of
the Plaza quarter and the Head of the Village quarter. Many people were killed on
both sides. The war broke off at the door of
the congregational mosque during the
months of 1093. When the war had become
silent, the people of righteousness mourned
one another and prayed over the bodies
of the fallen.*

—DESCRIPTION OF INTRAURBAN CONFLICT IN BAIHAQ
REPORTED IN IBN FUNDUQ, *TARIKH-I BAIHAQ*

The description in chapter 4 of the great surge of Islamic urbanization stressed the unusual circumstance that the growth of cities
seems to have been unaccompanied by any great population growth
in the countryside or by any profound improvement in the efficiency of agricultural production. One reason for this stress was to sub-
stantiate the importance of religious conversion as a factor stimulating rural-urban migration. Equally important, however, was the
contribution of this lopsided migration to the growth, in some
areas, of overlarge cities that existed in a very fragile economic relationship with their agricultural hinterlands. Just as I provided in
chapter 4 a physical context for describing the burgeoning of Islamic urban society in the ninth and tenth centuries, the purpose of this

129

chapter is to describe a deteriorating urban environment in Iran that stimulated an outward migration of crucial social and religious importance from the late eleventh century onward.

Quantitative data reinforce the descriptive accounts in the preceding chapters in portraying the Islamic cities of Iran as robust, prosperous, and intellectually vigorous communities in the tenth century and the first half of the eleventh. Hard times were clearly setting in by the late eleventh century, however, and demographic and economic deterioration is quite marked by the end of the twelfth. The seventeenth-century sample of 4,039 biographies of ulama from all over the Islamic world cited in chapter 4[1] to illustrate the phenomenal rise of Iranian cities in the ninth century, shows a decline of almost 50 percent in Iranian biographies between a peak in 985 and the year 1200, with most of the reduction occurring after 1080. Since the biographies are listed by date of death, this points to a definite tapering off of Iranian educational productivity in the second half of the eleventh century.

Iran's representation declines by half again during the thirteenth century when the country is under Mongol rule, but the figures make it clear that by the time the Mongol armies of Genghiz Khan overran the eastern parts of the caliphate in the early thirteenth century, Iran's major cities had already greatly declined, at least as centers of learning. Mongol depredations, including the destruction of whole cities, compounded the crisis, of course; but historians who blame them for all the ills of late medieval Islamic civilization too often ignore the earlier symptoms of deterioration and their causes.

Nor is this simply an inconsequential chronological matter. As will be detailed in the next chapter, the eleventh and twelfth centuries witnessed major changes in Islam. New institutions came on the scene; new forms of social organization developed; and a tendency toward religious standardization, or harmonization of religious differences, began to assert itself. The question is what prompted these changes? Since they coincide, in political history, with the rise and fragmentation of the Seljuq state, one common answer to this question is that they were an outgrowth of Seljuq policy, or at least the policy of the Seljuqs' Iranian viziers. Without discarding all aspects of this answer, I shall argue that a good share of the social and religious change of the period stems from reactions to deteriorating economic conditions, and, further, that the dissemination of the new outlook is attributable, in significant part, to the migration of Iranian ulama from Iran's declining cities to the non-Iranian provinces.

The nature of the problems that led to Iran's urban crisis becomes visible early. The caliphate was already experiencing economic difficulties in the ninth century, which is also the century of most rapid urban growth. Sporadic but consistent tax records indicate that the revenues of the Abbasid caliphate, which mostly derived from agricultural taxes, suffered a modest decline during the first half of the ninth century and then fell by 45 percent in the second half.[2] This sent the caliphs and their viziers scrambling for money to pay their professional army and made it very difficult for them to enforce tax collection in remote provinces, or even retain the loyalty of ambitious governors. But the retention of tax revenues in breakaway provinces—beneficial, of course, to the burgeoning provincial capitals—cannot explain entirely the bankruptcy of the central treasury because the tax yield from the agricultural districts of southern Iraq itself, the region most consistently controlled from Baghdad, shows a similar precipitous fall.

An archaeological survey of the agricultural district nearest Baghdad points to one underlying cause of the financial crisis. It indicates a 25 percent decline in the area under cultivation between the end of the pre-Islamic Sasanid empire and the middle of the ninth century, and a further 37 percent decline by century's end.[3] The same survey shows that Baghdad and the grandiose new city of Samarra, which served as the Abbasid capital in the second half of the ninth century, were each ten times larger in area than the pre-Islamic Sasanid capital, Ctesiphon, located just south of Baghdad.[4] The implication of these figures is clearly that the uncontrolled growth of these two capitals stripped the surrounding countryside of population. A similar process focusing on Basra in southern Iraq most probably explains the large-scale importation of East African slaves in that area for use as rural laborers, a practice that led to a fifteen-year slave revolt starting in 869. The cost of importing, controlling, and maintaining thousands of slaves to clear salinated topsoil from dead land, which would enjoy a tax abatement once it was brought into production, would have been unreasonable if an adequate pool of rural labor had been available in the region.

A dramatic increase in agricultural productivity could have compensated, of course, for any loss of agricultural manpower through migration to the cities; but as demonstrated in chapter 4, the evidence for such an increase is weak. On the other hand, a concern for the provisioning of the growing cities reveals itself even in hadith. The Prophet allegedly said, "Whoever imports food to one of the cities (misr) of the Muslims, for him is the reward of a holy martyr."[5] This hadith is patently fabricated since the institution of the misr, meaning a Muslim army encampment, had not yet been established in Muhammad's day. Placing these words in the Prophet's mouth, however, reveals the seriousness of the concern in later years. Convert migration, unsupported by overall population increase or major improvement in agricultural efficiency, certainly could have caused at least some cities—the largest and least easily provisioned—to outgrow their agricultural bases.

This risk would have varied widely from region to region. In principle, higher prices should have induced people with means to invest in intensified production or put new land under the plow. The tax abatements granted in Islamic law to people bringing dead land into production would have had the same tendency. But manpower and water supply posed serious obstacles. The slaves in southern Iraq were, indeed, set to work stripping the saline topsoil from dead land to make it productive; but nonservile labor was apparently too scarce to restore full production on already cultivated lands. Moreover, just as today, it is difficult to persuade recent urban migrants, even under the impetus of hunger or falling living standards, to return to a life of agricultural labor. Iraq's widespread dependence on expensive irrigation systems made it impossible for people to undertake farming on their own, and laboring for someone else would have meant a resumption of the arduous peasant life they left behind when they migrated to the city. As for long-term city residents, they were too lacking in skills and familiarity with agriculture to revert easily to peasant life.

In the Arab provinces, the largest cities could stave off the problem of food supply by importing food. In Iraq, Baghdad, Samarra, Basra, and Kufa were conveniently situated on or near rivers. Foodstuffs grown in northern Iraq and Syria were rafted downstream to the more northern cities, and Basra was able to import food by sea to compensate for any local shortfall in supply. The same was true of Fustat in Egypt—enlarged after 969 by the adjoining construction of the new capital complex of Cairo. The Nile River provided an inexpensive means of provisioning. As for Arabia, the holy cities of Mecca and Medina were supplied by caravans carrying donations from other Muslim lands. And Syria's numerous small agricultural districts did not rely so heavily on elaborate irrigation works as Iraq and Iran did.

In contrast to the Arab lands, Iran was extremely vulnerable. Though the Zagros mountain borderland with Iraq enjoyed enough winter precipitation to make farming possible without elaborate irrigation systems, the arid regions of central and eastern Iran used underground water channels called *qanats* for irrigation. Each Iranian village in these areas depended upon a single qanat. To establish a village, a specialist was employed to dig a "mother well" on the slopes above the village site and determine the depth of the water table. He would then calculate the course and slope the qanat would have to follow to deliver water to the village. This calculation had to be very precise because too great a slope would cause the rushing water to erode the underground tunnel and make it collapse, whereas too shallow a slope would make the flow sluggish and the qanat prone to silting. The specialist would then direct the digging of a string of wells along the calculated qanat line and the excavation of the earth between the wells to form a tunnel. The finished qanat, up to fifteen kilometers in length, delivered a steady stream of water by gravity flow from the water table on the hillside to the village, and thus satisfied all of its agricultural and household needs. Winter rain and snow in the mountains regularly replenished the water table. The only maintenance required was periodic cleaning and, under certain soil conditions, internal buttressing with ceramic hoops.

Qanat irrigation set economic, social, and political parameters that were very different from those of the riverine irrigation systems of Egypt and Iraq. The Nile flooded at a propitious time in the late summer of every year. The villagers had only to impound the water, allow it to soak into the ground, and plant their crops. Virtually everyone lived within a mile of the life-giving river, which served as the main conduit for communication and for governmental control. In Iraq, however, the annual floods were more destructive and came inconveniently at the start of the torrid summer season. The flood water destroyed irrigation works and, if drainage was ineffective, produced marshes and areas of caked, saline soil useless for agriculture. Crops, therefore, were commonly grown in the winter and watered from long canals that diverted some of the perennial flow of the Tigris and Euphrates. Major canal construction required centralized planning and investment, and canal maintenance depended upon all of the villages cooperating in the annual dredging of channels, raising of levees, and repairing of wiers.

In the qanat-dependent parts of Iran, the investments of labor and money required to establish a village had little connection with the needs of the neigboring villages. Irrigation was sophisticated and expensive, but it required little regional cooperation or centralized planning. Many villages were founded by wealthy individuals and bore their name. For example, a man named Mu'adh built the village of Mu'adhabad outside Baihaq, and his son continued to invest in it and its qanat even after he moved into Baihaq to live the life of a landed gentleman.[6] Each village was thus autonomous in water supply, and the steadiness in the flow from its qanat put a distinct limit on the number of acres the villagers could cultivate. This limit, in turn, acted as a rough determinant of the number of people who could be sustained by the village's agricultural production. If a village outgrew its water supply, it had either to dig a second qanat, or hive off part of its population to establish a new village or migrate to town.[7]

In some respects, the Iranian system was less vulnerable to widespread catastrophe than that of Iraq, where a breached or silted-up canal could render dozens of villages uninhabitable, or of Egypt, where a low flood could threaten the entire country with starvation. As in those other provinces, however, it was essentially impossible for a single family to set itself up in farming. Without water, most of the land was good only for grazing; and bringing water to the land was too expensive and laborious an enterprise for a single family.

One peculiarity of the qanat system of irrigation, namely, that a fixed and consistent water supply dictated a practical limit to every village's size, makes it possible to demonstrate the fragility of urban growth in Iran, or at least in the northeastern region of Khurasan. The technology of qanat building, like that of Iranian agricultural technology in general, was the same in the 1950s, before the beginning of agricultural modernization, as it was in early Islamic times. Hence, it may be assumed that the average water flow per qanat was also basically unchanged. And from this it may further be inferred that the average number of irrigable acres per village, as, indeed, the average number of people per village, was little changed from medieval times. If these assumptions are roughly correct, counts of villages, whether modern or medieval, should be broadly translatable, at least as rough estimates, into population counts on the basis of modern figures for average village size.

This measure does not have to be particularly precise to yield useful estimates of order of magnitude. For example, reference was made in chapter 4 to a list naming sixty-five villages that were incorporated into the city of Nishapur as it grew. Taking 350 as the average population of an Iranian village,[8] the above assumptions would indicate that a local population of almost 23,000 villagers was absorbed into the city. Since at its maximum extent, judging from aerial photographs and surface observations, Nishapur had a population somewhere between 160,000 and 220,000, this is quite a plausible number for the local nucleus population.[9]

The susceptibility of Nishapur, or any other city, to a food supply crisis depends upon the city's sources of food and the productivity of the region it is dependent upon. In Nishapur's case, medieval geographical sources indicate that the agricultural hinterland of the city in the tenth century covered 12,728 square miles and included either 1,671 or 1,871 villages, an eminently plausible number given that in the 1950s exactly the same region contained 1,763 villages. Using the average village size mentioned above and multiplying by a number midway between the two tenth-century figures, 600,000 emerges as the rough estimate of the rural population of Nishapur's hinterland. Given the high and low estimates of Nishapur's urban population, this would imply a ratio of villagers to city dwellers of either 3.7:1 or 2.7:1.

Even the larger of these ratios points to a dangerously thin agricultural base. Assuming that two-thirds of the villagers were actively engaged in food production, the ratio suggests that every four farmers produced enough food to feed themselves, two nonproductive villagers, presumably children and elders, and one-and-a-half city dwellers.

The work of the demographic historian J. C. Russell provides some illuminating comparative figures.[10] Focusing on the thirteenth century, Russell estimated the populations of the ten largest urban communities in each of several large, geographically discrete European regions, and then calculated the percentage of each region's total population that lived in these ten cities. The resulting "urbanization index" showed that in most regions the top ten cities aggregated about 4.9 percent of the total population. The major exceptions were the regions centered on Florence, with an urbanization index of 26 percent, Venice with 23.4 percent, Milan with 19.1 percent and Ghent with 14.1 percent.

Taking all of Iranian Khurasan as a single region, Nishapur was unquestionably its foremost city. In applying Russell's urbanization formula, the population for Nishapur itself may be estimated at 150,000, a number slightly smaller than the low end of the estimate given earlier in order to allow for semi-urbanized residents supporting themselves in part or entirely from garden farming. The estimate of the region's overall population, based on counts of villages, will be taken as approximately 2.3 million.[11] These figures yield an urbanization index of 21.3, or roughly that of Venice in the thirteenth century.

While it is regrettable that the near absence of concrete statistics for the tenth and eleventh centuries necessitates a resort to such convoluted and imprecise techniques of estimating rural and urban populations, the outcome of the exercise comes as no surprise. Historians familiar with both medieval Europe and medieval Islam would probably have assumed that a vigorous manufacturing, trading, and intellectual center like Nishapur would most resemble the bustling cities of northern Italy and the Low Countries, which underwent great commercial expansion in the thirteenth century. What is troubling about the comparison is not the degree of urbanization per se, but the fact that Milan, Florence, Venice, and Ghent had easy access to the sea and therefore to foodstuffs imported from abroad. By comparison, Nishapur, like almost every other Iranian city of the eleventh century, was well inland with no possibility of receiving provisions by water.

In the early fourteenth century, the city of Florence, with an urbanization index of 26 percent, produced only enough food in its rural hinterland to supply the city for five months of the year. The remainder had to be imported. Studies of nearby cities during the same period have even suggested that malnutrition caused by the pressure of population upon local food resources exacerbated the severity of the Black Death that struck in 1348.[12] When bad weather or political disorder caused a significant shortfall in a particular year, the only choices were increased importation from untroubled areas or malnutrition with its attendant problem of epidemic disease.

In landlocked northeastern Iran, the implications of this situation reveal the magnitude of the provisioning problem. Not only was water transportation out of the question, but wheeled vehicles had long since disappeared from the countryside. The pack camel was the standard means of heavy transportation.[13] Consequently, if Nishapur did have 150,000 nonfarming inhabitants, and they all consumed grain at the rate indicated by European medieval records for active working people, namely, 2.5 lbs. of bread or its equivalent per day,[14] then more than a quarter million camel-loads of grain per year would have been needed to keep the city supplied, an average of several thousand camels per day during the harvest season. To accommodate loads of other sorts, from other foodstuffs, animal fodder, firewood and sun-dried bricks to caravans of silk and luxury goods, one should probably double this estimate of the number of pack animals entering the city to get a proper impression of the logistics of supplying a large city.

If the rate of urbanization of Tuscany compelled the Florentines to import almost 60 percent of their food, where did the food come from to feed the landlocked cities of Khurasan? Part of the answer probably comes from higher agricultural productivity since irrigated land typically yields more crops than rain-fed land. Another part can be attributed to intensive garden and orchard development on the city fringes, which enabled part of the population to feed itself and have a surplus to sell. Still a third part must come, indeed, from imports, even though the cost of overland transport was much higher than water transport.[15] But even with these allowances, it is hard to avoid the conclusion that the exuberance of Islamic urbanization so altered the ratio between rural and urban population that the cities found themselves in a very precarious economic situation by the beginning of the eleventh century.

When Abu Sa'd al-Isma'ili died in 1007, as mentioned in chapter 6, he had just lost all of his wealth, a fact that his biographer attributed to God's blessing. Among his losses was the folowing: "He had some wheat being shipped to him from Khurasan; a group of people fell upon it and plundered it."[16] Where in Khurasan the wheat was coming from isn't mentioned, but the roads to Gorgan from Khurasan, whether from the south or from the east, are mountainous and difficult. Why was Abu Sa'd importing a bulky commodity like wheat from beyond the rich Caspian plain surrounding Gorgan? Furthermore, why did "a group of people" fall on the caravan and plunder it? The first question is best answered by high prices caused by shortages, and the second by hunger.

Since Muslim chronicles of the eleventh century are mostly oriented toward capital cities and the deeds and interests of rulers, there is no indication of how often famine and epidemic disease struck in Khurasan. Hence, it cannot be proved beyond doubt that cities like Nishapur were by then approaching the economic limits of their growth and entering a period of economic and nutritional fragility. In most years Nishapur probably did reasonably well. Approaching the limits of growth means not that people are starving, though malnutrition may have become common among the poorer citizens; it means, rather, that the occasional bad year, or run of bad years, which are inevitable occurrences in the arid zone that stretches from North Africa to northern India, can produce devastating results. When the limits of growth are reached, no margin remains to cushion the population against hard times, whether meteorological or political.

In Nishapur, the one terrible famine that is reported in detail must stand for all of the lesser crises that remained unrecorded.[17] In 1011 a severe winter caused famine in both Iraq and Khurasan. Nishapur was hit hardest, the number of dead being put at an unbelievable 107,000. One eyewitness reported that more than 400 people (a common way of expressing "a large number" in medieval Islamic rhetoric[18]) were carried off to the graveyard from his part of town alone. Stories of bones being dug up from graveyards for food and of parents eating their children—standard literary images in medieval Muslim accounts of severe famines—signal that this was, indeed, a great catastrophe. Though the details are murky, it would appear that the initial starvation caused by the failed crop was compounded by epidemic disease. Even after food supplies finally became available, many people died because malnutrition was no longer their primary affliction.

How frequently lesser catastrophes befell in the following years is difficult to say, but there is evidence of an epidemic in 1057,[19] and biographical sources confirm that the coming of the Turkomans, the pastoral tribes who infiltrated Khurasan over a period of years and eventually supplied the Seljuq sultan's armed forces, caused great hardship by disrupting rural life. One ulama family that had played a major role in Nishapur from the early ninth century onward suffered particularly badly. Famine and tribal depredations caused the destruction of their homes and the ruin of their family enclave (*khitta*).[20] The year is not stated, but family death dates suggest that it was probably not long after the famine year of 1011.[21] And conditions were again bad when the Seljuqs finally made their bid for power in the 1030s. One prominent scholar was waylaid and killed by bandits,[22] and another by Turkoman marauders.[23] Conditions around the nearby town of Baihaq were reportedly so bad that for seven years the only crops that could be harvested were those grown within a walled precinct, and people had to do without meat entirely.[24]

Unlike the nontribal armies that vied for control of Khurasan in the ninth and tenth centuries, the Turkomans needed extensive pastureland for their sheep and their horses. Moreover, they were wedded to their nomadic, pastoral way of life. While they may not initially have interfered too much with the farming villages the cities depended on, their presence in the countryside must have made wealthy people think twice about investing in new qanats to bring dead land under production. Village lands that fell out of production because of rural labor shortage reverted to a natural vegetation that afforded sparse pasture. Persuading the Turkomans to relinquish such newly occupied pasture lands so that more productive farming could resume must have been a daunting prospect.

Though conclusive quantifiable evidence of the here hypothesized urban population decline of eleventh-century Khurasan remains elusive, there is no evidence of further urban population growth in the region after the year 1000. Not only are no new names of quarters recorded for Nishapur after that date, but the number of Khurasani village names preserved in the family names of ulama drops from twenty-five in the tenth century to only five in the eleventh. Rural-urban migration had run its course. The limit of urbanization set by agricultural productivity had been reached, if not exceeded, at least for the largest cities. A dry winter that did not adequately replenish the water table, or an unusually cold winter that stunted crops just beginning to grow, could produce a famine. So could the political insecurity produced by Turkoman incursions, or of the sort that saw Abu Sa'd al-Isma'ili's qanats filled in by an envious ruler in 1007. Warfare and rebellion had buffeted Iran repeatedly from the seventh through the tenth centuries, but they had not seriously damaged its prosperity or stemmed the tide of urbanization. The eleventh century proved to be different.

Nor did conditions improve with time. The potential for Turkoman disruption was fully realized in 1153 when an agent of the Seljuq sultan Sanjar sought to collect a tribute of 50,000 sheep from a newly arrived group of nomads.[25] Disagreement led to a show of force by Sanjar, and that, unexpectedly, led to Sanjar's defeat and capture. The Turkomans celebrated their victory by sacking Marv, Sanjar's capital, and Tus, the second-ranked city in the Nishapur region. Then they attacked and plundered Nishapur itself, burning one of its largest mosques. Bodies lay in heaps, 15,000 of them allegedly being counted in two quarters alone. After taking away whatever valuables they could find, including many women and children, the nomads attacked the smaller cities of Juvain and Isfara'in. Then they returned again to Nishapur and took the inner city, which had previously been able to hold out behind its formidable walls. After the Turkomans came bandit looters (*ayyarun*).

Famine followed, and in 1157 prices were still extraordinarily high, indicating that agricultural production had fallen below the critical level needed to support the city. These prolonged crisis conditions undoubtedly contributed to the most violent outbreak of factional violence between the Hanafis and the Shafi'is on record. Civil war broke out in 1158 within the city, and partisans from nearby cities joined the fight. The two sides set fires in one another's quarters. Meanwhile, the Turkomans attacked once again and plundered Nishapur for a third time. But this did not bring an end to the factional fighting. Mosques and schools were destroyed, and the citadel was besieged. Then came a temporary truce, only to be followed in 1161 by a new and even more ferocious outbreak of fighting. For Nishapur, this was the end. The greater part of the city was abandoned in ruins, and most of the remaining population moved to a new settlement in the suburbs. A militant faction that continued to hold out in the citadel was finally forced to surrender by the use of catapults in 1162. With that, the greatness of the greatest of Khurasan's cities came to an end. A historian of the period wrote: "Where had been the assembly places of amity, the classes of knowledge, and the circles of scholars were now the grazing grounds of sheep and the lurking places of wild beasts and serpents."[26]

The number of survivors of this devastation reveals something of the period that preceded it. Shadyakh, the suburban quarter to which the survivors relocated, was walled, unlike the much larger city that preceded it. Applying the residential density estimates utilized earlier, the total population living within these walls should have been between 24,750 and 33,000.[27] Since the likelihood is slight that a great numer of people continued to live in the abandoned ruins completely at the mercy of returning Turkoman marauders, it would appear that Nishapur's population had shrunk by 85 percent from its peak around 1000.

Despite the severity of the Turkoman raids and internecine fighting, a population loss of this magnitude cannot conceivably be attributed to these calamities alone. It is evidence, rather, that Nishapur had already lost some substantial portion of its population before the decade of disaster that began in 1153. The city that the factions fought over at the end must already have been substantially depopulated, that being a factor, perhaps, in its inability to defend itself against nomad raiders. Nishapur's violent end was the climax of a long period of deteriorating conditions and waning population, not simply an unpredictable by-product of political instability.

Of course, all of Iran's cities did not suffer Nishapur's fate. Yet no city took Nishapur's place as the intellectual capital of the eastern provinces. As the data on ulama cited at the beginning of this chapter show, by the twelfth century Iran's scholarly enterprise was clearly declining despite the fact that from approximately 1040 until 1093 the Seljuq sultans provided, at the imperial level, the most stable period of government in Iran since early Abbasid times. The root of the region's decline from its tenth and early eleventh century position as the preeminent intellectual center of the Islamic world was economic rather than political. Certain of Iran's cities had grown too large to be sustained by the remaining rural labor force. Unlike in Iraq, where a determined government might—but by the twelfth century rarely did—order new canals dug or old ones reclaimed to bring land back into production, economic revival in Iran depended upon a multitude of individual investments in building new qanats. And that, in turn, depended both upon a supply of villagers ready to retill fallow lands and upon a degree of security from nomad incursions that could hardly be expected from a government that depended militarily upon those same nomads.

The possible impact of hyperurbanization on other regions must be left to other historians. However, the story of Iran's cities in crisis goes beyond provincial history. As in the Italian Renaissance, culture in Iran initially flourished in the face of growing economic and social problems. In fact, the eleventh century marked a pinnacle of intellectual and religious achievement in Iran, and particularly in Khurasan. However, the achievements of this period were conditioned by a growing sense of hard times, just as the weakening financial base of the major ulama families threatened their stability and independence as a class.

Yet just when some ulama responded to hard times and economic insecurity by migrating to other provinces—a development to be discussed in the next chapter—the late eleventh and twelfth centuries saw other ulama patricians pursuing a different trajectory, one that sought to respond to urban hard times by seizing political control of their cities. What this amounted to was an effort to establish patrician-dominated city-states in several important cities in the northeast.[28] Only the Burhan family succeeded. Using the religious title sadr, this family of ulama patricians essentially ruled Bukhara from the late eleventh to the early thirteenth century, accepting as necessary the overlordship of various imperial pretenders and warlords while keeping order in Bukhara and focusing its citizens' energies on the welfare of the city.

Elsewhere, there was a popular revolt and seizure of power in Herat in 1098 led by that city's paramount religious leader. His short-lived movement was quashed the following year. The year 1098 also witnessed the deposition and execution of an important scholar and would-be king who had built an independent position for himself in Samarqand. His biography reads, in part:

> He did not cease to raise and elevate his status until his rank reached that of a king (malik). He raised himself up against the Khan, and the demon of sovereign rule laid an egg in his head and hatched it. In his soul was a delusion of grandeur which made it manifest that his soul would not be satisfied except by dominion (mulk). I even heard that he ordered coins struck in his own name. He exercised the powers of government [literally, "he drew together and split apart"] until his time ended and the measure of his days was filled.[29]

While the frustration and tension arising from deepening urban crisis undoubtedly fueled these bids for patrician autonomy during the decades of Seljuq family squabbling following the death of Sultan Malikshah in 1093, single cities could not realistically hope to stand up long to the army of a sultan or a warlord. Some scholars sought refuge from hard times in suddenly popular madrasas, or Islamic

143

colleges, that became the most notable institutional development of the late eleventh century. Others, whose educational tradition of collecting hadith inclined them toward travel anyway, and who knew that visiting scholars were well accepted anywhere in the Islamic world, chose to emigrate. The next chapter will deal with the development of religious institutions and attitudes in eleventh-century Iran and with the ensuing Iranian diaspora that carried these institutions and attitudes into other regions and thereby helped trigger the emergence of a more cohesive and homogeneous Islamic society.

9

THE IRANIAN DIASPORA: THE EDGE CREATES A CENTER

If knowledge were located in the Pleiades,
one of the sons of Persia would go
there to get it.
—Hadith quoted in ABU NU'AIM, *AKHBAR ISBAHAN*

Sunni Islam is commonly portrayed as a comparatively uniform religion built around the Quran, an agreed upon corpus of hadith, an all-encompassing legal tradition, a generally accepted theology, and some widely spread institutions, notably the Islamic college (*madrasa*) and the Sufi brotherhood. Another part of the common portrayal is the notion that much of this uniformity goes all the way back to the early community around the Prophet Muhammad in Medina. Told from this perspective, the story of Islam necessarily treats deviations from the assumed norms during the first five centuries as anomalies, distortions, or short-lived wrong turnings. Or else they are not discussed at all. Uniformity is viewed as primordial rather than achieved, not so much because of an ignorance of history as because of the inherent need of all people who root their authority in tradition to regard that tradition as everlasting and unchanging, or at least anchored in the ways of a great founder.

I have argued thus far that Islam was actually quite variously understood from place to place in the early centuries. Even assuming that the muhaddithun were successful in refining the pure metal of historical truth datable to the time of the Prophet from the vast ore-field of hadith, it is apparent that millions of early Muslims,

145

many of them profoundly devout, included in their understandings of Islam lore and practices embodied in hadith that circulated only locally, or that were ultimately rejected as weak. The underpinnings of modern portrayals of Islam as a comparatively consistent and homogeneous religion go back only to the period of the twelfth through fourteenth centuries.

Reimagining all the lost diversity of the earlier Islamic centuries will be a task for future historians. My purpose here is to suggest why and how Islam achieved the degree of uniformity reflected in today's introductory primers. The view from the center addresses this question with difficulty because the time period involved encompasses the final fall of the marcescent caliphate with the destruction of Baghdad by the Mongols in 1258. Nevertheless, the theory of a Baghdad-centered reawakening of traditionalism, often dubbed a "Sunni revival," attempts an answer that is faithful to the view from the center. In fact, however, many of the practices, beliefs, and institutions most characteristic of the period when Islam invented a uniform identity for itself are rooted in the urban Muslim communities of eleventh-century Iran, communities that evolved from the local consolidation of societal edges rather than from a centralized religious tradition or authority symbolized by the caliphate.

The idea of a "Sunni revival" takes the Abbasid caliph al-Qadir's promulgation in 1017 of a creed espousing Sunni traditionalism as the beginning of a counterattack against Shi'ism and speculative theology in general.[1] Ulama of the Hanbali law school, a local Baghdad rite with few followers elsewhere, at least at that time, are argued to have been the storm troopers of the movement, and the Seljuq sultans, assumed, as Turks, to be ardent Sunnis, are portrayed as the commanders. Discussions of the "Sunni revival" do not always agree on its traditionalist character, but they are in accord in seeing it coming to a head during the century or so of Seljuq rule.

The primary instrument of this revival, the madrasa, was an endowed, residential institution dedicated, most often, to the study of Islamic law, but also giving instruction in such ancillary disciplines as hadith and Quran reading. The spread and standardization of the madrasa is commonly attributed to the Seljuq vizier Nizam al-Mulk. In the second half of the eleventh century, Nizam al-Mulk established a madrasa bearing his name, a Nizamiya, in most major cities under Seljuq control. The best known of these colleges is the one in Baghdad, but the Nizamiya in Nishapur antedated it by five or six years and rivaled it in importance.

Since the theory of "Sunni revival" hinges on the convergence of Sunni Turkish overlordship in Baghdad with the popularization there of the madrasa as an educational institution, the origins of the madrasa call for examination. The Nizamiya built in 1063 in Baghdad was the first madrasa in the Arab world. Iran was different, however. Nishapur counted at least twenty-five madrasas of greater antiquity than Baghdad's Nizamiya, and even the comparatively small Khurasani urban center of Baihaq had at least five pre-Nizamiya madrasas.[2]

The first references to madrasas in Khurasan date to the early tenth century, but they proliferate in the eleventh century. Literally "places of study," these early madrasas seem sometimes to have concentrated on law, sometimes on hadith study, and sometimes on Sufism. Some were built with private funds, and some were built by governors or rulers. Some were devoted to the educational activities of a single prominent scholar or family of ulama. Some, but not all, were dedicated to teaching a single legal doctrine. At least one pre-Seljuq Khurasani madrasa is specifically identified as Shi'ite.

Since Nizam al-Mulk was born in Khurasan and received his education there, he was obviously familiar with the idea of madrasas at the time of his assumption of administrative power in Khurasan. This occurred in 1058 when Alp Arslan, Sultan Tughril Beg's nephew, succeeded to power in his father's eastern Iranian appanage. Five years later, on the death of his uncle, Alp Arslan succeeded to the sultanate as well. Nishapur in 1058 was in the throes of turmoil because of the persecution of the Ash'aris inspired by Tughril's vizier Amid al-Mulk al-Kunduri. Aware that as the vizier of a subordinate member of the Seljuq family he did not have the power to countermand al-Kunduri's persecution, Nizam al-Mulk sought to quell the city's raging factional discord by endowing a private institution dedicated to legal, rather than theological, study and recalling the famous Ash'ari thinker Imam al-Haramain al-Juvaini from exile to direct it.

The first Nizamiya in Nishapur set a pattern for Nizam al-Mulk's educational endowments in other cities.[3] The Nizamiyas were privately endowed and dedicated to the teaching of Shafi'i law as the central focus of study. Nizam al-Mulk personally controlled all appointments. Scholars may debate whether Nizam al-Mulk's primary goal was sponsorship of Shafi'i and/or Ash'ari doctrines, patronage of specific scholars whom he admired, or manipulation of the ulama factions through financial dependency, the latter being, in my view, the preferable interpretation.

It is beyond debate, however, that the religious orientation of the Seljuq family, and of their Turkish followers, played little or no role in the rise of the madrasa. Not only are Turkish professors and students rarely mentioned, but the idea embodied in the notion of "Sunni revival" that the Seljuqs and their famous vizier were so fanatically anti-Shi'ite that they propagated the institution to indoctrinate Sunni loyalists for state service is belied by several facts: first, few Nizamiya-trained officials in Seljuk service have ever been identified—scholars, as a rule, did not work in government offices; second, Nizam al-Mulk and Sultan Malikshah, Alp Arslan's son and successor, both gave daughters in marriage to Shi'ite notables; and third, several Shi'ites held the office of vizier under Seljuq sultans. Furthermore, the madrasa was not exclusively a Sunni institution. A Shi'ite source lists six Shi'ite madrasas built in Iran during the Seljuq period, some of them under royal patronage.[4]

The spread of the madrasa from the late eleventh century on cannot be explained by a putative "Sunni revival" rooted in the religious policies of the rulers in the center. Why, then, did the number of madrasas in Baghdad increase from one to thirty within a century of the Nizamiya's founding? Or why in Damascus? The first madrasa there—not a Nizamiya since Damascus was not ruled from Baghdad—was founded in the 1090s. By 1200 there were more than twenty, and by 1260 another fifty-three.[5] The new institution arrived in Cairo in the 1170s. By the early fifteenth century there were seventy-three in the Egyptian capital, thirteen of them dating to before 1200. Mecca's first madrasa was founded in 1175 and was followed by two others before the century's end. Five more were built in the first half of the thirteenth century. Further west, the first madrasa was built in Tunis in 1252 and in Spain in the following century. As for the east, India's earliest madrasas date to the beginning of the Delhi sultanate in the first decade of the thirteenth century.

Truly a revolution in education! The rapidly spreading madrasa network reoriented students and teachers alike. Teaching long remained personalized, and much of it still took place outside the new institutions. But as residences for students and scholars, endowed sources of income for those ulama who gained positions in them, and symbolic public manifestations of the cultural importance of religious scholarship, the madrasas marked a distinct change in the religious life of Islamic cities. Moreover, the range of books studied in the madrasas tended, over time, to become standardized. The six famous collections of sound hadith compiled in the ninth century became canonical during this period, and a number of books written in the fourteenth and fifteenth centuries gained wide acceptance throughout the Islamic world. Many students still studied with family members or noted local scholars in less formal settings, but residence in a madrasa, where financial support was available, shaped student careers in new ways. The days of uncontrolled proliferation in Muslim scholarship were over. So were the days of ulama independence, at least to the extent that scholars holding appointments in madrasas, whether privately and royally patronized, were subject to dismissal.

Part of this revolution in education is attributable to rulers, the main financial patrons. Presumably, they saw the new institution as an instrument for promoting their pious reputations and for putting religious scholars in their debt, no doubt firm in the expectation that the recipients of royal largesse would not countenance agitation against the government. But no patron would have founded a madrasa had there been no scholars around who knew what one was and how it should function.

This is where the learned emigrants from the depressed and increasingly chaotic cities of Iran played a crucial role. Many of them knew exactly what a madrasa was because madrasas had long been known in Iran even though they had occupied a comparatively minor niche in the educational environment. The central educational relationship of the madrasa movement in its initial phases involved Iranians demonstrating to non-Iranians the educational techniques of their native land.

Six of the first ten law professors at Baghdad's Nizamiya, covering the period 1063–1123, were from Iran or studied in Iran.[6] Out of a total of twenty-three known law professors, twelve were Iranian or Iranian-trained. In the field of theology, eight out of eleven known professors were Iranian or Iranian-trained, including all of the first seven. At the student level, however, though the data are much more fragmentary, it appears that fewer than a quarter of the students were from Iran.

Any suspicion that the dominating presence of Iranian professors in Baghdad's Nizamiya might derive simply from Nizam al-Mulk's own Iranian origins can be laid to rest by looking at the situation in Damascus, where madrasas did not take root until after Nizam al-Mulk's death. Of eighteen madrasas founded in Damascus before 1175, nine included Iranians among their first three professors.[7] More tellingly, out of the nine earliest madrasas, founded between 1097 and 1145, seven had Iranian professors, five of whom were the inaugural professor. The very earliest Damascus madrasa started out as a conventional teaching circle in the Great Mosque but came to be called a madrasa after the famous Iranian scholar Abu Hamid al-Ghazali, formerly a professor at the Nizamiya in Baghdad, took up teaching there in 1097. In another Syrian city, Aleppo, the pattern recurs. The first three madrasas, founded between 1116 and 1149, were all inaugurated by Iranian professors, as was the sixth madrasa, founded in 1169.

The conclusion from all of this is clear. During the first two generations of madrasa proliferation outside Iran, founding patrons in Arab lands turned often to scholars from Iran to organize their new foundations. As time went on, of course, the pool of local scholars exposed to the madrasa environment and familiar with the madrasa's functions rapidly increased, and Iranians became less visible. But at the onset of this educational revolution, the availability of expatriate Iranian scholars familiar with madrasa practice in their homeland was crucial. They embodied what rapidly came to be seen as a superior educational perspective. In striking contrast to this sudden abundance and prominence of Iranian professors pursuing their careers outside their homeland, scholars from the Arab world are rarely mentioned in connection with the hundreds of madrasas in Iran.

Nor was the madrasa the only scholarly institution of Iranian origin that spread during this period. Two new regions gradually opened for Muslim settlement during the eleventh century: northern India, pummeled into submission by repeated invasions from the Ghaznavid and then Ghurid rulers of Afghanistan, and Anatolia, the heartland of Islam's Byzantine foe, which lost military protection after Alp Arslan defeated Emperor Romanus IV Diogenes in 1071 at the battle of Manzikert. Over the following two centuries, Persian became the literary and scholarly language of the Muslim populations in both areas. In accordance with the view from the center, this monumental language transformation is usually attributed to a preference for Persian on the part of the new Turkish warlords, but rulers have no way of imposing a language without an abundance of native speakers available to teach it and use it.

The key to the spread of Persian, which is particularly impressive in Anatolia since Arabic-speaking Syria and Iraq were more proximate than Iran, is the same diaspora of Iranian scholars that brought madrasa professors to Baghdad, Damascus, and Aleppo. Scholars have long agreed that thousands of Iranians fled their homeland after the Mongol invasions that began in 1218 and inaugurated a century of Mongol rule in Iran. But the economic fragility of Iran's cities prompted many Iranians to emigrate long before the Mongols appeared on the horizon. Though information on the nascent Muslim societies of India and Anatolia is scarce, the names that appear in educational and religious contexts are almost exclusively Iranian.

Moreover, the organization of scholarly and religious affairs in these regions followed a model that originated in Khurasan. From the turn of the eleventh century onward, the largest cities in Khurasan each had a personage titled the Shaikh al-Islam or, in some instances, the Sadr al-Sudur. This office apparently evolved in the tenth century in the process of the ulama consolidating their positions of social and religious leadership at the local level. The Shaikh al-Islam was not a governmental appointee, but no city had more than one at a time. He was normally chosen by the local ulama and was almost invariably an eminent and respected scholar. His duties seem to have involved oversight of religious education in all its forms. The first Shaikh al-Islam in Herat, for example, is reported to have been "the first to establish in Herat the custom of examining credentials (*takhrij al-fawa'id*) and investigating (*sharh*) and certifying (*tashih*) men."[8] His successor was noted for "the ordering of madrasas, teachers (*ashab*), and [Sufi] lodges and the holding (*nuwab*) of classes."[9]

After the eleventh century, the titles Shaikh al-Islam and Sadr al-Sudur spread widely and came to refer to several different functions: religious leader of local Muslim communities in Mongol-ruled China, chief jurisconsult in the Ottoman Empire, dispenser of royal patronage to scholars in the Delhi sultanate in India, and so forth. Their earliest spread, however, seems to have been to pre-Mongol Anatolia where, just as in Khurasan, a Shaikh al-Islam functioned in each city as the chief Muslim educational figure.[10] In all likelihood, the office reached India before the Mongol invasion as well. Under the Delhi sultanate, the royal largesse distributed by the Sadr al-Sudur made him "not so much controller of opinion as guardian of learning."[11] Though it is not known when this office was first filled in India, it at least dates back to the sultanate's founder, Iltutmish, who as a youth had been the slave of a man related to the Sadr al-Sudurs of Bukhara, the local ruling family of ulama.[12] Iltutmish came to the throne in 1210 and appointed a succession of Iranians to the position of Shaikh al-Islam in Delhi.[13] As in the later Safavid dynasty in Iran, the Shaikh al-Islam during the Delhi sultanate was presumably the chief religious figure in a single city with the Sadr al-Sudur functioning at the imperial level.

Twelfth-century India and Anatolia were flooded with Iranian scholars who brought with them both their language and an institutional outlook forged in the urban milieu of eleventh-century Iran. The number of Iranians who came to the Arab lands was doubtless smaller, but there, too, they had an impact in the field of religious education. Iran was second only to Syria-Palestine as the point of origin of foreign scholars in fifteenth-century Egypt, and Iranian scholars were highly respected there.[14] But the impact of the Iranian diaspora went beyond institutional changes. It affected the content of religious thought and practice as well.

It is generally accepted that from the twelfth century on Sunni Islam moved rapidly toward theological uniformity.[15] But unlike earlier episodes of theological dispute, such as al-Ma'mun's mihna and Amid al-Mulk al-Kunduri's persecution of the Ash'aris described in chapter 7, the new impetus toward theological consensus came not from the political institutions of the center, but from the scholarly milieu of the new madrasas. What is surprising in this is that madrasas fashioned on the model of the Nizamiya defined themselves by school of legal rather than theological interpretation. Shafi'is, Hanafis, Hanbalis, Malikis, and Shi'ites normally had separate madrasas, although eventually some important madrasas were established with chairs for each of the four Sunni law schools. In all of these institutions, theology was either a secondary subject or topic of preaching.

A historian of ideas might well argue that Ash'ari theology eventually prevailed because it affirmed certain deeply held popular beliefs about God and His creation—for example, the uncreatedness of the Quran and God's power to perform miracles—by arguing their validity in a rigorously logical fashion. Looked at this way, the Ash'aris afforded a compromise betweeen the bloodless intellectuality of the nu'tazilis and the unreflective traditionalism of the Hanbalis. Yet Ash'ari theologians had been refining their viewpoint for more than two centuries before it suddenly began to catch on in the twelfth century. For the timing of the rise of ash'ari theology we must look to the Iranian diaspora, even though this look will necessarily involve us in a plethora of names.

Al-Ash'ari himself, the eponym of the school, lived and worked in Iraq and died in 935. Within a century of his death, however, the locus of Ash'ari thought shifted to Khurasan. A study of early Ash'ari thought by Michel Allard charts sixteen important thinkers down to the beginning of the twelfth century.[16] Eleven of them, including all who flourished in the eleventh century, spent the better part of their careers in Nishapur.

The earliest of these was Abu Sahl al-Su'luki (d. 979),[17] a man remembered as a paragon of piety, while a teacher in Isfahan, for

153

having given his only cloak to a beggar while heading for his class in Shafi'i law. Forced to teach wearing a woman's robe, he had no choice but to throw an outer garment over it and go along when a delegation of scholars arrived to summon him to the court of Isfahan's Buyid ruler, Imad al-Dawla. "Does he make light of me?" exploded the prince when he caught sight of Abu Sahl. "The imam of the city riding dressed in a woman's robe!" By way of reply, Abu Sahl defeated the assembled scholars in debate and more than proved his scholarly excellence.

Abu Sahl al-Su'luki moved to Nishapur where his son Abu al-Tayyib, who is also included on Allard's chart of major Ash'ari thinkers, succeeded him as a Shafi'i legist. Abu al-Tayyib (d. 1013) adopted the nine-year-old son of a Hanafi who had converted to the Ash'ari belief after seeing the Prophet Muhammad in a dream. He had subsequently been murdered in factional fighting. The orphan, Abu Uthman al-Sabuni (d. 1057),[18] grew up to become Nishapur's paramount scholar and first Shaikh al-Islam. Moreover, he married his daughter to Nishapur's "head" (ra'is), Abu al-Fadl al-Furati (d. 1054), one of the four leaders later singled out for arrest by Amid al-Mulk al-Kunduri during his persecution of the Ash'aris.

The leader of Nishapur's Shafi'i-Ash'ari faction while Abu Uthman al-Sabuni was Shaikh al-Islam was Imam al-Muwaffaq (d. 1048), a grandson of Abu al-Tayyib al-Su'luki. It was Imam al-Muwaffaq who advised the Seljuq Sultan Tughril Beg to take his young protégé al-Kunduri into his service, and Imam al-Muwaffaq's son Abu Sahl Muhammad (d. 1064) was another of the four Ash'ari leaders targeted by al-Kunduri during his vengeful persecution. Abu Sahl Muhammad mustered a force of personal retainers to free Abu al-Fadl al-Furati from prison, and the two of them fled into exile, Abu al-Fadl dying en route.

Further extending the web of Ash'ari family connections, Abu Sahl Muhammad's nephew married the daughter of a third Ash'ari leader singled out for arrest, Abu al-Ma'ali al-Juvaini (d. 1086), better known as Imam al-Haramain, or "Imam of the Two Holy Places." He earned the title teaching in Mecca and Medina while in exile from Khurasan. Imam al-Haramain and his father Abu

154

Muhammad al-Juvaini (d. 1046) are both on Allard's list of major Ash'ari thinkers. Abu Hamid al-Ghazali (d. 1111), the man who has come to be revered as Islam's greatest theologian, was a student of Imam al-Haramain and a teacher in the Baghdad Nizamiya and in a madrasa in Damascus.

This linking together in a single family of four of Allard's prominent Ash'aris and three other major Ash'ari leaders does not complete the network of interconnections in Nishapur. Another man on Allard's list, Abu Bakr Muhammad ibn Furak, known simply as Ibn Furak (d. 1030),[19] was attracted to Nishapur from the Iranian city of Rayy specifically to teach Ash'ari theology, which he had learned in Iraq from al-Ash'ari's pupil al-Bahili. Ibn Furak's grandson, Abu Bakr Ahmad al-Furaki (d. 1085), married a daughter of the eminent Sufi Abu al-Qasim al-Qushairi (d. 1073), whom Allard also numbers among the Ash'ari worthies. Abu Nasr al-Qushairi (d. 1120) was another of Abu al-Qasim's children and a student of Imam al-Haramain al-Juvaini. In 1077 he electrified Baghdad by his frank exposition of Ash'ari theological views, and the ensuing riot between Ash'aris and Hanbalis caused deaths on both sides.[20] The dozens of scholars related to the al-Qushairi family constituted a long-lasting lineage of Ash'ari teachers in Nishapur. The last of them, indeed, the last of Nishapur's notable Sunni scholars of any sort, died in the general slaughter when the Mongols overran the city in 1221. He had studied under a grandson of Abu al-Qasim al-Qushairi.

As for the five other Ash'ari thinkers from Nishapur discussed by Allard, al-Hakim al-Naisaburi (d. 1015) was instrumental in persuading Nishapur's governor to invite Ibn Furak to Nishapur from Rayy. Abu Ishaq al-Isfara'ini (d. 1027) was a teacher of Abu al-Qasim al-Qushairi. Abd al-Qahir al-Baghdadi (d. 1038) taught in the same mosque as Abu Ishaq al-Isfara'ini. Abu al-Qasim al-Isfara'ini (d. 1060) was a teacher of Imam al-Haramain al-Juvaini. And Abu Bakr al-Baihaqi (d. 1066) made the pilgrimage to Mecca with his friend Abu al-Qasim al-Qushairi. In other words, the Ash'ari theological circle was very closely knit and concentrated overwhelmingly in Khurasan, particularly in Nishapur. Yet it was a large circle. Allard's listing of major thinkers obscures the fact that

155

hundreds of closely connected scholars can be identified as part of Khurasan's Ash'ari camp.

Ash'ari theology, therefore, was an Iranian export to the Arab world in the late eleventh century. Abu Hamid al-Ghazali looms historically as the definitive codifier and paramount disseminator of Ash'ari thought; but scores of lesser Iranian scholars carried the message abroad, not just to Iraq and Syria, but to Anatolia and India as well. And the new madrasas, supervised by expatriate Iranians or their students, provided the institutional environment for exposing people to the new theology.

A famous example of how Ash'arism spread comes from the life of Ibn Tumart (d. 1130), the founder of the Almohad movement that established a powerful empire in Morocco and Spain. Ibn Tumart came to Baghdad as a student in 1108. According to some sources, he met al-Ghazali there and was singled out by him for later greatness.[21] For chronological reasons, other sources are skeptical about the meeting; but whether Ibn Tumart studied with al-Ghazali in person, or only with one of his Iranian successors at the Baghdad Nizamiya, it is apparent that the Iranians in Baghdad taught him his Ash'arism and that al-Ghazali was already a name to conjure with in the twelfth century when the stories about Ibn Tumart were written.

Moving from institutional, academic, and intellectual manifestations of the Iranian scholarly diaspora to questions of social outlook and organization, a strong Iranian imprint can be seen on the Sufi brotherhoods that proliferated in the twelfth century. Scholars have long recognized the preeminence of Iran in the development of Sufism during the tenth and eleventh centuries. The twelfth century, however, is a watershed in this development. What began in individual strivings for "union" with God took on increasing elaboration as disciples sought guidance along the same path from renowned masters. The next step was the institutionalization of Sufism in the form of geographically extensive brotherhoods dedicated to the spiritual method and social praxis of a particular master. Ecstatic utterances and poetic exaltation of Sufi experience continue as literary forms, but they are joined by rules and codes stipulating not just the proper behavior for the Sufis of a particular brotherhood, but proper behavior for their admirers as well.

Stories about Iranian Sufis are legion, but a convenient place to begin examining standardized codes of behavior is with Abu Sa'id ibn Abi al-Khair (967–1049), a flamboyant Sufi from the town of Mayhana in Khurasan. Abu Sa'id sojourned in Nishapur and met there the most famous Sufis of the day, people like Abu Abd al-Rahman al-Sulami, the first collector of Sufi biographies; Abu Ali al-Daqqaq and his daughter Fatima; and Fatima's husband Abu al-Qasim al-Qushairi, the previously mentioned Ash'ari thinker. Though the Nishapuris did not always appreciate Abu Sa'id's style, they could not help being impressed by him.

One day whilst Shaykh Abu Sa'id was preaching at Nishapur, he grew warm in his discourse and being overcome with ecstasy exclaimed, "There is naught within this vest [jubba] except Allah!" Simultaneously he raised his forefinger, which lay on his breast underneath the jubba, and his blessed finger passed through the jubba and became visible to all. Among the Shaykhs and Imams present on that occasion were Abu Muhammad Juwayni [the Ash'ari theologian], Abu 'l-Qasim Qushayri, Isma'il Sabuni [the Ash'ari Shaikh al-Islam], and others whom it would be tedious to enumerate. None of them, on hearing these words, protested or silently objected. All were beside themselves, and following the Shaykh's example they flung away their gaberdines [khirqaha]. When the Shaykh descended from the pulpit, his jubba and their gaberdines were torn to pieces [and distributed]. The Shaykhs were unanimously of opinon that the piece of silk [kazhpara] which bore the mark of his blessed finger should be torn off from the breast of the jubba and set apart, in order that in the future all who came or went might pay a visit to it.[22]

Hagiographic marvels are as commonplace in the history of Sufism, of course, as in the lives of Christian saints; but Abu Sa'id is also one of the first Sufis to have composed, according to his twelfth-century biographer, a rule of behavior for the disciples who frequented his lodge (*khangah*):

I. Let them keep their garments clean and themselves always pure.
II. Let them not sit in the mosque or in any holy place for the sake of gossiping.

157

III. In the first instance let them perform their prayers in common.

IV. Let them pray much at night.

V. At dawn let them ask forgiveness of God and call unto Him.

VI. In the morning let them read as much of the Koran as they can, and let them not talk until the sun has risen.

VII. Between evening prayers and bedtime prayers let them occupy themselves with repeating some litany.

VIII. Let them welcome the poor and needy and all who join their company, and let them bear patiently the trouble of [waiting upon] them.

IX. Let them not eat anything save in participation with one another.

X. Let them not absent themselves without receiving permission from one another.[23]

Though Abu Sa'id's lodge in Mayhana survived and perpetuated his practice and memory for several generations, no network of khangahs came into being in conformity with his rule. He should be seen, therefore, as a precursor of organized Sufism rather than as the founder of a brotherhood. The first true Sufi orders (Arabic *tariqa*, pl. *turuq*) appeared within a century of Abu Sa'id's death, however. Their eponymous founders were Iranians working and preaching in Iraq, Abu Najib al-Suhrawardi (d. 1168) and Abd al-Qadir al-Jilani (d. 1166). The Suhrawardiya and Qadiriya established khangahs in dozens, eventually hundreds, of locations, the latter continuing as a widespread and vital organization to the present day.

Abu Najib al-Suhrawardi's manual setting forth the proper behavior for dedicated Sufis, as well as for those people who admired the Sufis and wanted to share their aura of saintliness without committing themselves to the full Sufi regimen, illustrates the codification of Sufi practice that had taken place by the early twelfth century and that was essential to the building of extensive brotherhoods. Starting with the affirmation that "Sufis agree that one should learn the ordinances of the shari'a so that praxis (*'amal*) would be in conformity with the teachings of the religious-legal science (*'ilm*),"[24] al-Suhrawardi goes on to stipulate, among many other rules, that:

The Sufi should associate with people of his kind and those from whom he can benefit. . . . He should not associate with people who are opposed to his religious affiliation even if they are related to him. . . .

The Sufi should undertake to serve his brethren and companions . . . and help them in obtaining their sustenance. He should endure their offence and should not rebuke them unless they transgress the law. . . .

Companionship with young men is reprehensible because of the harms involved in it. Whoever is tried by this experience should safeguard his heart and body from them and should prompt them to undertake exercises of self-discipline . . . and ethical training, and he should avoid informal behavior with them. . . .

Every limb has its own special ethics. . . . The ethics of the tongue. The tongue should always be busy in reciting God's names (*dhikr*) and in saying good things of the brethren, praying for them, and giving them counsel. . . . The ethics of hearing. One should not listen to indecencies and slander. . . . The ethics of sight. One should lower one's eyes in order not to see forbidden things. . . . The ethics of the hands: to give charity and serve the brethren and not use them in acts of disobedience. . . .

The Sufi should not travel for amusement, vanity, ostentation, or to seek worldly things. . . . He should not travel without the consent and permission of his parents and his master. . . .

The Sufi should prefer walking to riding except in case of pressing necessity, because his travelling is for self-discipline and for the sake of enhancing his religious state. . . .

When the Sufi enters a town, he should visit the Sufi shaykh, if there is one. If not, he should go to the meetingplace [sic] of the Sufis. If there are several such places, he should go first to the most important of them. . . . If there is no Sufi brotherhood and no Sufi meetingplace in town, he should stay with one of the people of the town who loves the Sufis and inclines to them most. . . .

The Sufis should not have a set time for eating, they should not make much ado about it and should not prefer plenty of food which is unclean over little which is clean. . . .

The Sufis do not disapprove of conversation during the meal. More of their rules of conduct in eating: to sit on the left leg, to use the formula "In the name of God," to eat with three fingers, to take small bites and chew well, to lick the fingers and the bowl. One should not look at the morsel taken by a friend.[25]

Al-Suhrawardi's rules give an overall impression that is quite different from that of Christian monastic rules because the Sufis did not live cloistered lives and were not prohibited from having families. But they convey an ideal of pious social behavior that was all the more influential for being manifested daily in public. Recognizing this public role for the Sufis, al-Suhrawardi went beyond regulating their own behavior to stipulating, as dispensations (*rukhas*, sing. *rukhsa*), behavior for those people who admired them:

It is allowed by way of [dispensation] to possess an estate or to rely on a regular income. Their [the Sufis] rule in this matter is that one should not use all of it for himself, but should dedicate this to public chairities and should take from it only enough for one year for himself and his family. . . .

There is a [dispensation] allowing one to be occupied in business; this dispensation is granted to him [sic] who has to support a family. But this should not keep him away from the regular performance of prayers. . . .

There is a [dispensation] allowing one to joke. The rule in this matter is to avoid slandering, imitation, and nonsense. . . . It is improper, especially for persons of high rank, to do much jesting. It is said: "Do not jest with a noble man lest he bear malice against you, and do not jest with a base person lest he behave impudently toward you." . . .

There is a [dispensation] allowing one to love leadership. The ethics of this matter are that one should know one's own capability and should not have aspirations beyond it. . . . One of the shaykhs said: "The fault which is the last to leave the heart of the righteous is the love of leadership." . . .

There is a [dispensation] allowing one to revile insolent persons by disparaging their ancestors. The rule is that one may resort to this [dispensation] only in retort to ill-behavior, and it should be done by indirect expressions and not by explicit ones. . . .

There is a [dispensation] allowing one to watch all kinds of amusement. This is, however, limited by the rule: What you

160

are forbidden from doing, you are also forbidden from watching. . . .

There is a [dispensation] allowing one to visit old women. The purpose of such a visit should be to seek God's favor and blessing and to pray. . . .

There is a [dispensation] according to which one may show a smiling face to a person whom he dislikes in his heart. The purpose of such an affected manner should be the quest of peace rather than ostentation or hypocrisy. . . .

There is a [dispensation] allowing one to behave with riffraff in a manner which is compatible with their worth and intellectual capacity, in order to keep safe from their dangers. . . .

He who adheres to the dispensations and accepts the rules which govern them is one of the truthful simulators [of the Sufis], about whom the Prophet said: "Whoever makes the effort to resemble a group of people is one of them." This is so, if he observes the three essential principles. The Sufi masters are unanimous in asserting that to violate these principles or one of them is to transgress the rules of Sufism. These principles are: to perform the religious duties, to avoid that which is forbidden, and to relinquish worldly possessions, except what is absolutely necessary. . . . Whoever adopts the dispensations is one of the beginners, and he should strive to enhance his inner state. . . . Whoever falls below the level of the "dispensations" thereby renounces Sufism and is forbidden to enjoy the gifts and endowments which are made for the Sufis, and the Sufi congregation should excommunicate him.[26]

These and other stipulations by al-Suhrawardi constitute a code of civility that is generally observed by religiously sensitive people to the present day. Organized Sufism was not simply a network of religious clubs engaged in spiritual exercises as part of a mystic quest. It was a systematized expression of a way of life intended for all levels of pious citizenry, from the saintly ecstatic to the craftsman or merchant who enjoyed the company of Sufis and fancied that their elevated spirituality might somehow rub off on him.

Though Sufis from many regions contributed to the intellectual and emotional definition of the Sufi mystic experience, and to the formulation of rituals designed to prepare the devotee for it, the

more prosaic aspects of organized Sufism represented by the provisions of al-Suhrawardi's rule, and especially by the dispensations for
people at the lowest level, come particularly from the urban milieu
of Iran in the tenth and eleventh centuries.[27] Their widespread
adoption in non-Iranian lands from the twelfth century onward, like
the spread of madrasas and of Ash'ari theology, is partly a function
of the emigration of Iranian scholars and Sufis from their troubled
homeland. When the title Shaikh al-Shuyukh begins to be used for
the preeminent Sufi in a major city, it is no coincidence that the first
Shaikh al-Shuyukh of Baghdad, and founder of one of two important Sufi lodges there, was an Iranian from Nishapur who was a
close friend and defender of the Qushairi family.[28]

A fourth and final manifestation of the twelfth-century Iranian
diaspora comes from the history of young men's organizations that
spread and flourished simultaneously with the proliferation of
madrasas and Sufi orders. The word *futuwwa* in Arabic denotes the
quality of being a young man, a *fata* (pl. *fityan*). In pre-Islamic Arabia, and in poetry in the early Islamic centuries, futuwwa had what
might now be called romantic overtones: bravery, impetuosity,
nobility, poetic temperament. Tradition deemed Muhammad's son-
in-law Ali, the first of the Shi'i imams, the perfect fata. "There is no
fata like Ali, and no sword like Dhu al-Fiqar [Ali's sword]."

As, with the passage of generations, non-Arab converts and
detribalized Arabs came to reflect on this constellation of manly
virtues within the firmament of peaceful urban life, a new understanding grew up alongside the old: the nobility of young manhood
could be as well exemplified by fraternity, hospitality, athleticism,
loyalty, and celibacy as by more overtly martial qualities. Not surprisingly, these reformulated virtues dovetailed nicely with the qualities expected of a novice Sufi. Both evolved in answer to pious
questions about proper Muslim behavior for people of different sta-
tions and aptitudes. A vigorous, unmarried young man could bond
fraternally with other males and engage in athletic pursuits, including weapons training, while maintaining his piety by revering and
emulating the dedicated Sufis. More worldly than a fully committed
young Sufi immersed in a quieter, more mature society and sworn

to obey a Sufi master, the fata was a younger version of the marginal member of the Sufi world visualized by al-Suhrawardi.

The earliest treatise on futuwwa in the context of Sufism was written by Abu Abd al-Rahman al-Sulami (d. 1021), the noted Nishapur Sufi mentioned earlier. Al-Sulami's formulation is replete with generalities:

> Listen to good discourses, participate in good conversations, and abide by the prescribed behavior upon these occasions. Having good manners means showing respect to those who are superior to you; loving friendship and agreement to those who are your equals; kindness and compassion to those who are lower than you; obedience and modesty to your mother and father; and compassion in the education of children. It means caring for your womenfolk; visiting and doing good deeds for relatives; loving your brothers and eliminating all and everything that may prevent you from loving them; offering good-hearted smiles and generosity toward all humankind; knowing the values of the Sufis and respecting their rights; not showing any need toward the rich; accepting the knowledge [sic] from men who know; humbly obeying men of wisdom without negation; and fleeing from the dogmatic ones, heretics, profiteers, and men who wish to enslave others.[29]

Al-Sulami's devotees of futuwwa do not appear to be organized into fraternities, but futuwwa organizations probably already existed in Khurasan at the time he wrote. They were certainly there a generation later when Abu al-Qasim al-Qushairi wrote his famous manual of Sufism, the *Risala*. Al-Qushairi lists futuwwa among the Sufi virtues and describes it in generalities similar to al-Sulami's, but some of his anecdotes betray at least informal organized activity. One story al-Qushairi transmits from al-Sulami describes a man as "a cunning 'bandit' [*ayyaran shatiran*] who was the head of the fityan in their town."[30] Another relates that "a group of fityan went to visit someone who claimed to be a fata. The man said [to his servant], 'Boy, lay the tablecloth.' But he didn't do it. So the man asked him a second and a third time. At this some of the visitors looked at each other and said, 'It's inconsistent with futuwwa for a man to have a servant who disobeys him this way in laying the tablecloth.' But the man said, 'I haven't delayed setting of the table. The servant says there were ants on the tablecloth. [Since] it is impolite to lay a tablecloth for fityan with ants on it, and it is contrary to futuwwa to brush the ants off, he was waiting for the ants to crawl away.' They replied, 'You're quite punctilious, Boy. The likes of you should serve the fityan.' "

A similar story goes: "Someone who claimed futuwwa for himself went from Nishapur to Nasa [another city in Khurasan] where a man who was with a party of fityan invited him in as a guest. When they finished eating, a slave girl went around pouring water on their hands. But the man from Nishapur shrank back from washing his hands. He said, 'It is contrary to futuwwa for women to pour water on men's hands.' Then one of them said, 'I've been coming to this house for years, and I never even noticed whether a man or a woman poured water on our hands.' "

Avoidance not just of women, but of sexual contact in general, is further suggested by al-Qushairi's story that "someone wanted to test Nuh al-Ayyar al-Nishapuri [a famous fata] so he offered to sell him a slave girl dressed up as a serving boy, stipulating that she was indeed a boy despite her comely face. So Nuh bought her, understanding that she was a boy, and she stayed with him for many months until finally she was asked, 'Does he know that you're a girl?' 'No,' she said. 'He hasn't touched me so he still imagines I'm a boy.' "

Anecdotes like these fall short of conveying a precise picture of Khurasani futuwwa in the late eleventh century, but they clearly imply that it had an organized dimension and a specific code of behavior, characteristics that also emerge from the occasional references to fityan in contemporary biographical dictionaries. One youth, for example, is called a fata "according to the Ash'ari doctrine." Another rose to political prominence through his leadership of the fityan in his town. A third is described as a member of the futuwwa who nevertheless didn't go along with their asceticism and special customs. And the father of a fourth young man is said to have forbidden his son to become a fata and live a celibate life.[31] Outside Iran, on the other hand, evidence for the existence of futuwwa organizations in eleventh century is entirely wanting.

The significance of these early traces of organized futuwwa becomes clear when we consider that between 1180 and 1225 the Abbasid caliph al-Nasir li-din Allah adopted organized futuwwa as a device for imparting new life to the flagging authority of the caliphate.[32] Although the stages by which the idea of futuwwa organizations left Iran and took root elsewhere cannot now be traced, they were clearly in place over a broad geographical area by the late twelfth century. And the mechanism for instituting them in cities outside Iran was surely migration. While some Iranians became madrasa professors or Sufi shaikhs, others (or possibly the same ones) involved themselves in organizing the local youth into clubs devoted to the principles of futuwwa. By the time of al-Nasir, these clubs had initiation rites and ceremonial garments, but their potential as a loyal network of religiously oriented youth with athletic and/or paramilitary training is what commended them to the caliph's patronage.

Though less successful over the long run than the Sufi brotherhoods, the futuwwa organizations survived well into Ottoman times, when they partially merged (as *akhis*) with the nascent guild organizations,[33] and partially merged (as *qabadays*) with the underworld. In Iran they survive to the present day as athletic clubs (*zurkhaneh*, "house of strength"), but they also had an impact upon the underworld.

Many different Islamic societies developed in the early centuries over the vast area conquered by the Muslim Arabs. Each society has its particular history of tradition making and accommodation to local conditions, but they have in common a high degree of non-formalized autonomy from the central political institution of the caliphate. In Iran, which is taken here as a case study, migration by converts to Arab governing centers and the consequent urbanization of those centers gave rise to a distinctive and self-consciously Muslim social milieu. Initially diverse and effervescent, the societies of the Iranian cities gradually converged upon a socio-religious pattern that conferred honor and moral leadership upon the ulama. Increasingly dominated by extensive lineages disposing of considerable wealth, power, and pious reputation, on a local scale, the ulama

165

also came to be riven by factions that were nominally legal in character but actually involved competing visions of Muslim social organization as well, perhaps, as different social origins tied to the chronology of conversion.

In the meantime, the burgeoning of the cities approached an economic and demographic limit. Hypertrophic development caused by too much uncontrolled migration from the countryside put them in danger of catastrophe. Bad winters, poor harvests, or political unrest could subject large cities to famine and disease. Yet the uncertain political climate of the Seljuq period, and the economic structure of irrigation agriculture in much of Iran, prevented the repopulation of the countryside and investment in new agricultural production that was needed to stem the deterioration. The increasing level of urban factional violence in the eleventh century is partly a testimony to the growing economic problems of the cities.

By the middle of the twelfth century, well before the Mongol invasions, Iran's medieval urban culture had passed its peak. The shrunken cities were still torn by strife, and the scholarly climate that had marked the tenth and eleventh centuries was rapidly dissipating. In response to this worsening of conditions, thousands of Iranians, particularly from the ranks of the ulama, emigrated to the Arab lands or to the recently conquered territories of Anatolia and India. As they departed their homeland, they took with them their stock in trade: knowledge.

What made the institutions and ideas of the Iranian emigrants so attractive to people in their newfound homes? The answer depends upon the as yet unwritten histories of the edges of Islamic society in those different lands. My purpose is not to claim that Iranian Islam was superior to Islam elsewhere, or to suggest that ideas and institutions from other regions played no role in the development of a comparatively uniform understanding of normative Islam that took place from the twelfth century onward. In fact, Iran's more conservative, or elitist, faction, centered particularly on nu'tazili theology, and opposition to Sufism, had much less success in transplanting itself than the populist current represented by Ash'ari theology, the Sufi brotherhoods, and the futuwwa organizations.

Once these qualifications are made, however, it remains apparent that the Iranian impact on Islam between the twelfth and fourteenth centuries was both profound and geographically located outside of Iran proper. The Iranian diaspora of this period was similar to, and at least as important as, the well-known diaspora of Muslims from Islamic Spain that transformed North African society from the thirteenth century onward. The difference between them is that the somewhat later Andalusian diaspora, though larger, did not affect central perceptions of Islam as a whole. The madrasas, the Sufi brotherhoods, and the thought and symbolic significance of al-Ghazali as Islam's greatest religious thinker all testify to the disproportionate contribution of local urban society in Iran, and particularly of the Ash'ari-Shafi'i-Sufi faction within that society, to the creation of a central and unified understanding of Islam that remains strong to the present day.

I am inclined to believe, though I can in no way prove, that the singular success of the Islamic social vision and institutional structure outlined in this chapter derives directly from the deteriorating conditions of Iran's eleventh-century cities. Times were hard; government was militaristic and more than ever remote under Turkish, tribe-oriented leadership. The ulama had enjoyed two centuries of eminence, but they hadn't the capacity to stem the growing disorder. Their occasional desperate attempts to seize the reins of power usually failed, and their financial resources were hard hit by urban unrest and rural decline. What they still had at their disposal was moral leadership, and what the populist faction recommended was communal self-help, close personal bonding, and adherence to a code of behavior that stressed philanthropy, sobriety, obedience to the religious law, and minimizing the social weight of economic disparities between rich and poor.

Under different global circumstances, the audience for this message of community bonding to endure hard times might have been restricted to Iran. But the Crusades and the Mongol invasions, punctuated by the symbolically important destruction of the caliphate in Baghdad, made hard times and political instability general. Thus, the worldview that originated with the rise and decline of the edge society of the Iranian cities found a warm audience abroad. For the first time, Islam developed a nongovernmental center in the form of a near-concensus on the basic beliefs and forms of Sunni Islam. The history of this center was then, understandably, retrojected to the earliest period in Islamic history. But, to a large extent, it was a center created by social currents that had originated on the edges of Islamic society in Iran.

10

NEW CENTER, NEW EDGES

Whoever makes himself like unto a people is
one of them.
—Hadith in praise of orthopraxy quoted by the Sufi
Hujwiri, *KASHF AL-MAHJUB*

My story appears to have lost its way. At the outset I promised an exploration of the edge, a dispersed, nongeographic, social terrain where Muslims created different localized models of Islam in relative isolation from the institutions of the center. But tracing the evolution of one particular edge over several centuries has brought us back to the center, albeit a religious center and not the historians' traditional political center symbolized by the caliphate. By and large, however, this has been a fortuitous development. A history of the edge of Islamic society in Morocco from the seventh to the twelfth century would not have led to the same result. The pre-twelfth-century religious and political movements of Islam's far west—those of the Idrisids, the Barghwata, the Almoravids—were little known and had little impact east of Tunisia. And even though the Almohad movement of the twelfth century embodied certain teachings of al-Ghazali, which its founder Ibn Tumart picked up on his travels to the East, the powerful state established by Ibn Tumart's followers induced no flow of influence in the opposite direction.

This does not mean, however, that the localized versions of Islam that developed in the West couldn't have been as influential as those of Iran during the period of Sunni recentering in the twelfth through fourteenth centuries. A case in point is that of Ibn al-Arabi (1165–1240), a Sufi from Islamic Spain whose views became as central to later Sufism as those of any Iranian mystic. Ibn al-Arabi was already thirty-five years old and embarked on a long career of writing before journeying eastward. Thereafter he spent the remainder of his life there, much of it in Anatolia, which was then in great religious ferment as conversion from Christianity to Islam gained momentum. (The situation of Anatolia in the early thirteenth century is analogous, in terms of conversion, to that of Iran in the early ninth century, when the bandwagon period of Islamization commenced.)

Ibn al-Arabi's orientation as a Sufi originated at the societal edges in Spain and North Africa, where miracles and pietistic extremes lent Sufism a more supernatural aspect than it had in the East. In two works where he recounts anecdotes concerning some seventy Sufis from the West, Ibn al-Arabi ascribes to them myriad miracles but few mystic aphorisms or demonstrations of divine ecstasy of the sort that crowd comparable collections from the East. He describes a companion of ten years, Abu al-Hajjaj al-Shubarbuli, for example, as "one of those who could walk on water" and tells of how thieves seeking to rob him while he was praying could not make off with his goods because the door disappeared every time they searched for it with loot in their hands.[1] Two other Sufis he depicts as normally traveling by spiritual projection rather than physical movement.[2] Yet another "succumbed to some impurity [and] God punished him on the spot by causing his head to be stuck in the earth, his feet in the air. His back stuck out an arm's length. Although he cried for help, no one was able to pull him out. When the matter was reported to his Shaikh, he came and ordered him to repent of his sin, which he did. Immediately his back returned to its place and the rest of his limbs were freed."[3]

The roots of Ibn al-Arabi's wonder stories lie in the West. One of his most notable predecessors in Spain, Ibn al-Arif (d. 1141), went beyond hagiographic miracle stories to raise miracle-working to a theoretical level. He dismissed the main Sufi qualities lauded by Eastern writers, such things as will to devote oneself to God,

asceticism, trust in God, patience, hope, and love, as commonplace virtues beneath the concern of a true Sufi. To the true Sufi
God granted miracles in this world and the next, including the following:

> Complete freedom regarding land and sea: if he wishes, he can
> walk either in air or on water, and so traverse the entire globe in
> less than one hour. Subjugation of animals, monsters and beasts:
> demons of the desert submit to him, and lions wag their tails at
> him. Possession of the keys to the earth's treasures: wherever he
> places his hands, there is a treasure, if he desires it; wherever his
> boot strikes, there is a spring of water, if he needs it; wherever he
> dwells, there is brought to him a table of food, if he intends to
> eat. . . . Some of the saints can simply point to a mountain, and it
> will disappear.[4]

This is a far cry from the rhetoric of wonder in the East, where stick-
ing one's finger through one's vest was enough to send the audience into transports of rapture.

Ibn al-Qasi, another Sufi predecessor, whose one surviving book
became the subject of a special treatise by Ibn al-Arabi, led an armed
revolt in Portugal during a period of weakened central rule in Muslim Spain. He declared himself a spiritual ruler and maintained his
state for nine years until his assassination in 1151. In keeping with
his teaching that in the hereafter Jesus and John the Baptist will
accompany Muhammad in the pulpit from which he will preside,
Ibn al-Qasi had two men, symbolizing Jesus and John the Baptist,
flank the preacher (*khatib*), representing Muhammad, at Friday
prayers in his principality.[5] There is nothing in the East with which
to compare this.

Historians of Sufism pay scant attention to the West prior to the
twelfth century because of a paucity of sources. Yet it would be
absurd to take the occasional mention of works by Iranian Sufis like
al-Ghazali and Abu al-Qasim al-Qushairi in Ibn al-Arabi's saints'
stories,[6] or Ibn al-Qasi's borrowing of material from al-Ghazali,[7] as
evidence that mystic contemplation and wonder working began in
the West only on stimulus from the East. Clearly, there was an earlier history, a history that developed at the edge in the West along

171

lines that appear to be heavily Christian in influence, but that need to be clarified by further study. In coming to the East, Ibn al-Arabi made this Western tradition known in much the same way al-Ghazali and other Iranian Sufis made known the spiritual traditions that had developed at the edge in the most eastern Islamic provinces.

That immigrant scholars from East and West played such a central role in the recentering of Sunni Islam, as well as in shaping Islamic norms and institutions in regions only recently opened to the faith, such as Anatolia and northern India, bespeaks a felt need for such recentering in the heartland of the caliphate. The efforts of the caliph al-Nasir to utilize Iranian Sufism and futuwwa organizations to revitalize or relegitimate his office show that this need was felt even at the very heart of the center. Yet it is hard to choose among all of the problems of the era which ones provoked the greatest feelings of unease, and hence of a need for change in the socio-religious sphere.

Iran fell upon hard times in the eleventh century with Iraq close behind. Then came the Mongol invasion of Iran in 1218, followed a generation later by the Mongol expansion into Iraq, Mesopotamia, and eastern Anatolia. In 1258 the Mongol leader Hulagu Khan sacked Baghdad and executed the last Abbasid caliph there. Over the next two years some people looked to the Hafsid ruler of Tunis or the sharif of Mecca for caliphal leadership, until the newly self-created Mamluk sultan in Egypt, building upon his success in stemming a Mongol advance into Syria, installed a member of the Abbasid family as caliph in Cairo. However, the Cairene caliphs exhibited none of the thought and energy that marked the caliphate of al-Nasir, and their effective authority was negligible.

Meanwhile, beneath the economic disorder and political upheaval, society was pulled and torn by chaotic population movements—Turkic, Mongol, and Kurdish tribes; Iranian immigrants; and a multi-ethnic flux of semi-Islamized groups along and across the old border zone between Anatolia, northern Syria, and Mesopotamia. In addition, in the fourteenth century, the Black Death struck.

I would suggest that the singular success that immigrant Iranian scholars met in spreading their religious ideas and institutions stemmed from the fact that they had been forged in the fragile and disordered environment of eleventh-century Iran. The strong elements of fraternity, mutual cooperation, localized religious authority, and institutional autonomy that characterized the Iranian religious outlook may have seemed to the Arabs, Turks, and Indians to be perfectly adapted to the onset of hard times in their territories. At a purely social level, this same yearning for local communal solidarity manifested itself in the crystallization of urban neighborhood identities as the bases for political leadership. Though rivalries between neighborhoods are mentioned frequently in the eleventh century, names of official neighborhood chiefs are not commonly mentioned until the fourteenth century.[8] To the same instinct might be attributed the otherworldliness of those Sufis who offered, on the one hand, a spiritual path to beatitude in the midst of an uncertain world and, on the other, a closely knit fraternity within which one could pursue that path. But these speculations cannot be pinned down concretely and are not essential to a discussion of the recentering of Sunni Islam and the consequent development of new sorts of edges.

It is commonly said that orthopraxy rather than orthodoxy is the hallmark of Islam. This, like so many other generalizations, seems to be most applicable to the post-Mongol centuries. Seen from the edge, Islam in the earlier centuries appears to have varied greatly in practice, and groups of Muslims struggled tenaciously to establish their own views as orthodox. The mutual tolerance of different legal and doctrinal interpretations of Sunni Islam that characterizes the later centuries belies the bitter factional conflicts between Sunni law schools that mark the tenth, eleventh, and twelfth centuries. As this doctrinal tolerance set in, it was accompanied by an increasing stress on orthopraxy as defined by the ever more uniform teachings of the ulama. At the same time, however, new variant practices were establishing themselves, sometimes in Sufi contexts, on the societal edges in the nascent Islamic communities of Anatolia, India, Southeast Asia, West Africa, and the Balkans. And in the Middle East proper, the final phase of conversion to Islam was manifesting itself in characteristically rural variants of Muslim behavior.

One striking aspect of religious practice in this period touches both upon the recentering of Sunnism and the rise of local practice. This is the increasing popularity of pilgrimages, both to Mecca and Medina and to hundreds of local, often rural, shrines throughout the Islamic lands. Though pilgrimage (*hajj*) to Mecca is one of the five pillars of Islam and is viewed as a personal obligation that every able Muslim should perform at least once in his or her lifetime, the salience of the hajj increases from the twelfth century onward until it becomes the dominant symbol of Islamic devotion that it remains today. Politically, this is manifested in the emergence of the sharifs of Mecca, hereditary governors descended from the Prophet Muhammad, as significant figures in the Islamic world, and by the emphasis the Mamluk sultans, and even more the Ottoman sultans, put on provisioning the holy cities and arranging the hajj caravans. The legitimacy imparted by these services continues in the present day to undergird the king of Saudi Arabia, who styles himself Servant of the Two Holy Cities (*khadim al-haramain*).

However, politics followed faith in this matter. Prior to the twelfth century, making the pilgrimage was a pious act, but seemingly not a transformative one. Mecca was comparatively unimportant as an educational center despite the fact that few people were more likely to perform the hajj than itinerant religious scholars.[9] Moreover, none of the tens of thousands of scholars surveyed in biographical dictionaries before this time is accorded the title al-Hajj or Hajji. By the end of the twelfth century, however, the title begins to signify religious merit and social distinction, as it does to an even greater degree today in regions such as Southeast Asia. Early examples of people dignified by their pilgrimage include Badr al-Din Abu Hamid Hajji Muhammad,[10] the governor of a town in Anatolia in 1210, before the Mongol invasion, and al-Hajj Abu Muhammad Abd Allah al-Burjani,[11] one of the saints Ibn al-Arabi wrote about in 1203. A generation later the semi-legendary founder of the Bektashi Sufi order in Anatolia is known only as Hajji Bektash.

The post-Mongol centuries also see the rise of pilgrimage narratives as an important literary genre abundantly attested from Morocco to India.[12] An early example is contained in the famous fourteenth-century travel account of Ibn Battuta, a native of Tangier in Morocco. Although most famed for the half of his book that covers his years in India, China, and Africa, Ibn Battuta devotes the other half of his account to the Middle East. Of that half, almost twenty percent concerns Mecca and Medina.[13] The mosques and pilgrimage sites of the holy cities are minutely described along with the local Meccan customs regarding high points on the Muslim religious calendar.

Pilgrimage is obviously an important religious concern for Ibn Battuta. He not only uses al-Hajj, "Pilgrim," as a name and a description, most often when speaking of India, Anatolia, and West Africa, where conversion to Islam was creating dynamic edge societies;[14] he also concerns himself with the fast-growing phenomenon of pilgrimage to local shrines, particularly ones devoted to Sufis and descendants of the Prophet Muhammad. He mentions the notable tombs of the historically important cities he visits—Damascus, Basra, Kufa, Baghdad, Shiraz—and sometimes gives specific directions for locating them. Looking for the tomb of the Prophet's Companion Anas ibn Malik at Basra? It is "six miles from [the tomb of Abu Bakra] beside Lion Creek . . . [but] there isn't any fountain there for devotions, except for a crude waterhole, because of the abundance of lions and the absence of human settlement."[15]

Here Ibn Battuta represents another new category of literature from the period of Sunni recentering: the guide to local pilgrimages. Abu al-Hasan al-Harawi, at the end of the twelfth century, devoted an entire book to the subject, particularly singling out the tombs of the Prophet's family and Companions, and mentioning Christian pilgrimage sites as well.[16] The popularity of this particular catalog of tombs is attested to by the survival of fourteen manuscripts copied in the thirteenth, sixteenth, seventeenth, and nineteenth centuries. In extreme forms, this genre of literature degenerates into unadorned cemetery lists designed to guide pilgrims to the correct spot in abandoned or ruined cities.[17]

The nature of this efflorescence of local shrines is indicated by whose grave is visited and whose is not. In Damascus, for example, Ibn Battuta mentions five visitation sites named for relatives or Companions of the Prophet and one site of the thirteenth century, with nothing in between. For Basra he similarly singles out six graves of the Prophet's family and Companions, and seven other early figures, including an important early Sufi. "On each of these graves is a dome on which is written who is buried there and his date of death. All are inside the old walls, there now being some three miles between them and the [inhabited] city."[18] For the last six he gives no information beyond the buried person's name. He clearly assumes his readers will recognize them. He adds that there are many other early graves as well, but they are apparently not pilgrimage spots.

Moving on to Baghdad, Ibn Battuta lists the tombs of the following: two descendants of Ali, the Abbasid caliphs, and the founders of the Hanafi and Hanbali law schools. Beyond that, he singles out six graves of early Sufis as pilgrimage sites that are visited on a weekly basis by the people of Baghdad. The thousands of other scholarly and saintly figures buried in the former Abbasid capital are passed over in a single sentence.[19]

Finally, Ibn Battuta gives a flavor of what a local pilgrimage was like in recounting his visit to the old Iraqi city of Wasit:

> When we stopped at Wasit . . . it occurred to me to pay a visit (ziyara) to the tomb of the saint (wali) Abu al-Abbas Ahmad al-Rifa'i. It is in a village called Umm Ubaida, a day's travel from Wasit. . . . We arrived at noon on the second day at the reception tent (riwaq), which was a great Sufi lodge (ribat) in which were a thousand Sufis. We encountered there the gallant Shaikh Ahmad Kuchik, the grandson of God's Friend Abu al-Abbas al-Rifa'i, whose pilgrimage we were set upon. He had come from a place we had visited in Anatolia to make the pilgrimage to his grandfather's grave and had ended up as shaikh of the lodge. . . . When the afternoon prayer was finished, drums and tambourines sounded and the Sufis began to dance. Then they prayed the evening prayer and had dinner, which was rice bread, fish, milk, and dates. . . . [Later] they began listening to recitations. Having already piled up loads of wood, they set them alight and entered, dancing, into the midst of the fire. Some of them anointed themselves with oil in it. Some put it in their mouths until it was entirely extinguished. This is their habit, the thing the Ahmadiya Order is especially known for.[20]

Ibn Battuta sharply delineates the religious landscape of the fourteenth century in which pilgrimages, both to Mecca, and to the
tombs of Sufi saints and the Prophet's kinfolk and Companions,
loomed ever larger. The hajj proper played a key role in recentering
Sunni Islam after the onslaught of the Mongols and the demise of
the Baghdad caliphate. It was only natural, therefore, for Mecca and
Medina to grow as intellectual and educational centers. Of the eighteen madrasas known to have been built in Mecca between 1200
and 1600, three were founded by rulers of Yemen, five by Ottoman
sultans, one by a Mamluk sultan of Egypt, and one by a ruler of
Bengal, who also founded a madrasa in Medina.[21] From the sixteenth century on, the teachers and madrasas of the holy cities were
famous throughout the Islamic world. Pilgrims from Indonesia,
Malaysia, India, and West Africa met there to imbibe the doctrines
and ways of recentered Sunnism, and then returned to their home-
lands to serve as beacons of orthopraxy (if not orthodoxy), showing
the "right" way to peoples at the edge whose Islam was dangerously encrusted, in their view, with local custom and syncretic belief.

As for the great and growing popularity of more local pilgrimages, these became centers for the continuing development of Islam
at the edge. Devotions at the minor shrines of saints and Sufis often
had distinctive characteristics stemming from the particular religious history and customary ritual practices of the locality, as the
case cited from Ibn Battuta demonstrates. Change occurred even in
regions that had been Muslim for many centuries. In Khurasan, for
example, a tombstone from the tenth or eleventh century conveys a
standardized message: name, genealogy, date, maybe a pious phrase
or two. But at some point in the post-Mongol era, the style
changed. Along with the name and date there began to appear a
schematic representation of a comb—teeth on one side for a male,
on two sides for a female—and next to the comb, a circle for the
pious visitor to mark with a pebble after saying a prayer.

Center and edge remain, therefore, in tension during the post-
Mongol centuries, though both evolve. The new center of Sunni
Islam coalesces around madrasa and mosque teachers guiding their
students through a fairly standard repertoire of books, and around
the increased importance of the hajj and of the holy cities as educa-

tional centers. In outlying and newly Islamizing regions, the pull of the center is attenuated; and educational institutions, if they exist at all, diverge in the form and content of their teachings.

But even in those regions that entered the Islamic orbit the earliest, there is change along the edge. Pilgrims to Mecca in the sixteenth century customarily became initiated by their professors into one of the Sufi orders that stressed obedience to religious law and strict observance of Sunni behavioral norms. At the same time, a colorful feature of Muslim life in rural areas of the Middle East—Syria, Iraq, Iran—was the wandering Sufi dervish (*qalandar, kalender*), not a member of any established order, dressed in rags with matted locks, begging bowl, and symbolic hatchet. Sufism covered such a broad range of religious experience that it flourished, in different forms, both at the center and at the edge.

Recentered Sunnism provided the social and religious solidity that underlay the establishment and longevity of the Ottoman Empire after 1400. Many ulama were coopted into government service as religious officials—qadis, law professors, etc.—ranked in a hierarchy under the head of the religious establishment, the Shaikh al-Islam. Their careers focused on Istanbul, Bursa, and other major Ottoman cities. Other ulama remained local: in residence, allegiance, and professional networking. Whether a madrasa trained official ulama under royal patronage in Istanbul or functioned at a local level under local scholarly leadership made little difference to the content of the teaching.

Oddly enough, the same is true after 1500 of the newly rising Safavid Empire in Iran. When Shah Isma'il, the empire's founder, declared Shi'ism the state religion at the outset of his reign, Iran had already been experiencing a growth of Shi'ite sentiment for several centuries. To be sure, there were comparatively few Shi'ite scholars in the country, and properly trained ulama had to be imported from Bahrain and Lebanon. But there were comparatively few properly trained Sunni ulama either. The decline in Iran's prosperity that began in the eleventh century and accelerated after the Mongol invasions induced scholars and Sufis of all sorts to leave the country. The society they left behind became increasingly influenced by customs and beliefs drawn from wellsprings of rural piety that had been

178

little tapped in the heyday of the great Iranian Muslim cities. By the fourteenth century, one local ruler of both Shi'ite and Sufi persuasion decreed that a caparisoned mount should be stationed at the city gate each day to receive the messianic Mahdi upon his return. Other Sufis ran, or sought to run, religious principalities on what seemed like the reasonable presumption that people would answer a call to arms made by a wonder-working shaikh.[22]

When Shah Isma'il Safavi eventually capitalized on the religious ferment of the times to establish his empire, he also saw that stability could not be guaranteed without a base in the recentered institutions surviving in the country's diminished cities. He installed a Sadr al-Sudur parallel in function to the Sunni Ottoman sultan's Shaikh al-Islam, and each city was headed religiously by a Shaikh al-Islam under the Sadr al-Sudur's jurisdiction. The Shi'ite scholars he imported from the Arab world taught in urban madrasas that fostered later generations of Iranian Shi'ite ulama bent upon establishing, in Shi'ite guise, the same kind of politically subservient religious atmosphere that the Ottoman ulama had already achieved.

For all their political and religious differences, the Ottoman and Safavid empires were remarkably similar in social and religious structure, at least at court and in town. But this does not mean that nothing changed over the next few centuries. The narrative of Ottoman and Safavid political and institutional developments revives the view from the center after the long, confusing interval following the dissolution of caliphal power in the tenth century. In addition, historians have recently been paying increasing attention to the institutions of recentered Sunnism.[23]

If I were true to my training and calling as a medieval historian, I might reasonably end my story at this point. To the degree that my goal has been to provide, through a view from the edge, an explanation for the evolution of Islamic society, from the unity of the early community inspired by the personal charisma of the Prophet, through the diversity of the early centuries after the Arab conquests, to a recentering through institutional and doctrinal homogenization after the twelfth century, I have completed my argument. Islamic society certainly did not remain static or uniform from the fourteenth to the nineteenth century, but the forms that were almost universally adopted between the twelfth and fourteenth centuries proved remarkably stable. Institutional stability, the solidity of communal norms, dense and overlapping networks of belonging, and strong legal and doctrinal reinforcement of personal and communal identity made Middle Eastern Islamic society of the Ottoman and Safavid period one of the most successful—though neither economically accumulative nor inventive—social syntheses in world history. But my concern has been to account for its coming into being rather than to detail its workings in these later centuries.

Yet one major task remains unaccomplished. That is to demonstrate the importance of this retelling of medieval Islamic history for the world of today. Though this will be the burden of my concluding chapter, one religious phenomenon of the early centuries needs to be highlighted here because of the change in form it undergoes in the post-Mongol centuries, and because it is integral to understanding the resurgence of Muslim political and social thought and action at the present time.

Islamic society originally formed itself at the edge through an iterative process of question and answer. New Muslims sought to discover what it meant to be a Muslim, and Muslims from families of longer standing in the umma sought to refine the understandings they had inherited from parents and teachers, and to answer the questions of others. No one was uniquely gifted, by virtue of office or sacrament, with the right answers. This absence of incontrovertible religious authority at the local, quotidian level distinguished Islam from the other religions in the conquered lands; but the examples of those other religions, particularly as felt by Muslims newly converted from them, continually restimulated the desire for authoritative answers to questions.

If no person held title to religious authority by right, could such authority reside categorically in a body of lore? As we have seen, the answer to this question was doubly yes: yes from the outset in terms of the authoritative text of the Quran, and yes through localized development in terms of the hadith of the Prophet. In some measure, the hadith came to fill the function of the absent clerical establishment; and the ulama, or that large proportion of them whose claim to learning rested on hadith study, came into being to deal with the creative efflorescence of hadith. They weeded them, pruned them, and trained them to the trellises of their uninstitutionalized educational networks. Ultimately, they turned the chaotic overgrowth into an orderly garden containing only known species of proven pedigree. The rest were discarded.

Yet the need to answer questions did not go away. Nor did the gradual trend toward formalizing the training of ulama through the madrasas turn the ulama into clergymen. Despite the comparative homogenization of social and religious institutions during the post-Mongol centuries, the spiritual and social needs of ordinary people still required satisfaction; the government was no more legitimate a locus of authority in such matters than it had been under the caliphate. Shi'ite Islam responded to personal needs in the later centuries by evolving, not without strenuous debate, the doctrine that every believer should choose a living *mujtahid*, or authoritative religious guide, to answer his or her questions. Thus Shi'ism, by formally preserving for its most educated ulama the capacity of *ijtihad*, or exercise of personal authority in a religious matter, came close to establishing a clergy. Even here, however, there was no formal binding of the believer to a particular mujtahid, or even a way of telling, without asking, which mujtahid any particular believer followed.

In Sunni Islam adherence to one or another Sufi brotherhood filled some of the gap in authority stemming from the purgation and standardization of hadith. Most brotherhoods either required or expected members to be obedient to the commands of their shaikhs, known as *murshids* or *pirs*, and the sage counsel of the Sufi shaikh became a leitmotiv of later Islamic society continuing down to the present day.[24] But how were the non-Sufi ulama to maintain the authority they had gained over the earlier centuries? To be sure, they could serve as qadis and as imams of mosques. And their education assured them of respect, especially if they were scions of well-known ulama families or favored students of important teachers. But none of these things imparted the measure of authority enjoyed locally by the eminent ulama of the tenth and eleventh centuries.

The spread of the understanding that Islam was totally embodied in the law of the shari'a strongly buttressed the question-answering authority of the later Sunni ulama. Though the shari'a remained poorly known in the villages in which most Muslims actually passed their lives, the later ulama never tired of stressing the central importance of the law even though many, if not most, of the important ulama of the early centuries did not specialize in law. It also became a commonplace of Western understandings of Islam that the shari'a was the keystone of the Islamic religious edifice, even though it was quite apparent that prior to the eleventh century legal study per se was not particularly pervasive or influential in shaping people's beliefs and behavior.

In part, the shari'a came to be stressed because it afforded an avenue for authoritatively responding to people's questions. Legal scholars had always been able to offer opinions on legal matters, of course. Such an opinion is called a *fatwa* (pl. *fatawa*) and normally has no binding power on the person, whether litigant or judge, who seeks it. The function performed by a scholar issuing a fatwa is that of *mufti*, but there is no indication that the mufti was an office during the pre-Mongol centuries. Exactly when and how the transition took place from mufti as a function performable by any legal scholar, to mufti as an official government post issuing opinions that represented government-supported legal authority in a given area is not entirely clear.

It is abundantly clear, however, that fatawa become immeasurably more important in the later centuries than they had been earlier. The *Fihrist* of al-Nadim, a late tenth-century bookseller's compilation of books in circulation in Baghdad, includes scores of titles of legal treatises, but none are labeled collections of fatawa. By comparison, many collections of fatawa were made by legal scholars in the post-Mongol centuries and referred to by later generations of legists. The typical fatwa would contain a question, called an *istifta'*, possibly posed by a named individual in a specific context but also framable in terms of John Does (Amr and Zaid), an explanation of the pertinent legal dicta, and a yes-or-no answer. So prevalent did the recourse to legal scholars for answers to questions become that in some parts of the Islamic world, notably West Africa and Morocco, faqih supplanted alim as the normal term for religious scholar.

The integration of the office of mufti into the religious bureau-
cracy of the Ottoman Empire, symbolized by the Shaikh al-Islam
serving as mufti to the sultan, accentuated the mutual dependency
of legal and governmental authority during the post-Mongol centuries. The fatawa of the Shaikh al-Islam legitimized the deeds of
the sultan while the sultan's recognition that even his imperial will
was subject to the constraints of the religious law legitimized the
claim of the ulama that the shari'a was the sole cornerstone of Islamic society. But the rise in status of the mufti, and the collection and
preservation of the legal opinions of eminent jurists, testify as well
to the persistence of question and answer as the dominant mode of
religious discourse from the earlier to the later period.

Of course, Islam is not the only religion that pays special attention to answering the questions of believers. What makes the question-and-answer motif distinctive in Islamic religious history is the
variability over time of the parties deemed capable of answering
questions authoritatively. In the earliest period, the Companions of
the Prophet, and those who heard hadith directly from their lips,
shared this capacity with local holy men and pietists, as was demonstrated in chapter 3 through the story of the family of Dinar. By the
tenth century, the concentration upon hadith study as the best way
to understand the faith had prompted the rise of the hadith scholar
as the individual believer's chief resort for authoritative answers to
religious questions. Then, in the madrasa era, with the corpus of
reliable hadith more or less restricted to the canonical collections,
authoritative answers to questions were sought variously from Sufi
shaikhs, from legal scholars and official muftis through fatawa, and,
in the Shi'ite case, from mujtahids.

The questioning persists, but the authoritative respondents
change. As we move in the next chapter to the contemporary era,
this persistent motif of Islamic religious history will take on new
importance as fresh answerers arise to respond to the questions
posed by people on the new edges that appear in the twentieth century.

11

THE VIEW FROM THE
EDGE TODAY

Islam is the answer.

—CURRENT POLITICAL SLOGAN

In Bengal and Malaysia, Rama and Sita, the principal characters of
the Hindu epic the Ramayana, are absorbed into Islamic culture.[1]
In African-influenced societies from the Persian Gulf to Morocco,
demonic possession by or of females provides catharsis in popular
Islamic cults.[2] Tuareg men from the southern Sahara desert ritually
shroud their faces while their women go proudly unveiled. A nineteenth-century Shi'ite potentate in the Indian state of Awadh cere-
monially dresses as a woman and "gives birth" to a doll, claiming
thereby to be the symbolic mother of the Shi'ite imam whose birthdate he is commemorating.[3] In eastern Turkey a youthful American
traveler comports himself as a Sufi and is generously received
despite his ignorance of the local language, of Islam, and of the
Quran. All he knows is that Sufism is a form of "Eastern" mysticism
and that *hu* means "He" and stands for Allah.

Every student of Islam knows of local beliefs and practices that
deviate more or less substantially from what is taught in the
madrasas of Cairo and Mecca. Sometimes they refer to them as "little" traditions, as opposed to the "great tradition" preserved and
propounded by authoritative scholars and embodied in time-hon-
ored texts. Though anthropologists often view them as important
religious and social phenomena, historians more often ignore
them.[4] Each society and each pattern of religious behavior has a

separate history, but their histories are local and seem to most historians not to contribute to the history of Islam as a whole.

In largely illiterate societies where most people live in dispersed farming communities, things could hardly be otherwise. Every expansive religious movement has developed edges with localized beliefs and practices to some extent. And the "central" authorities within every religious movement have striven, in one way or another, to rein in, minimize, normalize, purify, reform, or eliminate the most unacceptable manifestations of such developments.

Two things stand out in the history I have recounted in the preceding chapters. First, during its first five centuries, Islam was singularly lacking in mechanisms for controlling developments on the edge. And second, the homogenization or normalization of institutions, beliefs, and practices that took place during the period of religious recentering from the twelfth to the fourteenth century was extraordinarily successful in formalizing and inculcating religious understandings that are still taken to represent a "great tradition" going back to the Prophet Muhammad's own community. The variegated forms of Islam that dotted the Middle East and North Africa prior to the twelfth century have passed away, leaving little trace except in old manuscripts. The "little traditions" of the later centuries have shallower chronological roots.

The history of Islam, therefore, divides in half during the period of recentering: the edge developments that came before are largely forgotten; those that come after are more conspicuous and influential outside the Middle East than within it, and are generally disregarded or disparaged by proponents of recentered Islam. The later edges evolve, as the earlier ones did not, within a broader Islamic community that has developed both homogeneous doctrines and instruments for promoting compliance with those doctrines. To be sure, there is still no papacy or ecclesiastical hierarchy, and the power and will of Muslim governments to enforce religious uniformity on their heterogeneous populations remains weak even after the development of modern means of propaganda and communication. Moreover, the instruments working to suppress local variation and promote uniformity— scholarly suasion, missionary preaching, and some, but not all,

Sufi codes—are slow and lack powers of enforcement. But they steadily progress.

India, Indonesia, China, and Africa all have felt the impact of madrasa-trained scholars and moderate Sufi reformers, whether natives returning from pilgrimage and study in Mecca and Medina or immigrants from other Muslim lands. As early as the sixteenth century, and gaining momentum in the eighteenth and nineteenth centuries, itinerant scholars have issued fatwas against local practices they have deemed abhorrent, such as rule by queens in Indonesia,[5] and preached obedience to the shari'a, membership in moderate, law-abiding Sufi brotherhoods, and adoption of the social norms of educated, urban Muslims living in Arab and Iranian lands.

The slow but persistent campaign by madrasa-trained scholars against "aberrant" local custom has been an important current of Islamic history during the last few centuries, and it continues to be so today. Whether referred to as reform (*islah* in Arabic), renewal (*tajdid*), religious summoning (*da'wa*), or even holy struggle (*jihad*), it has inspired thousands of men to return to their home districts, or penetrate unfamiliar territory, to teach, cajole, inspire, and lead local peoples into a more "proper" observance of the faith. One such movement, the Tablighi Jamaat, originated in the effort to purify the faith of Muslims in the rural Mewat district of India in 1927. Today it is the largest Muslim organization in the world, capable of attracting over a million participants from many countries to its periodic congregations.

Any consideration of the current movement of Islamic political and social reassertion must keep this long-term campaign in mind, not simply because of its proven ability to inspire individuals and effect mass religious reorientation, but also because, through the written word and the impassioned sermon, it tirelessly extols a model of social, legal, and institutional life based on Muslim experience of the past few centuries, but retrojected, for the sake of legitimacy, into the earliest period of Islamic history.

Nevertheless, despite its long pedigree and undeniable success, the campaign to reform Islam in the image of recentered Sunnism cannot alone explain the seemingly sudden emergence of Islam as a political force in the last quarter of the twentieth century. A second, more recent current must be considered as well. Unlike the first, it relates to the political center of Islam, though in its second incarnation in the Ottoman and Persian empires.

The Ottoman sultans paid little heed to the content of teaching in centers of religious learning like the Zaituna Mosque in Tunis, al-Azhar in Cairo, the many madrasas of Mecca and Medina, or even in the madrasas in Bursa and Istanbul from which so many of the empire's top religious officials came. If Indian, African, Indonesian, or Chinese pilgrims and students learned things in their dominions that led them to preach reform to their fellow countrymen upon their return home, it was all the same to the Ottoman government.

Within the empire, however, and beyond the purview of textbooks and classroom instruction, the sultans were very concerned with the real and potential power of the ulama. The political bargain by which the ulama gave religious sanction to the sultan's rule in return for the sultan recognizing his subjection to the shari'a, and thus implicitly to the ulama who defined and preserved the shari'a, constrained the government's freedom to follow whatever course it wished. To take but one example, when Ibrahim Müteferrika, with the sultan's blessing, set up the first Ottoman printing press at the beginning of the eighteenth century, his publications were limited to subjects that did not offend or threaten the ulama, and the experiment was not repeated for a hundred years.[6]

Beginning in the late eighteenth century, however, pressured, challenged, and enticed by the growing power and success of Christian Europe, a succession of Ottoman rulers struggled to reinterpret this bargain in favor of increasing state power. In so doing they took steps to undermine the institutional infrastructure of the ulama. Though no one at the time could have predicted the impact of their policies, they initiated a process of change that eventually fostered a new Islamic political current, emerging after World War II, that is defined both by its hostility to secular government and its comparative freedom from the doctrinal and institutional constraints of recentered Sunnism. In effect, Ottoman "Europeanization" and post-Ottoman "modernization" inadvertently created new edges where Muslims began to ask questions they had not asked before, and to ask them of a different group of people.

I maintain that the complexity and potential of today's Islamic resurgence can best be seen in terms of a contest among three parties: secular, "modernizing" governments; ulama and lay people dedicated to making universal the norms of recentered Sunnism, and of similarly normative Shi'ism; and new Islamic organizations developing along the social edges created by massive rural-urban migration and by secular state education systems in the post-World War II period. Emphasis here will be placed upon the last of these factors, however, because the overall purpose of this book is to demonstrate the dynamism and impact of developments at the edge rather than to give a comprehensive treatment of aspects of Islamic history that have been well told elsewhere.[7]

Relationships between governments and ulama in the nineteenth and early twentieth centuries are difficult to disentangle because multiple viewpoints and interests were at play on either side. Napoleon's easy conquest of Egypt in 1798 and, even more, his career in Europe as a mighty emperor backed by a nationalistically inspired army, profoundly impressed would-be government reformers. They visualized a series of measures that would raise their military power to European levels and elevate the personal role of the ruler above what was accorded him in Islamic political theory.

Muhammad Ali, the essentially independent Ottoman viceroy over Egypt from 1805 to 1848, was the first to succeed. He conscripted peasants into a massive new army. He sent young men of the Turco-Circassian elite that had controlled Egyptian affairs for centuries to France for specialized training, and then directed them to set up European-style schools for military training. And he built factories to manufacture uniforms and equipment for his army. To pay for it all, he confiscated the pious endowments upon which most religious institutions depended and ordered the peasantry to sell their produce to the government at fixed prices for profitable resale abroad. By 1839 he was in a position to challenge the Ottoman sultan for power and was only prevented from overthrowing his suzerain by European intervention.

Sultan Mahmud II (1808–1839) and his successors in Istanbul—and belatedly and sketchily the shahs of the recently installed Qajar dynasty in Iran—imitated key aspects of Muhammad Ali's experiment after he and his family were leashed and largely disarmed by the European powers after 1839. They reorganized armies and equipped them with weapons and uniforms of European type. They trained military officers abroad or in new state schools with curricula modeled on European military academies. They established monopolies and other forms of economic control for the benefit of the crown. And they gradually redesigned their entire systems of government to conform to European practice.

Religious reaction to these changes was mixed and confused. Some ulama felt that increasing Muslim power vis-à-vis Christian Europe, which was then in imperial control of vast Muslim populations in India, Southeast Asia, and Africa, was worth almost any sacrifice. Others deplored what they saw as impious innovations in everything from posterior-revealing European trousers on Muslim soldiers to military band music. Still others paid little attention to matters outside the local sphere.

A simultaneous and related set of reforms affected the ulama directly, however. A powerful combination of pressures provoked a methodical and persistent attack on the bases of ulama power and influence. First was the pressure of European envoys who, from a Christian sense of mission to bring modern civilization to a benighted world, or at least from a desire to see Christians and Jews liberated from what they considered Muslim oppression, viewed the grip of Islam on society and government as archaic and superstitious. Second was the growing conviction among those few Muslims sent to study in Europe, or otherwise educated in schools with European curricula, that modernity required a total transformation of thought along European lines and was therefore incompatible with the pervasiveness of Islam.

As part of the assault on religious institutions, state schools with European curricula multiplied and penetrated downward to the elementary level. At all levels they competed with Islamic schooling informed and conducted by the ulama. In the legal field, without disavowing respect for the shari'a as the highest law, rulers used fiat power (*qanun*), previously employed for more limited purposes, to promulgate codes of European inspiration in such specific areas as commercial and criminal law. The shari'a was set aside in these areas, and the new courts and methods of pleading devised for the new codes rendered obsolete the legal training of the ulama. Furthermore, following Muhammad Ali's lead, governments progressively encroached on the pious endowments that supported the entire network of ulama-oriented institutions—mosques, shrines, madrasas, soup kitchens, Sufi lodges, and so forth.

At the same time, though in less purposeful fashion, increasing integration of Muslim economies into the European-dominated world economy undermined familiar forms of economic organization that were integral parts of religiously oriented community networks. Factories, European entrepreneurs (or local, often non-Muslim, entrepreneurs with European passports of convenience), and European-style business premises became ever more numerous. Corresponding to this was a steady erosion of craft production, of the social solidarity represented by the artisan guilds, and of the clustering of stores and workshops in the local *suq* or bazaar, the locus of merchant and artisan social and religious life. Along the same lines, government-sponsored refurbishing of major cities, in accordance with current trends in European urban design, as well as European advances in technology, e.g., streetcar lines, intruded on market areas and residential neighborhoods and sundered long-standing architectural, social, and communal environments.[8]

In retrospect, the results of the "Europeanization" policies of the nineteenth century suggest a purposeful assault on the power base of the ulama, a determined effort to alter radically the balance between imperial power and religious authority. Yet this objective may have been consciously present in the minds of only a few of the men who forged and implemented the reforms. Others no doubt saw their acts as strengthening Islam through enhancing the power of Muslim monarchs. A preview of a Middle Eastern state of the 1960s—an autocratic, secular, nationalist government; a population dressed like Europeans living in European-style cities; ulama confined to official mosque functions and largely excluded from public affairs—would have astonished everyone. What the state carried out in the legal, educational, and economic spheres was generally seen, throughout the nineteenth century, as being within the parameters of a centuries-old social and governmental pattern indelibly marked by Islam.

Moreover, the enhancement of government power to some extent served the interest of ulama bent on "purifying" Islamic practice along the lines of recentered Sunnism. The emotional hold of certain Sufi shaikhs on the most popular levels of the population, and some of the religious rituals observed in their honor, were deplored by ulama and reforming bureaucrats alike as retrograde, superstitious, and incompatible with modern life, however defined. Some ulama felt the same way about tomb visitation and veneration of the sainted dead. And in Iran, the charismatic and popular Babi and Baha'i movements smacked of heresy to conservative Shi'ite religious leaders.

Strong governments had the power to attack or suppress "backward," "superstitious," and "heretical" expressions of Islam and thus advance the penetration of normative Islam among the people. In Egypt, members of Muhammad Ali's dynasty curbed Sufi proselytization and worked to bring Sufism under government control.[9] In the Ottoman Empire, the abolition of the Bektashi Sufi order (not entirely effective) in 1826 as part of a military reform set a precedent for the eventual banning of all Sufi orders after World War I under the new, secular Turkish Republic of Mustafa Kemal Atatürk. In Arabia, the Saudi kingdom that rose, fell, reemerged, collapsed, resurfaced again, and finally discovered oil from the late eighteenth through the first half of the twentieth century militantly suppressed Sufi "excesses" and destroyed tombs and shrines that had become centers for local pilgrimage. In Iran, the Qajar shahs persecuted the Babis and Baha'is at the behest of conservative ulama.

In short, government power was an instrument that could undermine or support the interests of the mainstream of ulama, and it often did both at the same time. It was therefore not easily perceived that the trajectory of change was leading inexorably to a collapse of religious authority or, rather, a collapse of the institutional and economic infrastructure of that authority. Resistance to even such radical measures as Atatürk's abolition of the sacred Arabic script, prohibition on women veiling and men wearing turbans and skullcaps, and closure of the Sufi lodges took the form of grumbling rather than open rebellion. Prudent ulama began to send their sons to schools with European curricula and breathed thankful sighs that the cold wind of secularism was not chilling them as deeply as it was the dervishes and purveyors of superstition.

By the 1950s there seemed every reason to believe that the social role of Islam would continue to shrink, until it became either a biographical datum or, at most, a matter of private observance, like Catholicism and Protestantism among the European and American middle classes. Despite the proclivity of Western Orientalists for portraying Islam, following the script of the ulama themselves, as a comprehensive system of faith whose immutable law governed every aspect of the believer's life, it was difficult for secularists of Muslim family background—as it was for Western social scientists seeking to chart the future of the "non-Western" world—to see why Islam should not continue to fade. The shari'a, after all, was no more pervasive than orthodox Jewish law, but large numbers of Jews had emancipated themselves from orthodoxy and assimilated, to a greater or lesser degree, into secular civil society. And certainly Islam boasted no doctrinal power center with the resources and organization of the Roman Catholic church. But even the might of the papacy had faltered before the forces of modernization.

In light of these expectations, the reassertion of Islam in the social and political sphere came to world attention as one of the most unpredicted movements of modern times. Nevertheless, it has not only changed the face of politics from Morocco to Malaysia, but it has also eviscerated the models used by a confident America to predict the future in the aftermath of victory in World War II, and of subsequent American attainment of economic and political hegemony over the nonsocialist world. The unpredictability of Islam's reemergence is attested to by the fact that between the end of World War II and the onset of the Islamic Revolution in Iran in 1978–79, a bare handful of books about contemporary Islam were written by Americans.[10] Though Middle East studies as a part of the new academic discipline of Foreign Area studies grew rapidly in the 1950s and 1960s, the professors and graduate students who went to the Middle East to do research failed, for the most part, to take note of, or attach significance to, the growing interest, particularly among Muslim students in government schools and universities, in the writings of a new and militantly assertive group of Muslim thinkers: Sayyid Qutb of Egypt, Muhammad Baqir Sadr of Iraq, Ayatollah Khomeini and Ali Shariati of Iran, Abu al-Ala' Mawdudi of Pakistan, and others. Muslim assertiveness did not develop out of sight of non-Muslim observers; the observers simply failed to see.

The dominance of the view from the center helps to explain the apparent obtuseness of Western observers of the Muslim world in the third quarter of the twentieth century. The teaching that there is no distinction between state and religion in Islam led to a logical, though erroneous conclusion: in view of the all too apparent collapse of a state-embodied political expression of Islam following the fall of the Ottoman Empire, and the manifest secularism of the autocratic nationalist rulers who emerged in the 1950s and 1960s, Islam had surely lost its political vitality. Furthermore, the common portrayal of normative, recentered Sunnism of the post-Mongol era as the essential and unalterable embodiment of the faith as it had been prefigured in the days of the Prophet himself led observers to conclude further that if madrasas and Sufi orders were in decline, and if the shari'a had few remaining applications, then Islam, as a whole, must be losing its capacity to assert itself in the public arena.

The view from the edge that we have been tracing in this book affords a different perspective. As we have seen, those aspects of Islam that are so often deemed characteristic—the shari'a, the ulama, the wedding of state with religion through a commitment on the part of the state to uphold and abide by the shari'a of the ulama, the Sufi orders, popular piety manifested in pilgrimages and shrine devotions—were present only in embryo at the time of the Prophet. They all became elaborated over time, and their elaboration took place without the benefit, or burden, of an organized ecclesiastical structure or a centralized source of doctrinal authority. In the absence of patriarchs, archbishops, synods, councils, and suchlike religious authorities, local societies of Muslims largely found their own way, nominating their own local religious leaders through their willingness to follow those among them who seemed the most pious or learned.

194

The mechanism of elaboration was the dialectic of question and answer. Muslims on the edge wanted to know what Islam was and how it resembled or differed from the other religions they were familiar with. They wanted to know how Islam could solve their problems and assuage their pains. In the earliest phase of community, they often turned to ascetics and wonder workers for answers. Then, increasingly, they turned to the hadith scholars in their community, regardless of status or occupation, who could tell them about the words and deeds of Muhammad. Next, after the shari'a had developed sufficiently to answer a broad and diverse array of questions, they referred many of their questions to jurists, who answered them with fatawa. The fatawa of eminent legal personalities were collected and referred to, just as hadith had earlier been collected and used as sources of authority. As for questions of faith and pious behavior that could not be answered through the law, the worldwide proliferation of Sufi brotherhoods made saintly shaikhs the favored medium for providing authoritative answers.

Over the centuries, the qualifications of those individuals whom people trusted to give reliable responses to religious questions changed, but the pattern did not. Islam, to a greater extent than any other major religion, has been shaped by the questions Muslims have asked and by the willingness of Muslims to seek out their own religious authorities. The impetus for change in Islam has more often come from the bottom than from the top, from the edge than from the center. Prior to the thirteenth century, this tendency gave rise to a welter of local observances and religious understandings that only gradually succumbed to the gravity represented by the religious recentering of Sunnism. After the thirteenth century, recentered Sunnism, later paralleled by state Shi'ism in Iran, vigorously proclaimed the unity and homogeneity of Islam and combated, with limited effectiveness, the continuing eruption of new Islamic observances, not only on the far-flung edges of the growing Muslim umma, but even in the heartland of the Middle East itself.

Yet the ulama's constant reiteration of the refrain that Islam was an ordered, comprehensible, and homogeneous faith could not conceal that fact that millions of Muslims, in all good conscience, believed and acted differently. To an extraordinary degree, individ-

195

ual Muslims were, and still are, free to choose their religious mentors and exemplars, particularly on the edge.

This freedom is evident even in the most structured form of contemporary Islam, Iranian Shi'ism. A Shi'ite scholar who has followed the prescribed course of study in a madrasa and, subsequently, through his writings and personal probity, earned a high reputation for piety and learning may eventually come to be referred to by other mullahs as an ayatollah. As an ayatollah, this scholar may choose, or, more appropriately, be asked by others, to write a *risala*, a book stipulating proper religious conduct in all manner of situations, from prayer to sexual relations. Upon writing his risala, such an ayatollah becomes a potential spiritual mentor for individual Shi'ites, who, in the dominant school of contemporary Shi'ite thought, are expected to choose some living ayatollah as their religious guide.

But writing a risala does not make the author a guide. The initiative comes from the believers. This does not mean that every Shi'ite man and woman reads an assortment of risalas by living ayatollahs and chooses the one he or she feels most comfortable with, or is most impressed by, though many mullahs themselves surely do exactly this. More often, individual Shi'ites will go to a local mullah whom they respect and ask his opinion as to whom they should follow. And that mullah, if he does not already have a firm opinion, can consult the local representatives of various ayatollahs, normally their former students, to find out more about their masters' teachings. Upon receiving and accepting a recommendation to adhere to the risala of one specific ayatollah, the individual believer may then choose to make that commitment. But the commitment is neither irrevocable nor socially manifested by, for example, praying in one mosque instead of another. Thus, modern Shi'ites divide their allegiances among a handful of grand ayatollahs—those whose risalas command sizable followings—but this division is not normally reified at a social level after the fashion, say, of Christians choosing to become part of specific church congregations. No one needs to know to whom any particular Shi'ite has dedicated his or her religious allegiance. Nor do the grand ayatollahs, or their representatives, necessarily keep formal lists of members of their flock. Then, whenever a grand ayatollah dies, each person who followed him has to decide whom to follow next.

The purpose of this illustration is to demonstrate that even in this comparatively hierarchical and formalized branch of contemporary Islam there is great fluidity at the level of whom believers turn to for answers to religious questions, and great potential for independent action. In this way, contemporary Islam remains remarkably dissimilar from Judaism and Christianity, with their more formal congregational and ecclesiastical structures. And it is this dissimilarity that is at the root of the difference between Jewish and Christian reactions to the advance of "modernity" and the current Islamic reaction. Nineteenth- and twentieth-century ulama, with their dedication to the further spread of normative beliefs and practices within the parameters of recentered Sunnism and Shi'ism, absorbed blow after blow to the institutional infrastructure that sustained their authority, but they simultaneously witnessed even greater destruction being wrought upon popular Sufism and other manifestations of what they considered heterodox belief and behavior. The prospect they entertained, recognizing the obsolescence of the old balance of power between sultan and ulama, was of the final triumph of a unified, normative Islam, shorn of all excess and localism, within a political framework of religious subservience to some sort of "modern" state. This vision is today manifested in the system of religious absolutism with technological modernization devised by the kings of Saudi Arabia and their influential corps of ulama. At odds with this prospect was the eruption along newly developing social edges of reawakened religious questioning and of a fresh coterie of authoritative respondents.

Modern education in the Middle East begins with the military schools established by Muhammad Ali of Egypt.[11] As with so many of his undertakings, it is difficult to determine how much of his inspiration was European and how much derived from past models. In the case of education, Sultan Mehmed the Conqueror had established a palace school in Istanbul in the fifteenth century to train elite—but nominally slave—officials for military command positions and high bureaucratic posts.[12] The combination of elite education with a total dedication to serving the ruler's will links Sultan

197

Mehmed's palace school with Muhammad Ali's, and later Sultan Mahmud II's, academies for military engineers, artillerymen, surgeons, and bandmasters. It also lies at the heart of the subsequent development of modern schooling in the Middle East.

As the nineteenth century progressed, the Ottomans established secular secondary schools to feed their higher military schools, and then primary school to feed the secondary schools. After World War I, as they gradually freed themselves from European imperial control, the independent countries that rose from the ruins of the Ottoman Empire established comprehensive state school systems that for the first time brought literacy and awareness of the modern world to the mass of the population. The rationale for the new school systems, however, continued to be government service.

Unlike public education in the West, which grew from local roots, public education in the Middle East has always been state-sponsored, state-controlled, and dedicated to serving the interests of the state. Though American or European advisors, or people trained in Western schools of education, have often been employed to design curricula for the schools to ensure their modern character, government determination to make education an instrument of state policy has never wavered. Even today, the Egyptian government will publicize a decision at commencement time to employ so many thousand new university graduates, almost as if it had a duty to do so since all of the graduates had implicitly been educated for government service. In keeping with this ethos, the cost of education to the student is negligible, and private education is looked upon as potentially subversive. Aside from a few institutions founded by missionaries, such as the American University of Beirut and the American University in Cairo, there are virtually no private universities in Turkey, Iran, or the Arab world.

When Muhammad Ali sent students to Paris, he sent a few ulama along with them to oversee their religious conduct and keep them from straying. As more new schools were established during the course of the nineteenth century, however, the intrusion of the ulama, who usually were unfamiliar with the European-style curricula, became increasingly unwelcome. And as nationalism seized the popular imagination after World War I and fueled the ambitions of anti-imperialist politicians, Islam came to be seen by many as absolutely retrograde and undeserving of a significant place in the nascent state school systems.

Governments varied in the degree to which they minimized religion in the new curricula; overall, the deemphasis, or in the Turkish case eradication, of Islam in the schools, coupled with the decay, impoverishment, and eventual abandonment of many religious schools, particularly at the lower levels, led to a drastic decline in religious literacy. More young Muslims than ever before learned to read, write, and think along the same lines as European, American, and Japanese children; but they knew less than their parents or grandparents about their ancestral faith, and had far less contact with honored religious scholars. In addition, a new stress on learning European languages contributed, among non-Arabs, to a decline in literacy in Arabic, and thus of access to much of the Islamic literary tradition.

The difference between educational developments in the Middle East and in Europe and America does not, at first glance, seem particularly great. Secularism in education, whether centrally or locally controlled, progressed at least as far in the West as in the Islamic world during the nineteenth and twentieth centuries, with religious instruction largely relegated to Sunday schools, Hebrew schools, catechism classes, and the like. Yet the difference was actually profound. Secularism in the West was presented to students within a continuum of social and historical "progress" that portrayed it as the highest achievement of their own culture. Most European and American students accepted the teaching that what they were learning was more advanced than what their parents and grandparents had learned, but they did not at the same time cultivate disdain for the knowledge and outlook of those earlier generations.

By contrast, Arab, Turkish, and Persian students attending modern schools found themselves largely cut off from the learning and intellectual outlook of their forebears. Moreover, it was obvious, despite efforts to discover the roots of modernity in Islamic culture, that the modern world they were being trained to live and work in was not the end product of their own cultural history. Thus they were faced by an uncomfortable contradiction between the seemingly obvious value of becoming educated to take a place in the modern sector of their country's economy, and an awareness that the modern world they were preparing to enter had largely been created by the foreign imperialist culture their political leaders railed against.

This contradiction was not exclusively experienced by Muslims, of course. Third World students of many cultural backgrounds, as well as racial minorities in Western countries, were forced to think through the same dilemma. For young Muslims, however, a centuries-old pattern for dealing with personal quandaries was ready to hand. In effect, the generation of students that flooded the state school systems in the 1950s and 1960s became a new edge. Poorly educated in religious matters, but aware that as Muslims they were the inheritors of a culture that had once been a great force in the world, they began to ask questions: What does it mean to be a Muslim? What does it mean to be a Muslim in the modern world? What can I take from the historical culture of Islam that will enhance my life?

Ironically, the same secular policies that created the new systems of public education, as part of a broader effort to increase the power of the state, so diminished the status of traditionally trained ulama that when a new generation began to ask questions about Islam, they did not turn automatically to the shaykhs and mullahs their grandparents would have sought out for advice. Feeling free to bestow their religious allegiance upon whoever seemed best able to respond to their needs, the student generation eagerly consumed the teachings of assertive Muslim thinkers who, in many cases, had not received a traditional religious education. The fact that the answers these thinkers gave to the questions asked them were often at odds with traditional teachings, or manifestly predicated upon ideas deriving from Western academic study, did not deter the young men and women of the new edge from following them. The impression of being pious in one's personal demeanor and authoritative in one's answers to questions has always taken precedence over formal credentials or office holding on the edge of Islamic society.

Ali Shariati, whose writings had a powerful impact on Iranian students prior to the Islamic Revolution of 1979, acquired his education in Paris and used Western sociological concepts in his free reinterpretation of Shi'ite Islam as a force for change and revolution. Abu al-Hasan Banisadr, the first president of the Islamic Republic of Iran, was similarly educated in Paris, as an economist. Khurshid Ahmad, a major intellectual leader of the Jam'at-i Islami movement in Pakistan, was also trained as an economist and once served as Pakistan's Minister of Planning and Development. Hasan al-Turabi, the religious leader considered to be the eminence grise of the Sudanese Republic after the overthrow of the regime of Sadiq al-Mahdi, is an eloquent lawyer trained at the Sorbonne. His rival of earlier times, Mahmud Muhammad Taha, who was executed for heresy because of his unconventional analysis of the message of the Quran, was likewise trained as a Western-style lawyer. And Hasan Hanafi, a prominent religious intellectual in Egypt, is a professor of philosophy at Cairo University.

Below highly visible leaders such as these are thousands of younger activists who lead study groups, campaign for election to student councils, and recruit members on university campuses throughout the Muslim world. And not all of them wear headscarfs or beards. As one beleaguered left-wing secularist at Bursa University in Turkey said to me: "You see a girl, and she's wearing jeans and everything. So you talk to her, and she talks about her friends. Then she uses some words in her conversation—code words—and you realize she's one of *them*."

The religious ferment on the new edge is not greatly different from that of the eighth or ninth century in the Middle East, or of later centuries in Indonesia or Senegal. When, for whatever reason, people with little knowledge of Islam begin to think that being a Muslim might be an important part of their social and personal identity, they seek instruction. And they evaluate the guidance they receive by its relevance to their own backgrounds, and the pertinence it seems to have for their own lives. Today's pious engineer or economist who sets forth his personal interpretation of Islam bears a close relationship to the ascetic or wonder-worker of ninth-century Iran. Within the fluid structure of Islamic religious allegiance, both can attract followers, irrespective of their formal reli-

201

gious training, simply by being pious in manner, invoking the current language and symbols of Islamic discourse, and relating their words to the needs of their questioners.

A second edge of recent formation consists of villagers who have migrated to cities. Their story is simply told. Village life changes over time, but usually change is slow enough to leave undisturbed, at least in later memory, the illusion of stability and continuity. Migration to the city, however, is a profoundly disrupting experience. Even when there are previous migrants from the same village to cushion one's entry into urban life, the loss of the routines of the agricultural cycle, and of the village's closed society, is not easily compensated for. This disjunction was an important factor in the development of a distinct Islamic urban life in the ninth and tenth centuries, and it plays a similar role in today's Islamic movement. Urban newcomers, as well as earlier migrants who are dismayed by the difficulty of making their way in the city, seek help; and they seek help from the sources they have grown up revering.

The urban poor in the explosively expanding capitals of the post-World War II Islamic world do not understand the thoughts of the new brand of leader who tries to interpret Muslim beliefs and practices from the standpoint of Western sociology, economics, or legal argument. They are drawn much more to religious leaders who represent the older traditions that the students sometimes scoff at. But, like the students, they respond most strongly to leaders who speak to them about things that matter: access to jobs, provision of social services, curbing of government neglect and corruption, morality in public behavior, and so forth.

They also respond to holiness. In 1986 I was surprised, on walking through the cemetery adjoining the Süleimaniye Mosque in Istanbul, to see a new tombstone with an inscription in bright green Arabic script. There had been no new burials in the cemetery of the landmark mosque for two generations, and the use of the Arabic script had been prohibited by Mustafa Kemal Atatürk. The inscription, which was in Arabic rather than Turkish, identified the grave as that of a Naqshbandi Sufi shaikh. This, too, was surprising since all Sufi orders had been outlawed in Turkey in the 1920s. When I revisited the grave in 1988, two things were different. Beside the large stone was a smaller stone, inscribed in Turkish using Roman letters. It marked the grave of the mother of the president of the Turkish Republic, Turgut Özal. The second change was that while I stood there, several young men, dressed in workers' clothes, came up to the shaikh's grave and prayed, practicing a ritual veneration forcibly prohibited in the time of their grandfathers. Islam on the edge is still a creative force, at the highest and lowest levels of society, in the world's most militantly secular Muslim nation.

Enthusiasts of the contemporary Islamic movement sometimes portray it as a vast, unitary force ecnompassing everything from the Wahhabi movement of eighteenth-century Saudi Arabia and the Mahdist movement of nineteenth-century Sudan; through the Salafiya movement of turn-of-the-century Egypt and its later off-shoot, the Muslim Brotherhood; to Ayatollah Khomeini's leadership of Iran's Islamic Revolution and the recent electoral popularity of the FIS in Algeria.[13] Skeptical Muslims, and not entirely disinterested Western observers, incline more to taxonomies that single out this or that ripple in the current as "radical," "moderate," "reformist," "conservative," "fundamentalist," and so forth. Both approaches provide insight, but both concentrate on how the various leaders of today and yesterday articulate their goals, programs, tactics, and demands.

My intention in this chapter, as in this book as a whole, has been to complement other approaches to the history of Islamic society. There is no denying the important differences between modern Muslim thinkers. Mahmud Muhammad Taha's human rights interpretation of Islam, Ayatollah Khomeini's "governance of the religious jurist" (*vilayat-i faqih*), Muhammad Abduh's attempt to reopen the "gate of individual legal interpretation" (*bab al-ijtihad*), Sayyid Qutb's powerful analysis of Islam as a source of revolution, and the socialist economic policies incorporated into the constitution of the Islamic Republic of Iran betray radically different visions of how Islam can come to grips with a modern world that nearly succeeded in confining it to the narrow bounds of personal religious behavior.

The complementary view is one that looks at the continuity of Islamic history and recognizes that parallel moments of change have occurred before, and in much the same way. In the nascent period of Islamic society, between the eighth and tenth centuries, there were strongly competing loci of leadership. Muslims on the edge evolved local understandings of Islam and nominated, through seeking and accepting their guidance, a diverse array of religious leaders that only slowly shrank or coalesced into the group known as the ulama. Simultaneously, though sporadically, the political center, focused on the caliphate, tried and failed to understand, control, and normalize this dramatic evolution.

The period from the twelfth through the fourteenth centuries witnessed a second great transformation. Communal religious institutions, largely of Iranian origin, spread throughout the older parts of the Islamic world and some of the newly converting areas as well. Migration of scholars and Sufis played an important role in this change, but the desire of the general Muslim populace to be part of a broader consensus regarding proper belief and practice, to feel at one with other members of the universal umma in the dark period before and after the Mongol destruction of the caliphate, was a far more decisive factor than any particular scholar's writings or any government's religious policy.

And then there has been the ever expanding edge where converts from all manner of religious and cultural background make their decisions to join the Muslim community, and then seek to discover what that decision implies with respect to their earlier beliefs and customs. From the Philippines to Nigeria and from Bosnia to South Africa, Islam has responded to the needs of the most remarkable diversity of human beings, though often at the cost of informal compromises with local custom that appall the madrasa-trained scholars of Mecca and Cairo.

The locus of change in all these episodes has been local and popular. Unhaltered by sacramental and ecclesiastical entanglements, Muslims have repeatedly voiced their needs and discovered leaders who have been responsive to the times and circumstances of their petitioners. Today the process continues, because it has come, through historical development, to be an integral part of Islam.

Five popular forces tug at the fabric of Islam, trying to make it fit differing visions of modern life. One force is secular. Rooted in the nineteenth-century polemic that presented rationalism, unfettered by faith, as the sine qua non of modern life, secular Muslims fear that today's resurgence of Islam will destroy the Western lifestyles they have become accustomed to and doom their societies to benighted backwardness. Many of them support the neo-Mamluk dictatorships of countries like Iraq, Syria, Algeria, and Tunisia, which they rely on to combat any redressing of the balance in favor of religious power in society. Many others reject the dictatorships and long to see them replaced by secular, democratic governments that will successfully confine religion to, at most, a minority position in political life.

The second and third forces are the new edges described above. Sharing the religious ignorance of many secular Muslims, but convinced that Islam is all that can preserve their identity from being submerged by the tidal wave of Western culture circling the globe, a generation of students is providing an eager audience for a new breed of religious leader, often only half educated in conventional Islamic teachings, but determined to interpret the faith in ways that make sense to people with modern educations. In the slums and working class districts of the same metropolitan centers that house so many student activists, the underclass of poor workers and new immigrants from the countyside likewise turn to religious leaders for solace, guidance, and, increasingly, identification of those classes and political forces that perpetuate their poverty and powerlessness.

Fourth is the force of popular piety once represented by wonder-workers, wandering dervishes, and local pilgrimage rites. Unorganized, unorganizable, the masses of Muslims who believed they saw Ayatollah Khomeini's face in the moon, or who look expectantly for signs of the world coming to an end, or who dip pieces of cloth in the blood of the ram slaughtered on Id al-Adha and smear it on their children's faces, represent a volatile, occasionally politicizable, element that responds more to emotion and charisma than to specific doctrines and policies, however "orthodox" or "heterodox."

This leaves a fifth force, that represented by a nearly universal longing for the stability, community, and morality of a half-remembered past. Much of the remaining power of the ulama derives from the widespread belief that, as repositories of centuries of Islamic learning, they are still the best sources for answers to social and moral questions. Fatwa-issuing bodies that respond to believers' questions abound. Some are attached to madrasas and mosques; others speak through columns in Muslim magazines. All bespeak a desire for authoritative answers to questions. Not surprisingly, many questions deal precisely with those aspects of modern life most strongly identified with Western culture: the role of women, the nature of marriage, the permissibility of entertainments, the giving and taking of interest, and the proper role of government. More often than not, the answers given reflect the norms of recentered Sunnism.

It makes little difference that the arguments used to condemn rock music originated around the issue of Sufis using the intoxication of music to assist their spiritual trances, or that the *shura* (consultative council) invoked as a model for modern representative government functioned decisively only once, in the year 644. What is important is that the answers draw upon, or reflect continuity with, a presumed golden age somewhere in the past. It is hard even for secularists to deny the atavistic appeal of evocations of tradition and of a golden age. In the early days of the Islamic Republic of Iran, when the possibility seemed to exist that Ayatollah Shariatmadari might challenge Ayatollah Khomeini for popular leadership, one secular, Western-educated Iranian—a native Turkish speaker like most of Ayatollah Shariatmadari's followers—predicted that Ayatollah Khomeini would inevitably win the contest with his rival. He observed that photographs of Ayatollah Shariatmadari often showed him seated on a silk rug given to him by a follower, while photos of Ayatollah Khomeini showed him sitting on a straw mat obtainable for a few cents in the market. Iranians, he told me, would never give their hearts to a man on a silk rug over a man on a straw mat. Nor, to go back to the saying of the Prophet with which this book began, will they easily accept the religious leadership of the person who parades his qualifications and ostentatiously seeks a command position.

At present, I believe that the sheer abundance of people actively seeking answers to religious questions, in keeping with the engrained pattern of Islamic history, affords a better augury of the future of the Islamic world than the specific teachings or political policies of particular religious leaders. Nevertheless, finding accommodation between the faith of Islam and the reality of the modern world, between the warm appeal of a half-imaginary golden age and the necessity of coping with contemporary economic, demographic, and cultural challenges is a slow undertaking. There is no reason to think that any formulation currently being put forward, either radical or reactionary, will prove convincing or workable in the long run. Indeed, religious struggles within the Islamic world—for example, between the Saudi Arabian approach to Islam and the Iranian one—will almost certainly intensify in years to come. Eventually, however, a new Islamic synthesis will be achieved. We are currently living through one of the greatest periods of intellectual and religious creativity in Islamic—and human—history. But the final shape of "modern" Islam is still too distant to discern.

WA ALLAHU A'LAM

NOTES

Introduction

1. Hamza al-Sahmi, *Ta'rikh Jurjan aw kitab ma'rifa 'ulama' ahl Jurjan* (Hyderabad: Osmania Oriental Publications Bureau, 1967), pp. 78–79, 100, 176, 192, 196–97, 362, 431, 452, 542 (henceforward cited as Sahmi). At the other end of the Islamic world, Ibn al-Arabi, the twelfth-century Muslim mystic from Spain, wrote, "The Prophet said, concerning the office of Imam, 'If you are given it you will be assisted in it, but if you demand it you will not be assisted' " (*Sufis of Andalusia: The Ruh al-quds and al-Durrat al-fakhirah of Ibn 'Arabi*, translated by R. W. J. Austin [Berkeley: University of California Press, 1971], pp. 139–40). This saying of the Prophet is also included, with two separate isnads, in al-Bukhari's *Sahih* (Beirut: Dar al-Qibla, 1987), vols. 7–9, p. 703.

2. *The Patricians of Nishapur* (Cambridge, Mass.: Harvard University Press, 1972).

3. *Conversion to Islam in the Medieval Period: An Essay in Quantitative History* (Cambridge, Mass.: Harvard University Press, 1979).

209

1. Orality and Authority

1. The Arabic plural of hadith is ahadith. To avoid confusion, the word hadith will be used henceforward as both a singular and a plural.

2. The collections of hadith accepted as standard and reliable today are based on medieval research separating "sound" from "weak" traditions largely on the basis of the reliability of their isnads.

3. Al-Hakim al-Naisaburi, *An Introduction to the Science of Tradition Being al-madkhal ila ma'rifat al-iklil*, translated and edited by James Robson (London: Royal Asiatic Society, 1953), pp. 10–11.

4. Abd al-Karim b. Muhammad al-Sam'ani, *Kitab adab al-imla' w'al-istimla'* (Die Methodik des Diktatkollegs), edited by Max Weisweiller (Leiden: Brill, 1952), pp. 152–66.

5. Bulliet, *Patricians*, p. 234.

6. Ibid., p. 125.

7. Richard W. Bulliet, "The Age Structure of Medieval Islamic Education," *Studia Islamica* 57 (1983):107–9. Although some girls did learn hadith, often from their fathers, and some women transmitted hadith, their presence in formal hadith classes was so rare that I shall use masculine pronouns in speaking generally of hadith education.

8. Ibid., pp. 116–17.

9. Ibid., p. 107.

10. For examples, see the story of the Isma'ili family in chapter 6.

11. R. N. Frye, ed., The Histories of Nishapur (Cambridge, Mass.: Harvard University Press, 1965), contains, among its three facsimiles, two quite different condensations of Abd al-Ghafir al-Farisi's Al-Siyaq li ta'rikh Naisabur, a biographical dictionary of Nishapur compiled in the twelfth century. The manuscript in the middle of the book will be cited as Farisi II, and the other will be cited as Farisi I. Data on this embassy may be found in Farisi I, f12a–13b, Farisi II, f3a–b, and Sahmi, pp. 411, 413.

12. Al-Hakim al-Naisaburi, *Al-Madkhal*, p. 39.

13. Ibid., p. 41.

14. Sahmi, p. 168.

15. Al-Sam'ani, *Adab al-imla'*, pp. 27–28.

16. Ibid., pp. 28–34.

17. Ibid., p. 141

18. Al-Hakim al-Naisaburi's *Madkhal* contains a long catalog of possible deficiencies.

19. For a sophisticated Western analysis of the issue of fabrication and the doctoring of isnads, see Gualterus H. A. Juynboll, *Muslim Tradition: Studies in Chronology, Provenance and Authorship of Early Hadith* (Cambridge: Cambridge University Press, 1983). Muslim scholars were well aware of the prob-

lem. Ibn Adi's listing of unsound transmitters, *Al-Kamil fi du'afa' al-rijal* (Beirut: Dar al-Fikr, 1985), contains 2,700 names in seven volumes. I am grateful to Dr. Lawrence Conrad for bringing this source to my attention.

20. Their compilers were al-Bukhari (d. 870), Muslim (d. 875), Ibn Da'ud (d. 888), al-Nasa'i (d. 915), al-Tirmidhi (d. 892), and Ibn Maja (d. 886).

21. For a biography of al-Kushmaihani, see Sam'ani, *Kitab al-Ansab*, facsimile edition by D. Margoliouth in the E. J. W. Gibb Memorial Series, vol. 20 (London: Luzac, 1912), f484a.

22. It is reported of one important political figure that he was not known for the elevation of his isnad, but rather his eminence in hadith was a function of his rank as a ra'is. Farisi II, f28b. A more typical reference notes that a certain scholar had a high isnad, to wit, no more than four links between him and the Prophet. (Ibn Funduq, *Tarikh-i Baihaq*, edited by A. Bahmanyar, [Tehran: Foroughi, 1938], p. 145.) People rarely began to teach hadith classes before the age of fifty since their isnads were not considered high in their younger years. For quantitative evidence on the importance of young students studying from old teachers see Bulliet, "Age Structure."

23. Al-Sam'ani, *Adab al-imla'*, p. 4.

24. Ibid., pp. 6–7.

25. See, in particular, George Makdisi's *The Rise of Colleges: Institutions of Learning in Islam and the West* (Edinburgh: Edinburgh University Press, 1982); as well as his "Muslim Institutions of Learning in Eleventh-Century Baghdad," *Bulletin of the School of Oriental and African Studies* 24 (1961):1–56.

2. Prophet, Quran, and Companions

1. The foci of the debate are John Wansbrough, *Qur'anic Studies: Sources and Methods of Scriptural Interpretation* (Oxford: Oxford University Press, 1977); Patricia Crone and Michael Cook, *Hagarism: The Making of the Islamic World* (Cambridge: Cambridge University Press, 1977); and Patricia Crone, *Meccan Trade and the Rise of Islam* (Princeton: Princeton University Press, 1987). For a thoughtful analysis and response to this school of thought, see Christian Decobert, *Le mendiant et le combattant* (Paris: Editions Seuil, 1991).

2. Sahmi, p. 79.

3. Muhassin b. Ali al-Tanukhi, *The Table-Talk of a Mesopotamian Judge*, translated by D. S. Margoliouth (London: Royal Asiatic Society, 1922), p. 96.

4. "Garlic, leeks and onions, mushrooms and (all plants), springing from impure (substances), are unfit to be eaten by twice-born men." (*The Laws of Manu*, translated by G. Bühler, in *Sacred Books of the East*, vol. 25, chap. 5, verse 5, edited by Max Müller [Oxford: Clarendon Press, 1886]). I am most

grateful to my wife, Dr. Lucy Bulliet, for elucidating the Indian attitude toward garlic for me.

5. Hadith noting that Muhammad drank water standing up may be found in Bukhari, *Sahih*, vol. 7–9, p. 209. These hadith appear to relate to a taboo certain pre-Islamic Arabs had on drinking this way. There is nothing to indicate that the taboo applied to other beverages.

6. Scholarly inquiries into the lore concerning the Sahaba raise doubts about the identity and actual role as transmitters of various individuals, as well as about the possibility of local Muslim communities claiming certain Sahaba visited them and dispensed lore. (Miklos Muranyi, *Die Prophetengenossen in der frühislamischen Geschichte* [Bonn: Orientalischen Seminars der Universität Bonn, 1973].) Hard though it is to believe every alleged connection between hadith and Sahaba, however, it is harder to envisage the corpus of hadith coming into existence without this instrumentality.

7. Sahmi, p. 157.

8. Ahmad b. Yahya Baladhuri, *Kitab futuh al-buldan*, edited by S. D. Munajjid (Cairo: Maktaba al-Nahda al-Misriya, n.d.), p. 71.

9. Ibid., p. 82. These and other examples are discussed in R. W. Bulliet, "Conversion Stories in Early Islam," in M. Gervers and R. J. Bikhazi, eds., *Conversion and Continuity: Indigenous Christian Communities in Islamic Lands, Eighth to Eighteenth Centuries* (Toronto: Pontifical Institute of Mediaeval Studies, 1990), pp. 123–33.

10. Muhammad b. Jarir al-Tabari, *Ta'rikh al-rusul wa'l-muluk*, edited by M. Ibrahim (Cairo: Dar al-Ma'arif, 1960), vol. 7, 55. I am grateful to Dr. Jamsheed Choksy for drawing this passage to my attention.

11. At one point a group of people known as *qurra'* became politically important, and a debate has arisen over whether the word *qurra'* means "Quran reciters," its most obvious meaning, or something else. At the center of the debate is Muhammad Shaban's *Islamic History A.D. 600–750 (A.H. 132): A New Interpretation* (Cambridge: Cambridge University Press, 1971), pp. 50–55. Even if these qurra' were Quran readers, there is little in the episode to indicate their overall role in society.

12. Sahmi's biographical dictionary of Gorgan, for example, begins with the city's conquest by the Arabs, and then devotes three pages to naming the Companions who passed through, and another three pages to the generation of Followers who transmitted lore about Muhammad from the Companions. Only then does he speak in detail of the general who commanded the conquering army and of the deeds and visits of the Umayyad and Abbasid caliphs.

13. Juynboll, *Muslim Tradition*, pp. 10–23.

14. Abu Ja'far Muhammad al-Tabari, *The Reign of al-Mu'tasim (833–842)*, translated by Elma Marin (New Haven: American Oriental Society, 1951), p. 116; emphasis added.

15. Sahmi, p. 83.

16. Western doubts about the authenticity of hadith stem largely from Ignaz Goldziher's *Muhammedanische Studien* (Halle: Max Niemeyer, 1889–90) and Joseph Schacht's *Origins of Muhammadan Jurisprudence* (Oxford: Clarendon Press, 1950). For a Muslim analysis and refutation of their position, see Muhammad M. al-Azami, *On Schacht's "Origins of Muhammadan Jurisprudence"* (New York: John Wiley and Sons, 1985).

17. I am grateful to Dr. Lawrence Conrad for bringing this hadith to my attention.

3. The View from the Edge

1. Abu Nu'aim al-Isfahani, *Kitab dhikr akhbar Isbahan*, edited by S. Dedering (Leiden: E. J. Brill, 1931–34), vol. 1, p. 237. For a broader discussion of Muslim naming practices, though pertaining mostly to the post-Mongol period, see Jacqueline Sublet, *Le voile du nom: Essai sur le nom propre arabe* (Paris: Presses Universitaires de France, 1991).

2. For a detailed discussion of the method and implications of conversion curves based on this assumption, see my *Conversion to Islam in the Medieval Period*.

3. For nonquantitative discussions of what were apparently later episodes of conversion in Mamluk Egypt and Ottoman Syria, see Donald P. Little, "Coptic Converts to Islam during the Bahri Mamluk Period," in Gervers and Bikhazi, eds., *Conversion and Continuity*; and Robert M. Haddad, *Syrian Christians in Muslim Society: An Interpretation* (Princeton: Princeton University Press, 1970).

4. See details in Daniel C. Dennett, *Conversion and the Poll-Tax in Early Islam* (Cambridge, Mass.: Harvard University Press, 1950).

5. A particularly vivid example of some Arabs' horror at the thought of their fellow tribespeople intermarrying with non-Arab converts is provided by al-Jahiz in *Kitab al-qawl fi al-bighal*, edited by C. Pellat (Cairo: Mustafa al-Babi al-Halabi, 1955), p. 87, where a poem likens miscegenation between Arabs and non-Arabs to Arab women fornicating with donkeys and mules.

6. The evidence that educated non-Muslims knew almost nothing reliable about Islam is well reflected in the data gathered by Crone and Cook in *Hagarism*. Their interpretation of these data is entirely different, however. They assume literal accuracy and on this basis challenge the entire Muslim tradition dealing with Islam's origins. However, they do not deal effectively with the question of how the monks and rabbis they cite acquired their alleged knowledge of the religion of the Arabs.

7. Al-Baladhuri, *Futuh al-buldan*, p. 172.

8. Bulliet, *Patricians*, chap. 8.

9. For example, Sahmi relates that "Abu Ja'far al-Thumi is the one who called the people of Gilan to Islam, and they converted at his hands. All of those among the Gilanis who are on the path of the Sunna are his clients (*mawali*)" (p. 570). While it is unlikely that the mass conversion of the Gilanis implied by this statement actually took place, the passage probably does reflect some instances of group conversion in response to missionary activity in Gilan province.

10. Gorgan was first conquered in 639. Its ruler then was Ruzban Sul b. Ruzban, Sul evidently being the title of the local ruler. Ruzban Sul signed a treaty of submission preserving his people's lives and property, and his own rulership and legal authority (Sahmi, pp. 5–6). The Sul of this story is probably Ruzban's grandson since Yazid b. Muhallab's reconquest of Gorgan took place eighty years later (Sahmi, p. 10).

11. Sahmi, p. 247.

12. Abu Nu'aim, *Akhbar Isbahan*, vol. 2, pp. 186–87.

13. For a fuller discussion of this point see Bulliet "Conversion Stories," pp. 123–33.

14. Sahmi, pp.310–20.

15. Bulliet, "Age Structure."

16. Sahmi, p. 254.

17. Ibid., pp. 159–60.

18. Ibid., pp. 22–24, 254.

19. Bulliet, *Conversion*, chap. 6.

20. Yaqut, *Mu'jam al-Buldan* (Beirut: Dar Sader and Dar Beirut, 1956), vol. 2, pp. 182–83.

21. Sahmi, pp. 375–76.

22. Ibid., p. 376.

23. Ibid., p. 380.

24. Ibid., p. 382.

25. For a discussion of such rebellions, see B. S. Amoretti, "Sects and Heresies," in *The Cambridge History of Iran* (Cambridge: Cambridge University Press, 1975), vol. 4, pp. 481–519.

26. Sahmi, p. 75. This is almost certainly a spurious hadith since the office of qadi did not yet exist in Muhammad's time.

27. Bayard Dodge, trans., *The Fihrist of al-Nadim* (New York: Columbia University Press, 1970), vol. 1, 503.

28. Sahmi, p. 380.

29. Ibid., p. 255.

30. Ibid., pp. 20, 42, 524.

31. Ibid., p. 554.

32. Ibid., p. 22.

33. Sahmi has a separate entry (p. 275) for this Abd al-Rahman, but it contains no information other than the name of one of Sahmi's sources who transmitted lore from him.

34. Ibid., p. 22.

35. The basic ideas about the evolution of family history in this book are adumbrated in my previous books, *The Patricians of Nishapur* and *Conversion to Islam in the Medieval Period*.

4. Islamic Urbanization

1. Abu Nu'aim, *Akhbar Isbahan*, vol. 2, pp. 186–87.

2. Cambridge, 1983.

3. Ibid., pp. 129, 130.

4. Robert McCormick Adams, *Land Behind Baghdad* (Chicago: University of Chicago Press, 1965), pp. 98–99.

5. Watson, *Agricultural Innovation*, p. 132.

6. Richard W. Bulliet, "Medieval Nishapur: A Topographic and Demographic Reconstruction," *Studia Iranica* 5 (1976):87–88.

7. Abu Ishaq Ibrahim al-Istakhri, *Kitab masalik al-mamalik*, edited by M. J. de Goeje (Leiden: E. J. Brill, 1927), pp. 207–8.

8. Lisa Golombek, "Urban Patterns in Pre-Safavid Isfahan," *Iranian Studies* 7 (1974):18–44; al-Istakhri, *Kitab masalik al-mamalik*, p. 198.

9. Sahmi, p. 10.

10. Ibid., p. 19. *Afna'* should probably be read as *fina'* ("courtyard") or its plural, afniya. Dr. Lawrence Conrad informs me that "the fina' is the open space adjacent to a warrior's tent, and outsiders under his protection would pitch their own tents there. From this origin the term came to refer to those who, upon entering an Arab garrison town, found that their own tribe was not numerous enough there to have its own khitta, and so would camp in a special khitta reserved for members of such sparsely represented clans. Their security was assured by the strategy of claiming that they were under the protection of the larger Arab tribes as a whole, i.e., the less numerous ones all grouped together were in their fina' or afniya."

11. Sahmi, pp. 18–20.

12. Ibid., pp. 19, 238. Shuja' ibn Sabih served as market inspector (*muhtasib*) of Gorgan.

13. Ibid., pp. 42, 524.

14. Ibid., pp. 63, 160, 280, 303. The reference to the street ending at the river (p. 303) proves it was outside the walls. Carved and painted stucco was a major feature of interior and exterior architectural decoration in northeast Iran.

15. Bulliet, "Medieval Nishapur," p. 73.

16. Bulliet, *Patricians*, p. 90.

17. Jean De Menasce, "Problèmes des Mazdéens dans l'Iran musulman," *Festschrift für Wilhelm Eilers* (Wiesbaden, 1967), pp. 224–25, gives a Zoroastrian legal text confirming that the property of a convert to Islam could legally be seized by other Zoroastrians. Another passage bars a Zoroastrian from selling livestock to Muslims unless he has no other means of earning a living. B. T. Anklesaria, *The Pahlavi Rivayat of Aturfarnbag and Farnbag-srosh*, (Bombay: Industrial Press, 1969), vol. 2, pp. 137–38, 129, cites laws constraining Zoroastrians from purchasing goods in Muslim markets and from consorting with non-Muslims in caravanserais.

18. This is obviously a difficult generalization to prove without more data than has survived. There are many indirect indicators, however. Numismatics is one. Excavations conducted at Nishapur by the Metropolitan Museum of Art before World War II explored only a few parts of the city's enormous field of ruins. Nevertheless, the chronological distribution of coin finds, 269 from the late eighth century and 234 from the ninth and early tenth centuries—87 percent of the total—generally confirms the city's main period of construction.

19. Richard W. Bulliet, "Pottery Styles and Social Status in Medieval Khurasan," in A. Bernard Knapp, ed., *Archaeology, Annales, and Ethnohistory* (Cambridge: Cambridge University Press, 1992), pp. 75–82.

20. The data are drawn from Ibn al-Imad's *Shadharat al-dhahab fi akhbar man dhahab* (Cairo: Maktaba al-Qudsi, 1931–32), 8 vols. Ibn al-Imad selected the most prominent figures named in a broad selection of biographical sources available to him. The representativeness of his selection is supported by the fact that the work of a compiler who lived three and a half centuries earlier and belonged to an opposing religious faction yields almost identical percentages despite the fact that the total number of biographies per twenty-five-year period diverges greatly (al-Dhahabi, *Kitab al-'ibar fi khabar man ghabar*, edited by Salah al-Din Munajjid and Fuad Sayyid [Kuwait: Office of Printing and Publication, 1960–66], 5 vols.). For a fuller discussion see Bulliet, *Conversion*, chap. 2.

21. Abu Nu'aim al-Isfahani, *Akhbar Isbahan*, vol. 2, pp. 138–39, 186–87.

22. An Umayyad governor of Iraq estimated the number of mawali in Basra at 150,000 early in the eighth century. As the story of the Hamdani family illustrates, however, these included people from other provinces that had been brought to the Iraqi cantonments as prisoners of war. Julius Wellhausen, *The Arab Kingdom and its Fall* (Beirut: Khayat, 1963), p. 402.

5. *Question and Answer: The Roots of Religious Authority*

1. Sahmi, pp. 384–85.
2. Ibid., p. 386.

3. Ibid., p. 385.

4. Ibid.

5. Ibid.

6. Ibid., p.390.

7. Ibid., pp. 382, 398–99.

8. For Sul's descendants see ibid., p. 247; for Yazid's see pp. 13–14.

9. In response to a reservation made about Yazid's hadith, one transmitter said, "Yazid was the noblest person who lied about hadith" (ibid., p. 14).

10. Ibid., p. 396.

11. Or 245 out of 2,582.

12. No one from Muslim Spain is mentioned in the biographical dictionary of Isfahan, and only six Spaniards show up among the 4,397 biographies of scholars in Nishapur. As for travel in the other direction, only eleven Iranians, two of them from Khurasan, were included among the 3,612 scholarly biographies from Muslim Spain surveyed by Abdulghafour I. Rozi, "The Social Role of Scholars ('Ulama') in Islamic Spain: A Study of Medieval Biographical Dictionaries," Ph.D. dissertation, Boston University, 1983, pp. 99, 104.

13. Sahmi, p. 54.

14. Ibid., p. 58.

15. Ibid., p. 57.

16. Ibid., p. 136.

17. Ibid., p. 137.

18. Ibid., p. 113.

19. Ibid., p. 368.

20. Ibid., p. 486.

21. Ibid., p. 159.

22. Ibid., p. 175.

23. Ibid., p. 215.

24. Ibid., p. 213.

25. Ibid., pp. 43–44.

26. Ibid., p. 254.

27. Ibid., p. 264.

28. Ibid., p. 365.

29. Ibid., p. 464.

30. Ibid., p. 443.

31. The two occurrences of this word may be textual errors since rahib and zahid look somewhat similar in Arabic and since eschewal of priesthood and monasticism is a hallmark of Islam. One occurs in Isfahan, where Abu Nu'aim mentions a rahib (vol. 2, p. 54) as part of the brotherhood (*ikhwan*) of one al-Abbas al-Tamidhi. The latter is described as a zahid (Akhbar Isbahan, vol. 2, p. 140), and the same word is used in place of rahib in a second duplicate biography of the same disciple (vol. 2, p. 57). One might discount the word entirely

were it not for one Ahmad b. al-Mubarak of Nishapur being described in a different source both as a zahid and as "the monk of the people of his time" (*rahib ahl asrihi*) (al-Hakim al-Naisaburi, *History of Nishapur*, facsimile published in R. N. Frye, *The Histories of Nishapur*, f20b).

32. For Nishapur, see chart in Bulliet, *Patricians*, p. 41. For Isfahan, the numbers from Abu Nu'aim's biographical dictionary are 2 out of 377 for the period 844–897, 11 out of 733 for the period 898–951, and 18 out of 360 for the period 952–1028.

33. Abu Hayyan al-Tawhidi, *Kitab al-imta' w'al-mu'anasa*, edited by Ahmad Amin and Ahmad Al-Zain (Cairo: Matba'a Lajna al-Ta'lif w'al-Tarjama w'al-Nashr, 1939), vol. 2, p. 40.

34. Abu Abd al-Rahman al-Sulami, *Usul al-malamatiya wa ghalatat al-sufiya*, edited by Abd al-Fattah al-Fawi Mahmud (Cairo: Matba'a al-Irshad, 1985), pp. 145–46. I am grateful to Paul Hardy for bringing this work to my attention and undertaking a partial translation of it.

35. Ibid., pp. 182–83.

36. Much later the malamatiyya was ferociously vilified for allegedly advocating public performance of disgraceful acts, apparently to court censure as a way of proving they were not courting self-aggrandizing praise.

37. Afaf Abd-el-Baki Hatoum, "An Eleventh Century Karrami Text: Abu Hafs an-Nisaburi's 'Raunaq al-Majalis,' " Ph.D. dissertation, Columbia University, 1991, p. 185–86.

38. Ibid., and Clifford Edmund Bosworth, "The Rise of the Karamiyyah in Khurasan," *Muslim World* 50 (1960):5–14.

39. For a full discussion see Clifford Edmund Bosworth, *The Mediaeval Islamic Underworld: The Banu Sasan in Arabic Society and Literature* (Leiden: E. J. Brill, 1976).

6. Ulama

1. We shall discuss this questionable concept in chapter 9.

2. Sahmi, pp. 133–37.

3. Ibid., pp. 134–35.

4. One of the greatest sources for medieval Jewish history in the Islamic world is a geniza, or repository of disused manuscripts, preserved intact in a sealed room of a Cairene synagogue down to the nineteenth century. Piety dictated that papers possibly bearing God's name not be destroyed. Though no Muslim geniza has survived, the same sentiment was not unfelt among Muslims. In 1966, looking about a tiny village shrine in Khurasan, I happened upon a small room that was five feet deep, wall to wall, in discarded manuscripts. There was no way of guessing how old the books on the bottom of the pile were, or what they contained.

5. A book listing a person's teachers and serving as a guide to his class notes and texts was called a *mashyakha*. A number of these works still survive in manuscript libraries. See, for example, Georges Vajda, "La masyaha d'ibn al-Hattab al-Razi," *Bulletin d'Etudes Orientales, Institut Français de Damas* 23 (1970):21–99. The author names and makes a few comments about forty-seven of his teachers. The style and content of his entries is identical to that of thousands of notices collected in biographical dictionaries.

6. Of the 1,699 Nishapuri biographies compiled by al-Farisi, 207, or 12 percent, belong to only nine complex families. In three cases, the biographical notices of al-Farisi and other compilers extend over eight generations and in four cases over seven generations. See Bulliet, *Patricians*, part 2.

7. Similar distinctions between major and minor ulama have been described in nineteenth-century Tunisia and twentieth-century Morocco. Arnold H. Green, *The Tunisian Ulama 1873–1915* (Leiden: E. J. Brill, 1978), chap. 3; Dale F. Eickelman, *Knowledge and Power in Morocco* (Princeton: Princeton University Press), 1985, pp. 104–6.

8. Sahmi, p. 157.

9. Ibid., pp. 115–17.

10. Ibid., pp. 438–40.

11. Abraham Marcus, *The Middle East on the Eve of Modernity* (New York: Columbia University Press, 1989), pp. 210–11.

12. Sahmi, p. 130.

13. Ibid., pp. 85–96.

14. Among those he prayed over were two qadis (ibid., pp. 296, 488).

15. Ibid., p. 164.

16. Ibid., pp. 92, 521–22.

17. Ibid., pp. 198–99.

18. Ibid., pp. 519–20.

19. Ibid., p. 589.

20. Ibid., p. 92.

21. Ibid., pp. 235–36, 535–36.

22. Ibid., p. 523.

23. So says al-Jaulaki's biography. The son's biography (ibid., pp. 236–37) gives a birthdate that would make him twenty-two instead of eighteen.

24. Ibid., p. 108–9.

25. Bulliet, *Patricians*, p. 42. The overall ratio between identifiable Shafi'is and Hanafis in Nishapur is 7:3. The Hanafi eschewal of Sufism is underscored by the fact that four Sufis belonged to law schools with very few followers in the city. Two were Malikis, and two Zahiris.

26. The compilers of the biographical dictionaries of Nishapur and Gorgan were Shafi'is, Isfahan's primary historian a Sufi. The latter also compiled one of the first biographical dictionaries of Sufis. A similar work was put together at

about the same time by Abu Abd al-Rahman al-Sulami, a Shafi'i Sufi from Nishapur.

27. Most notably Shahristani's *Kitab al-milal wa al-nihal*, and Abd al-Qahir al-Baghdadi's *Kitab al-farq bain al-firaq*.

28. Farisi II, f17a.

29. For a study of the chronology and social significance of Nishapur pottery styles see Bulliet, "Pottery Styles."

7. Caliph and Sultan

1. See, for example, the origins of the Bahiri family in Nishapur in Bulliet, *Patricians*, pp. 192–93.

2. Abu Nu'aim, *Akhbar Isbahan*, vol. 1, pp. 274–76; Abi Shaikh [sic], *Tabaqat al-muhaddithin bi-Isfahan wa'l-waridin 'alaiha* (Beirut: Dar al-Kutub al-'Ilmiya, 1989), vol. 1, pp. 186–89.

3. There is some discrepancy between the two biographies noted above, but this is the most likely story. Al-Husain ibn Hafs's Arabic genealogy goes back several more generations, but it was not unknown for an Iranian mawla to adopt the genealogy of his Arab patron. See, for example, the genealogy of al-Husain's father-in-law (Abu Nu'aim, *Akhbar Isbahan*, vol. 2, p. 147).

4. Ibid., vol. 1, p. 274; vol. 2, pp. 147–48.

5. This sum is probably symbolic. The dirham was the standard silver coin of the Abbasid caliphate. Though price information for the ninth century is rare, at that time 100 kg. of wheat probably cost between five and ten dirhams. See Eliyahu Ashtor, *A Social and Economic History of the Near East in the Middle Ages* (Berkeley: University of California Press, 1976), p. 93.

6. Abu Nu'aim, *Akhbar Isbahan*, vol. 2, pp. 53–54.

7. Ibid., vol. 2, p. 210; Abi Shaikh, *Tabaqat al-muhaddithin*, vol. 2, p. 113.

8. Abu Nu'aim, *Akhbar Isbahan*, vol. 2, pp. 100–1.

9. Ibid., vol. 1, pp. 125, 145, 155–56, 282–83, 355; vol. 2, pp. 23–24, 88–89, 102, 115, 210–12, 263–64, 302–3, 310, 317; Abi Shaikh, *Tabaqat al-muhaddithin*, vol. 2, pp. 112–15.

10. Abu Nu'aim, *Akhbar Isbahan*, vol. 2, p. 210; Abi Shaikh, *Tabaqat al-muhaddithin*, vol. 2, p. 114.

11. In Egypt, for example, the qadi first ordered to implement the mihna, Harun ibn Abd Allah, agreed to examine the certified witnesses for doctrinal soundness but later asked to be excused when a new letter from the caliph called for the examination of all legal specialists. He was replaced by a new qadi sent from outside Egypt, Muhammad ibn Abi al-Laith, who zealously interrogated every legal scholar, hadith reciter, mosque official, and teacher and prevented those who failed to affirm the mu'tazili creed from entering or even coming near the mosques until the mihna ended (al-Kindi, *Kitab al-Qudat*,

edited by Rhuvon Guest [Leiden: E. J. Brill, 1912], pp. 443–58). I am grateful to Dr. Sam Gellens for bringing this information to my attention.

12. Abu Nu'aim, *Akhbar Isbahan*, vol. 2, p. 211; Abi Shaikh, *Tabaqat al-muhaddithin*, vol. 2, p. 113.

13. For biographies of the witnesses see Abu Nu'aim, *Akhbar Isbahan*, vol. 2, pp. 222–225; Abi Shaikh, *Tabaqat al-muhaddithin*, vol. 2, pp. 173–74, 242–43. In Abi Shaikh's version of the story there are only two witnesses.

14. Though his grandfather, father, brother, and nephew are all specifically called muzikki, Muhammad ibn Abd Allah is not. Obviously, however, Muhammad would have had access to his family's store of confidential and damning information about Isfahan's citizens.

15. Walter M. Patton, *Ahmed Ibn Hanbal and the Mihna* (Leiden: E. J. Brill, 1897), p. 59.

16. In Nishapur, biographical information is available for fourteen members of a single family who served as qadi between 987 and 1200 (Bulliet, *Patricians*, pp. 201–16, 257–59). One of them is specifically described as having been selected locally for the position (p. 206). A later report maintains that the family produced no fewer than seventy qadis (Ibn Abi al-Wafa', *Al-Jawahir al-mudiya* [Hyderabad: Nizamia Oriental Publications Bureau, 1332/1914], vol. 1, p. 262). A surviving document investing one family member with a judgeship adverts to the hereditary character of the post (*Atabat al-kataba*, edited by Abbas Eghbal [Tehran, 1329/1950], p. 10).

17. Richard W. Bulliet, "Local Politics in Eastern Iran under the Ghaznavids and Seljuks," *Iranian Studies* 11 (1978):35–56.

18. For a more detailed account see Richard W. Bulliet, "The Political-Religious History of Nishapur in the Eleventh Century," in D. S. Richards, ed., *Islamic Civilization 950–1150* (Oxford: Cassirer, 1973), pp. 80–85.

8. Cities in Crisis

1. Bulliet, *Conversion*, chap. 2.

2. David Waines, "The Third Century Internal Crisis of the Abbasids," *Journal of the Economic and Social History of the Orient* 20 (1977):282–306.

3. Adams, *Land Behind Baghdad*, p. 99.

4. Ibid., p. 98.

5. Sahmi, p. 55.

6. Ibn Funduq, *Tarikh-i Baihaq*, p. 149. A high proportion of medieval Iranian village names were compounded of personal names with the suffix "-abad" meaning "built by."

7. Numerous Iranian villages bear the same name as a neighboring village, the two being distinguished by the words "upper" and "lower," referring to the

slope of the land. This pattern may be caused by a second village hiving off from a first.

8. J. Behnam, "Population," in *The Cambridge History of Iran* (Cambridge: Cambridge University Press, 1968), vol. 1, p. 479. The author speaks of average sizes of larger and smaller villages. I have chosen to use the larger of the two numbers to guard against underestimating the rural population.

9. The estimate given in Bulliet, "Medieval Nishapur," pp. 87–88, is 110,000–220,000. This was based, however, on estimates of population density derived from other parts of the medieval Islamic world. Lawrence Potter ("The Kart Dynasty of Herat: Religion and Politics in Medieval Iran," Ph.D. dissertation, Columbia University, 1992, appendix 3) provides a more plausible range of figures based specifically on the urban building patterns of Khurasan. I have adjusted my earlier estimate in accordance with his figures.

10. Josiah Cox Russell, *Medieval Regions and their Cities* (Bloomington: Indiana University Press, 1972).

11. This broad economic region oriented toward the one major city of Nishapur is delimited by the agricultural hinterlands of Herat to the east, Marv to the northeast, Gorgan to the northwest, and Rayy to the west. The ranking of the top ten cities (1. Nishapur, 2. Tus, 3. Nisa, 4. Abivard, 5. Sarakhs, 6. Damghan, 7. Bistam, 8. Juvain, 9. Qa'in, 10. Semnan) is based on the frequency of appearance of individuals from those cities in the biographical dictionaries of Nishapur and of Baghdad. Given these assumptions, Russell's ranking formula predicts a population for Damghan, the sixth-ranked city, of 30,000. A published population estimate based on the area of medieval Damghan multiplied by a density factor is 25,000 (Shahriyar Adle, "Contribution à la géographie historique du Damghan," *Le monde iranien et l'Islam* 1971:69–104). The overall population estimate of 2.3 million comes from the 1956 Iranian census. This figure was used, as explained earlier in this chapter, because of the stability over time of village size in qanat-irrigated regions and the apparent comparability in number of villages between the 1950s and the tenth century.

12. David Herlihy, *Medieval and Renaissance Pistoia: The Social History of an Italian Town 1200–1430* (New Haven: Yale University Press, 1967), chap. 5.

13. For a full discussion, see Richard W. Bulliet, *The Camel and the Wheel* (Cambridge, Mass.: Harvard University Press, 1975).

14. Christopher Dyer, *Standards of Living in the Later Middle Ages: Social Change in England c. 1200–1520* (Cambridge: Cambridge University Press, 1990), pp. 64, 153.

15. Little had changed in Iranian transport technology by 1775 when an effort to relieve a famine in the southwest by bringing grain on camelback from the north, a trip of less than 500 miles, caused the price to multiply by seven

times. Cost of transport seems to have been the primary cause of this increase (John R. Perry, *Karim Khan Zand: A History of Iran, 1747–1779* [Chicago: University of Chicago Press, 1979], p. 241).

16. Sahmi, p. 135.

17. Ibn Funduq, *Tarikh-i Baihaq*, p. 176; Utbi, *Kitab-i Yamini*, pp. 314–18.

18. Lawrence Conrad, "Abraha and Muhammad," *Bulletin of the School of Oriental and African Studies* 50 (1987):230–32.

19. Bulliet, *Patricians*, p. 137.

20. Ibid., pp. 109–10.

21. For mention of the famine see Ibn Funduq, *Tarikh-i Baihaq*, pp. 175–76, and Wilhelm Barthold, *Turkestan Down to the Mongol Invasion*, 3d ed. (London: Luzac, 1968), pp. 287–88.

22. Farisi I, f90b; Farisi II, f133a.

23. Farisi II, f6b.

24. Ibn Funduq, *Tarikh-i Baihaq*, p. 268.

25. For a more detailed account of Nishapur's destruction see Bulliet, *Patricians*, pp. 76–80.

26. Muhammad al-Rawandi, *Rahat al-sadur wa ayat al-surur*, edited by M. Iqbal (London: Luzac, 1921), p. 182.

27. Bulliet, "Medieval Nishapur," pp. 85–89.

28. For further detail see Bulliet, "Local Politics," pp. 44–46.

29. Farisi I, f48a–b.

9. The Iranian Diaspora: The Edge Creates a Center

1. For an extended exposition of this idea see George Makdisi, *Ibn 'Aqil et la résurgence de l'Islam traditionaliste au xie siécle* (Damascus: Institut Français de Damas, 1963), chap. 4.

2. Bulliet, *Patricians*, pp. 249–53; Ibn Funduq, *Tarikh-i Baihaq*, p. 194.

3. The model for the Nizamiya itself was almost certainly the al-Sa'idi madrasa founded in the year 1000 by the brother of the Seljuqs' illustrious predecessor Mahmud of Ghazna. This madrasa was devoted to the teaching of Hanafi law (Bulliet, *Patricians*, pp. 250–51). Tughril Beg himself seems to have founded a madrasa in Nishapur, called the Sultaniya, in 1045, well before Nizam al-Mulk's Nizamiya. It, too, was Hanafi (ibid., p. 252).

4. Nasir al-Din Abu al-Rashid Abd al-Jalil Qazvini Razi, *Ba'd mathalib al-nawasib fi naqd "Ba'd fada'ih al-rawafid,"* quoted in Neguin Yavari, "Nizam al-Mulk Remembered: A Study in Historical Representation," Ph.D. dissertation, Columbia University, 1992, pp. 151–52.

5. Joan Gilbert, "Institutionalization of Muslim Scholarship and Professionalization of the 'Ulama' in Medieval Damascus," *Studia Islamica* 52 (1980):115.

6. All data on the Baghdad Nizamiya come from Asad Talas, *La madrasa nizamiyya et son histoire* (Paris: P. Geuthner, 1939).

7. Data on Damascus and Aleppo are from Nikita Elisséeff, *Nur ad-Din, un grand prince musulman de Syrie au temps des croisades (511–569H./1118–1174)* (Damascus: Institut Français de Damas, 1967), vol. 3, pp. 915–30.

8. There is substantial room for disagreement on the meanings of these and other terms connected with the conduct and oversight of education in the eleventh century. Roy Mottahedeh has proposed that the proper reading of this passage should be, "He was the first to establish in Herat the teaching of the implications of hadith, the description of its transmitters (*sharh al-rijal*) and the certification of hadith (*al-tashih*)" (review of *The Patricians of Nishapur* in *Journal of the American Oriental Society* 95 [1975]:493). While this is a possible reading, it implies, implausibly, that proper hadith teaching did not reach the major Khurasani city of Herat until the start of the eleventh century, a century and a half after hadith instruction and selection of "sound" traditions had developed elsewhere in the region.

9. For a full discussion of this topic see Richard W. Bulliet, "The Shaikh al-Islam and the Evolution of Islamic Society," *Studia Islamica* 35 (1972):53–67.

10. Mustafa Akdag, *Türkiye'nin Iktisadi ve İçtimai Tarihi* (Ankara: Türk Tarih Kurumu Basimevi, 1959), vol. 1, pp. 10–12.

11. Ishtiaq Husain Qureshi, *The Administration of the Sultanate of Delhi*, 4th ed. (Karachi: Pakistan Historical Society, 1958), pp. 176–77.

12. See supra chapter 8.

13. Khaliq Ahmad Nizami, "The Religious Life and Leanings of Iltutmish," in his *Studies in Medieval Indian History and Culture* (Allahabad: Kitab Mahal, 1966), pp. 13–40.

14. Carl F. Petry, *The Civilian Elite of Cairo in the Later Middle Ages* (Princeton: Princeton University Press, 1981), pp. 61–72. Prior to the twelfth century, Iranians seem to have been comparatively rare in Egypt (Sam I. Gellens, "Scholars and Travellers: The Social History of Early Muslim Egypt, 217–487/832–1094," Ph.D. dissertation, Columbia University, 1986).

15. W. Montgomery Watt's is a representative voice. "From this time on [the time of Nizam al-Mulk], until perhaps the beginning of the 8th/14th century, the teaching of the Ash'ariyya was almost identical with orthodoxy, and in a sense it has remained so until the present time" (*Encyclopedia of Islam*, new ed., 1960, vol. 1, p. 696). George Makdisi, a fervent proponent of the theory that the "Sunni revival" was primarily a traditionalist Hanbali phenomenon, argues to the contrary: "To my mind, Ash'arism cannot be said to have triumphed in Baghdad in the eleventh nor even in the twelfth century. Ghazzali had nothing official to do with its propagation there that we know of, and it remained, in its version from Khurasan, a hated importation which was repeat-

edly rejected, and especially so after the middle of the eleventh century and the foundation of the Nizamiya" ("Muslim Institutions of Learning in Eleventh-Century Baghdad," *Bulletin of the School of Oriental and African Studies* 24 [1961]:47). If ash'arism did not spread in Arab lands in the twelfth century, however, it is difficult to explain how, by the end of the thirteenth century, the noted Syrian Hanbali Ibn Taimiya came to be viewed as a critic of ash'ari "orthodoxy." It seems inconceivable that a century marked, as the thirteenth was, by fear or experience of Mongol invasion fostered widespread theological change.

16. Michel Allard, *Le problème des attributs divins dans la doctrine d'al-Ash'ari et de ses premiers grands disciples* (Beirut: Imprimerie Catholique, 1965). Allard's selection should be viewed as illustrative rather than definitive.

17. For information on him and his family see Bulliet, *Patricians*, chap. 9.

18. For information on him and his family see ibid., chap. 10.

19. For information on him and his family see ibid., chap. 11.

20. For details see Makdisi, *Ibn 'Aqil*, pp. 350–66.

21. Rachid Bourouiba, *Ibn Tumart* (Algiers: SNED, 1974), pp. 24–27.

22. Reynold A. Nicholson, *Studies in Islamic Mysticism*, reprint of 1921 ed. (Cambridge: Cambridge University Press, 1978), p. 73.

23. Ibid., p. 46.

24. Abu Najib al-Suhrawardi, *A Sufi Rule for Novices*, translated by Menahem Milson (Cambridge, Mass.: Harvard University Press, 1975), p. 34.

25. Ibid., pp. 45–58.

26. Ibid., pp. 73–82.

27. A third Sufi rule, composed by the Iranian Abd al-Allah al-Ansari of Herat in the eleventh century, has been studied by Gerhard Böwering in "The Adab Literature of Classical Sufism: Ansari's Code of Conduct," in Barbara Metcalf, ed., *Moral Conduct and Authority: The Place of Adab in South Asian Islam* (Berkeley: University of California Press, 1984), pp. 62–87.

28. Makdisi, *Ibn 'Aqil*, pp. 378–80.

29. Abu Abd al-Rahman al-Sulami, *The Book of Sufi Chivalry*, translated by Tosun Bayrak al-Jerrahi al-Halveti (London: East West Publications, 1983), p. 73.

30. Abu al-Qasim al-Qushairi, *al-Risala al-Qushairiya fi 'ilm al-tasawwuf* (Beirut: Dar al-Kitab al-Arabi, 1957), pp. 103–5. The puzzling relationship with the urban "bandits" know as ayyarun or shuttar has been explored by Claude Cahen, *Movements populaires et autonomisme urbain dans l'Asie musulmane du moyen âge* (Leiden: E. J. Brill, 1959). The two movements share a devotion to paramilitary training and a localized urban theater of action, but despite some personnel overlaps they are not identical.

31. Bulliet, *Patricians*, pp. 45, 123, 158, 161.

32. Angelika Hartmann, *An-Nasir li-Din Allah (1180–1225). Politik, Religion, Kultur in der späten 'Abbasidenzeit* (Berlin: de Gruyter, 1975).

33. Ibn Battuta, *Rihla Ibn Battuta* (Beirut: Dar al-Turath, 1968), pp. 275–76.

10. New Center, New Edges

1. Ibn al-Arabi, *Sufis of Andalusia*, pp. 81–83.

2. Ibid., p. 82.

3. Ibid., p. 156.

4. Ibn al-Arif, *Mahasin al-Majalis: The Attractions of the Mystical Sessions*, translated by William Elliott and Adnan K. Abdulla (Amersham: Avebury, 1980). The translators believe this quotation from the closing portion of Ibn al-Arif's work may be a later interpolation, but it is entirely in keeping with the spirit of Ibn al-Arabi's anecdotes.

5. David Raymond Goodrich, "A Sufi Revolt in Portugal: Ibn Qasi and his Kitab Khal' al-na'layn," Ph.D. dissertation, Columbia University, 1978, pp. 45, 56, 250, 315.

6. Ibn al-Arabi, *Mahasin al-Majalis*, pp. 51, 71, 136.

7. Goodrich, "A Sufi Revolt," pp. 316–18.

8. Ibn Battuta, for example, notes that Basra in his day had three quarters. "The first of them is Hudhail quarter. Its grandee (kabir) is Shaikh al-Fadil Ala' al-Din ibn al-Athir , who is among the virtuous and generous ones. . . . The second is the Bani Haram quarter. Its grandee is Sayyid Sharif Majd al-Din Musa al-Hasani, the possessor of fine qualities and virtues. . . . The third quarter is that of the Persians. Its grandee is Jamal al-Din ibn al-Luki" (p. 182). It's not hard to guess which of the three did not show hospitality to the author.

9. A tabulation of 2,582 instances of scholars from Nishapur studying under specific teachers in the eleventh century yields only nine students learning from two teachers in Mecca, as opposed to ninety-five students studying under fourteen teachers in Baghdad.

10. Claude Cahen, *Pre-Ottoman Turkey* (New York: Taplinger, 1968), p. 245.

11. Ibn al-Arabi, *Sufis*, p. 139.

12. Barbara Metcalf, "The Pilgrimage Remembered: South Asian Accounts of the Hajj," in D. E. Eickelman and J. Piscatori, eds., *Muslim Travellers: Pilgrimage, Migration, and the Religious Imagination* (Berkeley: University of California Press, 1990), pp. 85–107; Abderrahmane El Moudden, "The Ambivalence of Rihla: Community Integration and Self-Definition in Moroccan Travel Accounts, 1300–1800," in Eickelman and Piscatori, eds., *Muslim Travellers*, pp. 69–84.

13. Ibn Battuta, *Rihla*, pp. 108–78 (out of 682 total pages).

14. E.g., ibid., pp. 259, 301, 541, 662.

15. Ibid., p. 184.

16. Abu al-Hasan Ali al-Harawi, *Guide des lieux de pélerinage*, edited by J. Sourdel-Thomine (Damascus: Institut Français de Damas, 1953). Conforming to the pattern discussed in the previous chapter, al-Harawi's family came from Herat, in eastern Iran; but he lived his life in Aleppo in Syria where a local ruler built a madrasa for him.

17. Three cemetery lists of Nishapur are preserved in facsimile form in Frye's *The Histories of Nishapur*, f67b–71b of the manuscript Frye describes as the "Persian version" of al-Hakim al-Naisaburi's biographical dictionary of Nishapur epitomized by Ibrahim ibn Muhammad al-Sarifini. All three lists are much later than al-Hakim's tenth-century work. Internal evidence suggests that they date from the fourteenth to sixteenth centuries.

18. Ibn Battuta, *Rihla*, p. 184.

19. Ibid., pp. 218, 220.

20. Ibid., pp. 179–80.

21. Azyumardi Azra, "The Transmission of Islamic Reformism to Indonesia: Networks of Middle Eastern and Malay-Indonesian 'Ulama' in the Seventeenth and Eighteenth Centuries," Ph.D. dissertation, Columbia University, 1992, pp. 137–43.

22. Potter, "The Kart Dynasty," p. 73.

23. John Voll and Nehemia Levtzion, eds., *Eighteenth-Century Renewal and Reform in Islam* (Syracuse: Syracuse University Press, 1987); Azra, "The Transmission of Islamic Reformism to Indonesia."

24. The role of the shaikh in Nobel Prize winner Naguib Mahfouz's novel *The Thief and the Dogs* (Cairo: American University in Cairo Press, 1984) is both an evocation of and a commentary on this motif.

11. The View from the Edge Today

1. Shadow puppets of the Hindu epic heroes are popular craft products in the conservative Muslim state of Kelantan in Malaysia.

2. Vincent Crapanzano, *The Hamadsha: A Study in Moroccan Ethnopsychiatry* (Berkeley: University of California Press, 1973).

3. Juan Cole, *The Roots of North Indian Shi'ism in Iran and Iraq: Religion and State in Awadh, 1722–1859* (Berkeley: University of California Press, 1988), p. 190.

4. Reinhold Loeffler's *Islam in Practice: Religious Beliefs in a Persian Village* (Albany: State University of New York Press, 1988), is an example of an anthropologist's extensive inquiry into contemporary Islam on the local level.

5. Azra, "The Transmission of Islamic Reformism to Indonesia," pp. 396–99.

6. G. Káldy-Nagy, "Beginnings of Arabic-Letter Printing in the Muslim World," in G. Káldy-Nagy, ed., *The Muslim East: Studies in Honour of Julius Germanus* (Budapest: Lorand Eötros University, 1974).

7. For good accounts of the development of Islamic reform and of secularism in the nineteenth and twentieth centuries, see Albert Hourani, *Arabic Thought in the Liberal Age* (Cambridge: Cambridge University Press, 1983); Niyazi Berkes, *The Development of Secularism in Turkey* (Montreal: McGill University Press, 1964); and Hamid Enayat, *Modern Islamic Political Thought* (London: Macmillan, 1962).

8. Janet L. Abu-Lughod, *Cairo: 1001 Years of The City Victorious* (Princeton: Princeton University Press, 1971); Zeynep Çelik, *The Remaking of Istanbul: Portrait of an Ottoman City in the Nineteenth Century* (Seattle: University of Washington Press, 1986).

9. Fred De Jong, *The Turuq and Turuq-Linked Institutions in Nineteenth-Century Egypt* (Leiden: E. J. Brill, 1978).

10. Noteworthy exceptions to the rule include Richard Mitchell, *The Society of the Muslim Brothers* (London: Oxford University Press, 1969), and Morroe Berger, *Islam in Egypt Today* (Cambridge: Cambridge University Press, 1970).

11. J. Heyworth-Dunne, *Introduction to the History of Education in Modern Egypt* (London: Cass, 1967).

12. Barnette Miller, *The Palace School of Mehmet the Conqueror* (Cambridge, Mass.: Harvard University Press, 1941).

13. A representative example of this may be found in *Al-Khumaini: al-hall al-Islami w'al-badil*, by the Muslim Brother Fathi Abd al-Aziz.

INDEX

229

DATE DUE

GAYLORD   PRINTED IN U.S.A.